A Life of Courage

Sherwin Wine and Humanistic Judaism

A Life of Courage

Sherwin Wine and Humanistic Judaism

Compiled by

Dan Cohn-Sherbok
Harry T. Cook
Marilyn Rowens

The International Institute for Secular Humanistic Judaism
Farmington Hills, Michigan

A Life of Courage

Sherwin Wine
and Humanistic Judaism

Compiled by Dan Cohn-Sherbok, Harry T. Cook, and Marilyn Rowens

Published by the International Institute for Secular Humanistic Judaism and Milan Press, Farmington Hills, Michigan

Design Tracey Rowens
Typesetting Graphix Group

ISBN 0-9673259-6-X

For more information and a list of other publications contact:

The International Institute for Secular Humanistic Judaism
28611 W. 12 Mile Rd
Farmington Hills, MI 48334
Phone: 248-476-9532 Fax: 248-476-8509
Web: www.iishj.org
E-mail: iishj@iishj.org

Printed in the United States of America

10 9 8 7 6 5 4 3 2 1

To Sherwin,

It is a privilege to study a philosopher.
It is an honor to know one.

Thank you.
All of your students—and friends.

contents

contents

foreword

Dan Cohn-Sherbok

The first time I met Sherwin Wine was at one of his colloquia. I was sitting with my wife in the Birmingham Temple at the opening ceremony when she suddenly giggled. "That man is exactly like Mr. Toad," she said.

"Mr. Who?" I asked.

"Mr. Toad ... you know ... in *The Wind in the Willows*, Toad of Toad Hall."

I am ashamed to say I did not know and forgot the whole conversation. But when we had returned home, she took down a battered old book from our bookshelves, turned to the last chapter, and said: "Read this!" It was a program for a celebratory concert and I had to admit that it was not altogether dissimilar to what we had recently experienced in Detroit. It went like this:

Speech.......... By Toad
(There will be other speeches by Toad during the evening)

Address . . . . By Toad
(Synopsis included)

Song. . . . . By Toad
(Composed by himself)

Other Compositions . . . . By Toad
Will be sung in the course of the evening by the Composer

Over the course of the years I have come to know Sherwin better. I am not a Humanistic Jew; I remain by the skin of my teeth within the Reform movement. But I do recognize that Sherwin is an extremely significant figure in the history of Judaism in America—more important perhaps than any of us yet realize. For many today, belief in an omnipotent, omniscient, and benevolent deity has become an impossibility. Yet there is still a fascination with and a hunger for religious solutions. You only have to look round a twenty-first-century book shop. There are endless sections on such recondite subjects as crystal therapies for interior designers, zodiacal chart-making for credulous draftsmen, kabbalistic runes for B-list filmstars, and dreary self-help books for the emotionally retarded and terminally self-indulgent. It is a sorry picture.

Among all this, Sherwin stands as a beacon of rational intelligence. As he himself has written, what he offers is sanity in a crazy world. His whole life has been dedicated to the foundation and establishment of a new movement, Secular Humanistic Judaism. His ideas are firmly grounded in the proud tradition of Eastern European Jewish scholarship, but he is completely open to the ideas, influences, and discoveries of the modern world. Literally nothing is sacred.

To establish the new movement, Sherwin initially founded the famous Birmingham Temple in Detroit. Then, over the years, he has created other institutions, and the movement has spread. Today, through his energy and dedication, there are congregations in most sizeable cities in the United States, and the word has reached Europe and Israel as well. A new generation of rabbis has been recruited, trained with utmost vigor, and ordained. Sherwin has ensured that Secular Humanistic Judaism will survive him. It is more than Rabbi Wine's One-Man-Band. It is a fully formed branch of American Judaism, along with the Orthodox, the Conservative, the Reconstructionist, and the Reform.

This volume is an attempt to chart Sherwin's achievements. It is written by his friends and his disciples, by people who have worked with him, by people who care about him, and by people whose lives he has touched. It is hoped that its publication will encourage more interested students to learn more about Humanistic Judaism, but that is not its prime purpose. Ultimately it has been produced to give Sherwin pleasure, to express our admiration, and, at the moment of his retirement, to say thank you.

As my wife long ago observed, there is no doubt that Sherwin does resemble the immortal Mr. Toad. He shares his sleek handsomeness, his unabashed showmanship, his tireless enthusiasm, and his incorrigible desire to perform "just one last, little song." (You will notice that the editors have indulged him in this in the final few pages of this volume!) Nonetheless, over the years, I have come to realize that there is another character in English literature who far more nearly reflects Sherwin's real nature. That is Mr. Valiant-for-Truth in the great seventeenth-century spiritual classic *The Pilgrim's Progress.*

That is exactly what Sherwin is—he is valiant for truth. In *The Pilgrim's Progress,* Mr. Valiant-for-Truth is consistently brave, honest, and true-hearted. He is the ultimate seeker. What he says of himself when he departs from this life, can, with very little rewriting, be declared by Sherwin himself on his retirement:

> Then said he, I am going to my fathers, and tho' with great difficulty I am got hither, yet now I do not repent me of all the trouble I have been at to arrive where I am. My sword I give to him that shall succeed me in my pilgrimage, and my courage and skill

> to him that can get it. My marks and scars I carry with me, to be a witness for me that I have fought these battles.
>
> When the day that he must go hence was come, many accompanied him to the river-side into which he went.... So he passed over, and all the trumpets sounded for him on the other side....

Sherwin is a very great figure. We all love him, and it is hoped that, as he embarks on his retirement, this volume will be a small contribution to all the trumpets that sound for him.

acknowledgments

The International Institute for Secular Humanistic Judaism is grateful to all of the contributing authors of *A Life of Courage*. Their insightful essays provide the essential building blocks for the tribute and honor we bestow upon Sherwin Wine, the founder of Humanistic Judaism.

We thank Dan Cohn-Sherbok and Lavinia Cohn-Sherbok for collecting and compiling the essays, and Harry Cook and Marilyn Rowens for creating the biographical background.

We thank Richard McMains for providing the beautiful worldwide photographs he has taken over the last twenty-five years.

We thank Ron and Esther Milan for the special support that has made this publication possible.

We thank the staff of the institute—Susan Williams, Bonnie Cousens, and Charlotte Nelson—for their assistance and support.

We thank our editor, Judy Galens, for her skillful work.

We thank Marco Di Vita, typesetter extraordinaire.

We thank Tracey Rowens for creating the cover and page design.

contributors

Shulamit Aloni is an attorney, teacher, writer, and journalist. She was a member of the Israeli Knesset from 1965 to 1969 and from 1974 until 1997. Originally a member of the Labor Party, Ms. Aloni founded the Ratz Party, Israel's civil rights and peace movement. She served as Minister of Education and Culture and Minister of Communications, Science, and Arts. Ms. Aloni founded the Israel Consumer Council and Bureau of Civil Rights. Her publications include *Children's Rights in Israel* and *Women As Human Beings*, as well as a political autobiography, *I Can Do No Other.*

Khoren Arisian is Minister Emeritus of the First Unitarian Society of Minneapolis, where he served from 1979 to 1997. He is currently senior leader of the New York Society for Ethical Culture. Dr. Arisian helped found both the North American Committee for Humanism and the Humanist Institute. He was the associate dean of the Humanist Institute from 1990 to 1996, and he continues to serve on its board of governors. He is a distinguished member of the Humanist Institute faculty.

Yehuda Bauer is a world-renowned Holocaust scholar. He was born in Prague, Czechoslovakia, and immigrated to Palestine in 1939. He served in the War of Independence and joined Kibbutz Hoval in 1952. He was historical advisor to Claude Lanzmann for the film *Shoah* and to Abba Eban for *Heritage*. He is the academic advisor at Yad Vashem in Jerusalem. His books include *My Brother's Keeper*, *The Holocaust in Historical Perspective*, *Out of the Ashes*, and *A History of the Holocaust*. His most recent book is *Rethinking the Holocaust*.

Adam Chalom is a rabbi at the Birmingham Temple. He is assistant to the dean of the International Institute for Secular Humanistic Judaism. Rabbi Chalom was raised as a Humanistic Jew at the Birmingham Temple and went on to receive a B.A. in Judaic Studies from Yale University, rabbinic ordination from the International Institute for Secular Humanistic Judaism, and an M.A. in Hebrew and Jewish cultural studies from the University of Michigan, where he is completing his doctoral dissertation.

Joseph Chuman is currently the leader of the Ethical Culture Society of Bergen County, New Jersey, where he has served for twenty-eight years. He is visiting professor of religion and human rights at the Graduate School of Arts and Sciences of Columbia University. He teaches at the United Nations University for Peace in Costa Rica. He is a member of the faculty of the International Institute for Secular Humanistic Judaism, and he is on the board of the Humanist Institute and the International Humanist and Ethical Union.

Dan Cohn-Sherbok is currently professor of Judaism at the University of Wales. Educated at Williams College, he was ordained a reform rabbi at the Hebrew Union College–Jewish Institute of Religion and received a doctorate from Cambridge University. He has served congregations in Alabama, Illinois, Colorado, and Pennsylvania, and as far away as South Africa and Australia. Dr. Cohn-Sherbok is the author and editor of more than sixty books, including *The Jewish Heritage* and *The Future of Judaism*.

Harry T. Cook is the rector of St. Andrews Church in Clawson, Michigan. He is a graduate of Albion College and Garrett-Evangelical Seminary/Northwestern University. Harry Cook was the ethics and public policy columnist for the *Detroit Free Press* for many years. He is the author of *Christianity Beyond Creeds*, *Sermons of a Devoted Heretic*, and *The Seven Sayings of Jesus*. He is a distinguished lecturer at the Center for New Thinking.

Edd Doerr is the president of Americans for Religious Liberty, founded in 1981 by Sherwin Wine and Ed Ericson. He is the immediate past president of the American Humanist Association and author, co-author, or editor of more than twenty books. He and his wife Herenia translated into Spanish Rabbi Wine's book *Staying Sane in a Crazy World*. He is a founding board member of the Religious Coalition for Reproductive Choice and the National Committee for Public Education and Religious Liberty. He has lectured widely on religion and government issues in the United States and abroad.

Ruth Duskin Feldman is a writer, editor, teacher, and lecturer, and a longtime spokesperson for Humanistic Judaism. She is a graduate of the International Institute for Secular Humanistic Judaism, and she is certified as a *madrikha* (Secular Humanistic Jewish leader). She has been the creative editor of the journal *Humanistic Judaism* since 1983. She has been affiliated with Congregation Beth Or in Deerfield, Illinois, since 1968. Currently she is the congregation's *madrikha*, assisting the rabbi, and she serves on its board of directors.

Helen J. Forman is the immediate past executive director of the Birmingham Temple. In 1973 Helen and her family joined the Birmingham Temple, and she assumed her role as executive director in 1985. She retired from that position in 2001 but remains an important, active participant in the movement of Secular Humanistic Judaism by serving as the secretary of the executive board of the International Institute for Secular Humanistic Judaism and as the chair of the admissions committee.

Egon Friedler, born in Uruguay, is a senior journalist for *Identidad,* the mouthpiece of the Secular Humanistic Jewish group in Uruguay, called Corriente Judia Humanista. He also writes widely on subjects of Jewish interest for several publications in Argentina, Israel, the United States, and England. He has been closely associated with the international movement of Secular Humanistic Judaism since the 1980s and is its best-known spokesperson in Latin America.

Daniel Friedman is a graduate of Brandeis University and was ordained as a rabbi at the Hebrew Union College. He served for thirty-five years as the rabbi of Congregation Beth Or, a Humanistic temple in Deerfield, Illinois. Currently, he is rabbinic advisor to Kol Hadash Humanistic Congregation in north suburban Chicago. He is the author of *Jews without Judaism: Conversations with an Unconventional Rabbi* (Prometheus Books, 2002) and resides in Lincolnshire, Illinois.

Judith A. Goren, Ph.D., is a humanistic clinical psychologist and the author of three collections of poetry. Her work has appeared in many literary journals and several anthologies. Judith is a longtime member of the Birmingham Temple. She was a contributing editor to *Humanistic Judaism,* the first journal published by the movement, and she is the author of a Sunday school text on the subject of Jews of Eastern Europe.

Roger E. Greeley is Minister Emeritus of People's (Unitarian) Church in Kalamazoo, Michigan. He served the church for twenty-eight and a half years. He received his master's degree in education from Boston University. In 1985 he became the associate dean of the Humanist Institute in New York. Now in retirement, he writes, travels, counsels, and agitates for secularism and separation of church and state.

Miriam S. Jerris, Ph.D., is a rabbi and the community development associate of the Society for Humanistic Judaism. She was ordained as a rabbi in 2001 by the International Institute for Secular Humanistic Judaism. She is the co-owner of the Wedding Connection, a ceremonial and wedding planning company. For more than thirty years she has been instrumental in developing Humanistic Judaism, and she serves on the faculty of the institute.

Tamara Kolton, Ph.D., is a rabbi and the school director at the Birmingham Temple. She has a bachelor's degree from Hebrew University in Jerusalem. She has a master's degree in clinical psychology and a Ph.D. in Humanistic and Jewish Studies. Rabbi Kolton was the first rabbi to be ordained by the International Institute for Secular Humanistic Judaism, in October 1999.

Yaakov Malkin, Ph.D., is a professor of Aesthetics and Rhetoric at Tel Aviv University. He is the founder and academic director of Meitar College of Pluralistic Judaism. He is the founder and director of the first Culture Community Centers in Israel: Beit Rothchild and Beit Hagefen, the Arab-Jewish Center in Haifa. He has written more than eleven books on literature and theater. His books on secular Judaism include *Judaism As Culture* and *What Do Secular Jews Believe.*

Ronald Modras is a professor of theological studies at Saint Louis University. He received his doctorate at the University of Tuebingen, in Germany. He received the College Theology Society's Book Award for *The Catholic Church and Antisemitism: Poland 1933–1939.* He is an Annenberg Research Fellow and a recipient of the St. Louis American Jewish Committee's Micah Award.

David Oler, Ph.D., is the rabbi of Congregation Beth Or in Deerfield, Illinois, and the president of the Association of Humanistic Rabbis. He is a graduate of McGill University and was ordained by the Rabbinical Seminary of Canada. He received the Doctor of Ministry degree from Andover Newton Theological School. He is also a licensed clinical psychologist, having earned his Ph.D. from the University of Maryland.

Charles R. Paul is a past president of the Birmingham Temple (2000–2001). From 1977 through 2003 he was the editor of *The Jewish Humanist,* the internationally distributed monthly publication of the Birmingham Temple. He also served on the temple board of trustees for many years. He is the president of a marketing and training agency in Farmington Hills, Michigan, and produces videos, manuals, speeches, and presentations primarily for the automotive industry.

Felix Posen is a powerful voice for secular Judaism. His special life interest in higher Jewish education and primarily his quest to determine "what it means to be a Jew in a secular society" has led to the creation of the Posen Foundation, which is the foremost foundation active in the field of cultural, secular, and Humanistic Judaism in Israel and America. He is the energy behind the Felix Posen Bibliographic Project, today's leading world reference work on the subject of antisemitism. He is the cofounder of Alma Hebrew College and Meitar College of Pluralistic Judaism.

Michael J. Prival is a graduate of the International Institute for Secular Humanistic Judaism and a certified *madrikh*. He is one of the founding members of Machar, the Washington Congregation for Secular Humanistic Judaism. He is the author of *Learning Bible Today: From Creation to the Conquest of Canaan*, a work explaining how to present the Bible to children. He currently serves on the board of governors of the International Institute for Secular Humanistic Judaism.

Marilyn Rowens is the executive director of the International Institute for Secular Humanistic Judaism. She also serves as the Leadership Program director and the Rabbinic Program director. She was the ceremonial director of the Birmingham Temple for twenty years. She is the resident cartoonist for the monthly Birmingham Temple publication, *The Jewish Humanist*. She is also the author of many plays and short stories that reflect the human condition.

Peter Schweitzer is the leader of the City Congregation for Humanistic Judaism in New York City, where he has developed liturgy, including a Secular Humanistic Haggada and Shabbat and High Holiday services. He has also developed educational programs for children and adults. He is the vice president of the Association of Humanistic Rabbis. He was ordained as a reform rabbi from the

Hebrew Union College–Jewish Institute of Religion and received a master's degree in social work from New York University.

Mitchell Silver is the cultural director of Camp Kinderland and the educational director of the I. L. Peretz School of Workmen's Circle in Boston. Dr. Silver has taught philosophy at the University of Massachusetts in Boston since 1982. He is the author of *Respecting the Wicked Child: A Philosophy of Secular Jewish Identity and Education*, and he has published works on ethical theory, bioethics, and Middle East politics.

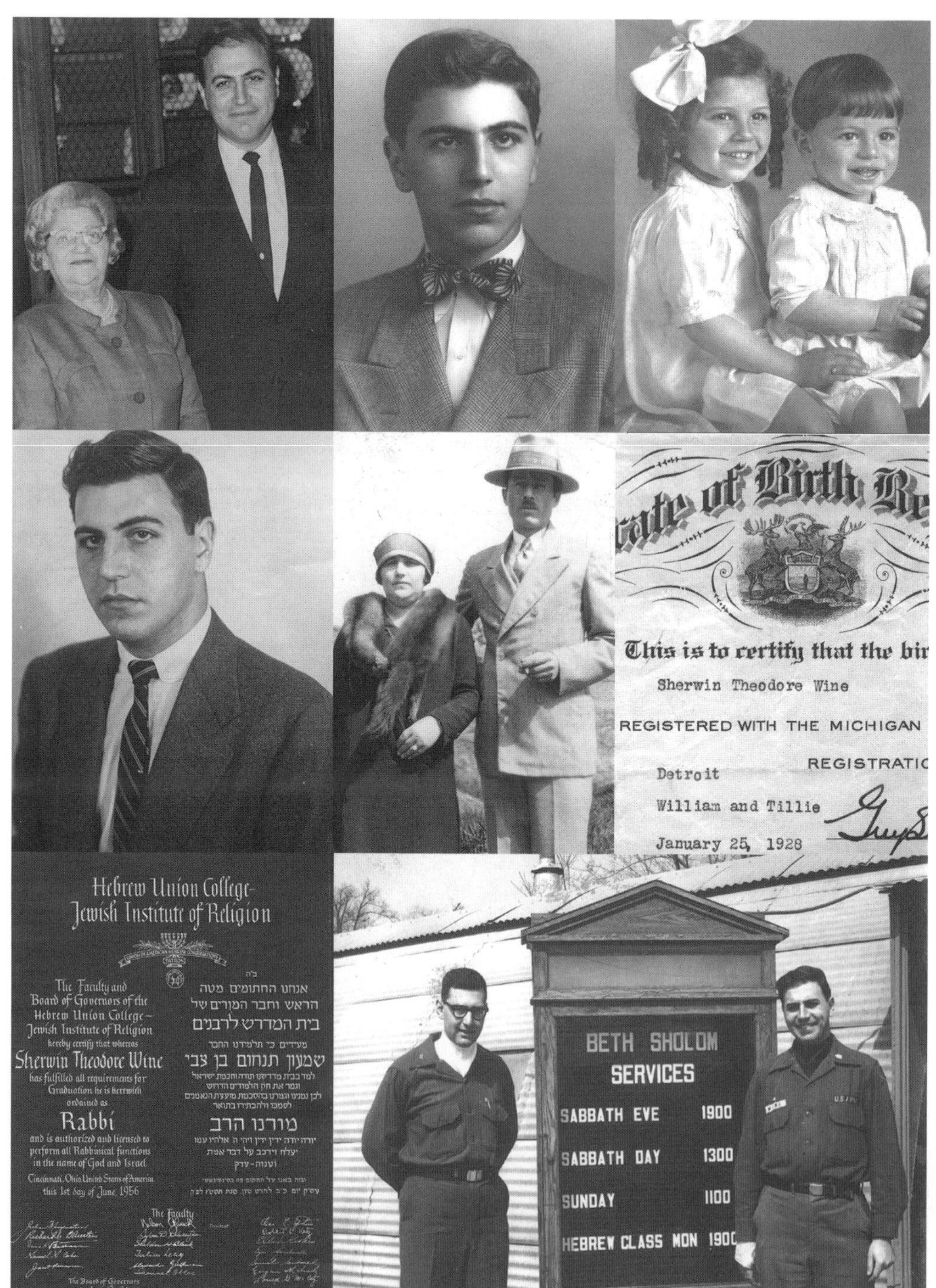

...cate of Birth Re...
This is to certify that the bir...
Sherwin Theodore Wine
REGISTERED WITH THE MICHIGAN
REGISTRATIO...
Detroit
William and Tillie
January 25, 1928
Hebrew Union College-
Jewish Institute of Religion
ב״ה
The Faculty and
Board of Governors of the
Hebrew Union College-
Jewish Institute of Religion
hereby certify that whereas
Sherwin Theodore Wine
has fulfilled all requirements for
Graduation he is herewith
ordained as
Rabbi
and is authorized and licensed to
perform all Rabbinical functions
in the name of God and Israel
Cincinnati, Ohio United States of America
this 1st day of June, 1956
אנחנו החתומים מטה
הראש וחבר המורים של
בית המדרש לרבנים
מעידים כי תלמידנו החבר
שמעון תנחום בן צבי
מורנו הרב
The Faculty
The Board of Governors
BETH SHOLOM
SERVICES
SABBATH EVE 1900
SABBATH DAY 1300
SUNDAY 1100
HEBREW CLASS MON 1900

The world we live in is ageless.
It has no beginning and no end.
It has no author and no conclusion.
It may explode and contract.
It may expand and shrink.
But it never dies.
It is simply there—with its infinite variety
and its never-ending change.

Sherwin Wine

biography

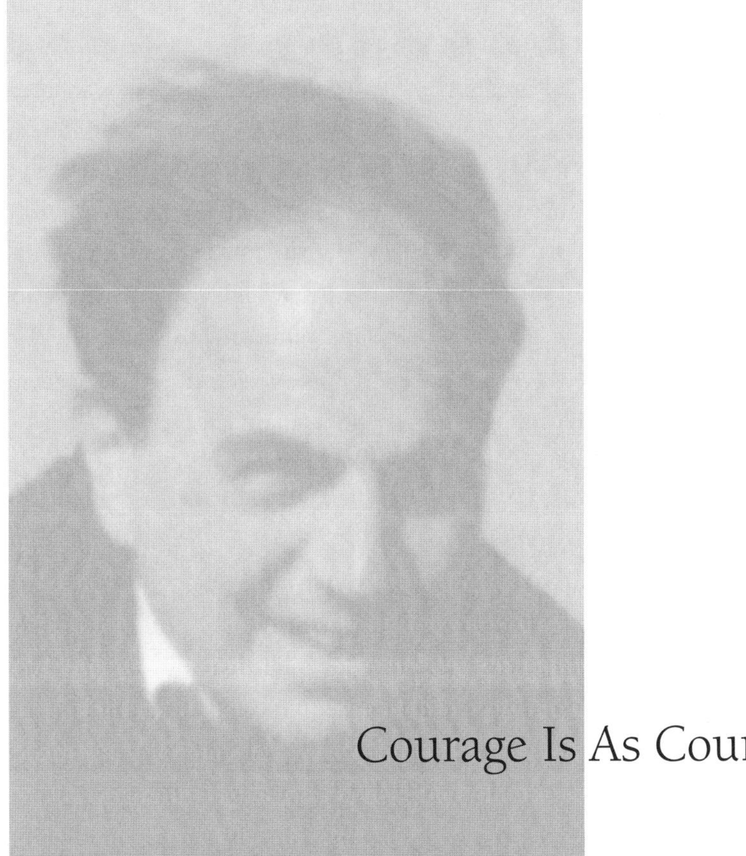

Courage Is As Courage Does

Harry T. Cook

The times and events during which one lives and works—the context of a life—in large part determine how one will be regarded and remembered by posterity. If fascism had not bid fair to absorb the world in the first half of the twentieth century, Winston S. Churchill might be known today as a slightly cuckoo and prolix writer. Neither Ulysses S. Grant nor Dwight D. Eisenhower would have even come close to being elected president of the United States had it not been for their participation in the wars during which they came to prominence. By contrast, the presidency of Lyndon B. Johnson would have been all the more remarkable—and maybe one term longer—for its domestic agenda had an anti-communist America not been so obsessed with repeating Korea's unwinnable war in Vietnam. If the stock market had not crashed and burned in 1929, Herbert Hoover would be much more favorably remembered as one of the most intellectually gifted men ever elected president of the United States.

Sherwin Theodore Wine is certainly not the first Jew—or rabbi, for that matter—to have and to express doubts about the philosophical and theological assumptions of normative Judaism. But the raw power of his intellect, the breadth and depth of his learning, and his courage and determination to make a difference converged at a very ripe juncture. By the early 1960s, America had come into its own as a world power. Its industrial wisdom and might was an unprecedented phenomenon. Its major universities, including Harvard, Yale, Columbia, and Stanford, had little to yield by way of reputation to Oxford, Cambridge, and the Sorbonne. Economically, America was the global powerhouse. Multiple chickens and cars in multiple pots and garages were, except for the very poor, symbols of widespread ordinary success enjoyed by millions. After the trauma of the Great Depression, World War II, and the McCarthy era, America had settled down to enjoy the fruits of its conquered frontiers. Even Alaska and Hawaii had by then attained full statehood. Space exploration was in the cards. Anything was possible.

By the early 1960s, religion in general, which up until that time had been a largely unquestioned aspect of society, was finding itself the subject of clear-eyed investigation and scholarly probing. Helped along by an Italian prelate by the name of Angelo Roncalli—who, as Pope John XXIII, was in the process of demythologizing the Roman Catholic Church—the beginning of the seventh decade of the twentieth century was, at least for organized religion, a time pregnant with possibility. Reform Judaism had become a major player in the American spiritual world. Its leading rabbis were no longer simply Jewish leaders with an immigrant aura but established national religious leaders of major importance. Reform Judaism had become assimilationist and philosophically compatible with twentieth-century intellectual life. Such avant-garde Christian theologians as Harvey Cox (*The Secular City*), Paul van Buren (*The Secular*

Meaning of the Gospel), and Thomas Altizer (*The Gospel of Christian Atheism*) were being widely read and discussed. Hugh Hefner, of Playboy Club notoriety, took famous note of this philosophical brew (and brouhaha) by inviting the English prelate John A. T. Robinson (*Honest to God*) and American Episcopal Bishop James A. Pike (*If This Be Heresy*) to an open forum in the Playboy mansion in Chicago. There had never been such a spectacle.

Onto this stage stepped Wine, a rabbi in his early thirties who was (and is) blessed with an operatic basso's voice, Demosthenes's eloquence, and a polymath's scope of knowledge. In addition, he was (and is) possessed of an intellectual honesty that requires perceivable data for the formulation of beliefs. In that respect, he may turn out to be one of a kind. He personified the sentiment expressed in Aleksandr Solzhenitsyn's landmark essay "Zhit ne po lzhi!" (live not by lies). Wine became the assistant rabbi of one of Detroit's most prestigious Reform Jewish congregations, and in his sermons he startled and engaged a generation of men and women who themselves were in their early thirties and riding the postwar crest of economic and social upward mobility. They had in large part become mildly impatient with the rote religion of their fathers and mothers but figured that the Judaism of their childhood would be the Judaism of their own children. So the constructs of American Reform Judaism would be handed down to a new generation. But Wine's approach changed all that. He could stand on the *bima*, or stage, in the rabbinical authority of his black gown and for all the world appear to be straight out of central casting as the up-and-coming young leader of an established religion. Yet his message was markedly different. It was intellectually challenging and bold in its approach. He posed questions, almost daring his audiences to take those questions seriously and to work out the answers, going wherever reason and logic led them.

Wine's natural charisma made his message all the more attractive, and he developed a following that was to become the core of a congregation called the Birmingham Temple. Perhaps just as significantly, Wine developed a movement that within the decade would become national and then international. The movement is denominated "Secular Humanistic Judaism," but that nomenclature does not do the reality sufficient justice. The title of one of Wine's major works says it best: *Judaism Beyond God.* One can fairly and accurately say that "God" became a casualty of a reason-based religious movement. So, in due course, did ritual prayers and observances that turned out to be empty of intellectually respectable content. With Wine's encouragement and nurturing, what became the Birmingham Temple, what became the Society for Humanistic Judaism, what became the International Institute for Secular Humanistic Judaism and—apart from any of those—what became an entity known as the Center for New Thinking are venues of critical thought, evolving belief, and practice grounded in common sense, logic, and practicality.

Often attributed to a famous Jew is the proposition that "the Sabbath was made for man, not man for the Sabbath." The religion that grew out of that Jew's brief public career has never owned up to the extraordinary promise of that insight. Neither has the Judaism that produced him. Wine—a latter-day Jew—and the movement of Secular Humanistic Judaism that his work helped create has taken the underlying meaning of that proposition seriously. Wine's life—and the lives of those who have peopled the temple and the movement that have grown up around him—is one of courage, for breaking out of the bonds of any long-entrenched ideology is never without its risks. As Wine's late mother once observed, "Sherwin, if you only believed in God, think how much larger your congregation would be."

The Birmingham Temple is not one of metropolitan Detroit's largest religious institutions. Secular Humanistic Judaism is very much a minority in the world of religions. But the impact of both, and of their undisputed leader and founder, is becoming apparent. A life of courage is remarkable not only for its infrequency among humankind, but also because its influence over time often far outweighs what may have been its modest inception.

ENTER SHERWIN WINE

Sherwin Wine first came into my life when I was an upperclassman at Albion College, a small mid-Michigan liberal arts college. At the time, Wine was a young rabbi fresh from a tour of duty as a U.S. Army chaplain in Korea. In the late 1950s Albion still had compulsory chapel twice a week. Usually the speakers were Protestant ministers, and most were crashing bores. Chapel was, in reality, a sea of open newspapers and fidgeting students.

Then one day, this slender, dark-haired, cinematic figure, robed in black, swept up to the dais. From the moment he opened his mouth until he sat down thirty minutes later, there was heard neither a crackle of newsprint nor a single suppressed whisper. All eyes were on Wine; most ears could hardly believe what they heard. What we were experiencing was a mighty gust of fresh air inundating the wasteland of bland midwestern Protestantism. What we were hearing was the not-so-tentative overture of what would, in a few years, become a full-blown secular, humanistic Judaism. Those of us who were philosophy majors freshly exposed to logical positivism and already nursing intellectual rebellion in our hearts were incited by Wine's talk and ready to mutiny. I cannot think of any chapel speaker in all my four years at the college who received the ovation that greeted Wine upon completion of his talk.

I followed the steep trajectory of Wine's career as he became the founding rabbi of the Birmingham Temple, as he bid Reform Judaism farewell, as the temple's ritual progressively dropped the Sh'ma, the Kaddish, and Torah reading—all thought to be absolutely essential to the Jewish religion and identity. The press was soon writing about the "atheist rabbi." As my own ministerial career was beginning, I became less and less connected with Wine and his movement. But when, in 1979, I was appointed religion reporter of the *Detroit Free Press*, I was immediately reconnected. The managing editor at the time, Neal Shine, told me my first day on the job that I was barred from giving Sherwin Wine so much as a drop of ink. "It only pisses off our Jewish readers and advertisers," Shine said.

> One can fairly and accurately say that "God" became a casualty of a reason-based religious movement.

Shine's admonition only excited my reportorial instincts, and I paid an unannounced visit to the Birmingham Temple. It was a Monday evening and Wine had set for the topic of his weekly forum lecture "The Emerging Religious Right." On hearing his piercing and perceptive analysis of the Right's bogus claims to superiority, I realized why this voice was of critical importance in an otherwise impotent and cloistered religious community. And so I wrote my first article about Wine, not treating him as the freak show my predecessors had. I think I helped *Free Press* readers understand that, while Wine might still be a novelty among so-called religious Jews, he was more fundamentally an *original.*

Presently he would organize Voice of Reason, an enterprise dedicated to blunt the preposterous claims and views of the Jerry Falwells and Pat Robertsons of this world. Then came the Conference on Liberal Religion, a kind of ecumenical rounding up of the usual suspects, with the intention of, among other purposes, showing that the religious right had its vigorous opponents.

Sherwin Wine and I were thrown together again in early 1995. We worked with temple member and Southfield attorney Mark H. Cousens and others to form Clergy and Citizens United—united to oppose the Gingrichian Congress's drive to reintroduce sectarian prayer in the nation's public schools. By then I had left journalism for good and had taken a suburban pulpit.

Over the last decade or so, Wine has generously invited me to speak at several Birmingham Temple functions; the most generous invitation was to be one of three speakers at his gala seventieth birthday party in January 1998. And with that event we begin to tell the story of one of the more original thinkers of our era.

■ ■ ■

A YOUTHFUL SEPTUAGENARIAN

The traffic was backed up in both directions along Twelve Mile Road between Inkster and Middlebelt, as agitated motorists attempted to maneuver their cars into the already crowded parking lot of the Birmingham Temple. A chill rain was falling on a queue of people pressing toward the entrance of the graceful building, by then twenty-seven years old. They were coming to a dinner and service to honor Sherwin T. Wine, founding rabbi of the Humanistic congregation, on the occasion of his seventieth birthday. It would be accurate to say that but for the absence of his late parents and a few other people who had been significant in his life, all those for whom Sherwin Wine had been an organizing principle across three-and-a-half decades were present. Crowded into the temple's pleasant "family room," at round tables seating ten, nearly 400 people dined on a salad of Romaine lettuce, dried cherries, toasted pecans, and assorted vegetables; mushroom chicken *en croute*; pea pods and shredded carrots; and twenty-four-carrot cake. The meal was accompanied by a piquant Chardonnay and a robust Cabernet Sauvignon.

A visibly excited Sherwin Wine, who enjoys a superb meal as much as anyone, soon abandoned his unfinished dinner to move from table to table. In every sector of the room could be heard his ringing baritone voice: "Hi! How *are* you?" There seemed to be no face he had forgotten, no name he did not remember. And at each table there were affectionate kisses from the women and firm, prolonged handshakes from the men.

> The temple's ritual progressively dropped the Sh'ma, the Kaddish, and Torah reading—all thought to be absolutely essential to the Jewish religion and identity.

Left behind at Wine's table were his sister and brother-in-law, Lorraine and Ben Pivnick, then–gubernatorial candidate Doug Ross, Jack and Marilyn Rowens—Marilyn being a long-time Wine associate and the temple's ceremonial director—and Wine's partner of twenty years, Richard McMains.

Before long there was general movement into the "meeting room" of the temple, where most of its services and programs take place. At the center of the raised dais was the impeccably groomed rabbi, dressed in one of the dark blue suits he favors, with a muted striped necktie against a white cuff-linked shirt. The meeting room vibrated with anticipation as the musicians assembled and began to play the introduction to the first song: "Shaaloo shalom yerushalayim"—"seek the peace of Jerusalem"—which, taken from Psalm 122, would be the sole biblical allusion of the entire service. Rabbi Wine himself wrote the service. Temple board president Michael Egren spoke lovingly of the rabbi and of "how much he has always taught us about the world and philosophy." Egren's affection and esteem for Wine were evident in his carefully chosen words and in the respectful sidelong glances in Wine's direction. Wine smiled and nodded again and again. Doug Ross, who had been one of Wine's students in the former's youth at Detroit's Temple Beth El, spoke glowingly of the rabbi's facility in making concepts clear and sharp. "You couldn't help but be engaged by the young Sherwin," Ross said. "At last temple was exciting. You couldn't wait to go instead of dreading your next trip there. It was a true privilege to have had Sherwin Wine as my teacher."

This writer also offered a tribute to Wine. Excerpts from it follow:

> I was just thinking of the irony we would experience on this of all nights if Sherwin had laryngitis and could only smile and nod as the rest of us spoke. I wouldn't wish it on him for the world, but the image makes me chuckle.
>
> This is a tribute to my older brother, Sherwin Wine, because he has become that to me. I represent a world far different from the one in which most of you live and move and have your being. I am not only part of the [non-Jewish world], but from a precinct of [that world] in which reason, liberality, intellectual adventure, and risk-taking are all considered by too many and to one degree or another subversive. For a long time I was a captive of all that and from a distance broke the 10th of the great commandments and whatever number of the other 603 it is. For a long time I have looked across the wasteland of middle class Protestantism toward the Promised Land of the emerging movement of Humanist[ic]

Judaism and wondered if I could ever attain unto anything like it in my own tradition.

The bishop who ordained me, the late Richard Emrich, told our class of young initiates that we were to avoid contact with people like Unitarians, like Bishop Pike (also now of blessed memory) and the atheistic rabbi known as Sherwin Wine. "Nothing good can come of your speaking with him," the bishop said.

Sherwin Wine is without a doubt the most singularly interesting figure in the general arena of religion in this community. He has said things that most only think and dare not say, but in saying them Sherwin has made it possible for the rest of us to say them, if only in muted tones. I owe the courage I summoned to write and publish my book *Christianity Beyond Creeds* (a natural sequel to his own *Judaism Beyond God*) to Sherwin, who has been encouraging and supportive of what he calls my gradual liberation from the shackles of tradition. He has helped me say what I really think and believe. And, Sherwin, believe me when I say that you give courage to others in our line of work out there who are discovering bit by bit that they are secular humanists, too. I don't know that many of them would come to your defense publicly—such is the general pusillanimous nature of the clergy—but if they didn't have you, they would have to invent you.

Sherwin Wine is without a doubt the most singularly interesting figure in the general arena of religion in this community.

The myth-laden language of the tradition from which I spring would express it this way: "Thank God for Sherwin." I shall not say that. Rather, I shall say, I celebrate the happy confluence of genes, intellect, experience, honesty, and courage that gives you to us, Sherwin: as a mentor, visionary, and—I do not use this word lightly—a hero. Happy birthday.

THE FORMATION OF SHERWIN WINE

Sherwin Wine's roots are in modern-day Poland and Eastern Europe, where once 80 percent of all the Jews in the world lived. The Holocaust changed that forever, but not before Wine's parents, Herschel Wengrowski and Teibele Israelski, had left for America—he in 1906 and she eight years later in 1914. Wengrowski was born the second of four children in the northeast Polish shtetl of Korczyz in 1884. His grandfather was a cobbler. Herschel attended a *heder*, a one-room school house where he studied Torah in Hebrew under the tutelage of a *malamed*, or teacher. From age twelve to eighteen he worked as a cobbler's helper.

"There was nobody famous or extraordinary in my family," Rabbi Wine said. "We're pure peasant stock." Yet, Wine pointed out, "My father was a born student who loved to read and had interests in many things. What he might have become under different circumstances we can't know now, but he would have made a great teacher or scholar."

When Wengrowski was 18, Russian authorities—who governed what is now Poland—approached him for army duty, which meant in essence that he was drafted. He was assigned to a Moscow garrison led by a commander named Sergei, the brother of Alexander III. Wengrowski was placed in the honor guard at the Kremlin, where occasionally he caught a glimpse of Czar Nicholas II. But what really made a lasting impression on the young Wengrowski was seeing the virulently antisemitic Sergei in action. Wine related his father's story: "If Sergei knew you were Jewish, you got a hard time. My father saw Sergei kick a man in the stomach so hard that he died right there." Wengrowski deserted the army in 1905 after going home on leave. Crossing the border, he came to England via Bremen and to New York City via Liverpool, arriving in 1906. Part of the largest flow ever of Jewish immigrants to the United States, Wengrowski joined his uncle and two cousins, who were already established in Detroit in a cap-making business. Informed that the family name was now "Wine," Wengrowski became William Harry Wine, took up residence in a boarding house, and went to work in his uncle's cap-making factory: Wine Brothers, at Woodward and Montcalm. In time the concern switched from making caps to trousers, and Bill Wine, as he came to be known, became a trouser cutter—a job done laboriously by hand—until he died in 1948, at the age of 64.

Sherwin Wine's mother, Teibele, was born in 1897, one of nine girls in a merchant-class family in Sztabin, not too far from Korczyz, in the general area of Bialystok. The business had to do with what contemporary Americans would call wheat brokering: the concern bought wheat by the wagon load from farmers and resold it to millers. "My mother told us she had memories of a huge wheat wagon that would ply the trade route between farm and shtetl," Wine said. "The family lived in a nice house, and everybody catered to my grandfather. What can you expect with one man in a house of ten women?" Teibele—Yiddish for the German *taube*, or dove—went to school mainly to learn fundamental literacy skills. But whereas the boys were taught in Hebrew, the girls were taught in Yiddish.

For some of the same reasons Wengrowski had fled the shtetl, Teibele's father decided, in 1914, on the eve of the Great War, to send Teibele and her sister Mashke to America. They came on the maiden voyage of the *Aquatania*—"she always pronounced it 'Achvtania,'" Rabbi Wine laughed—in June 1914. Cleared through Ellis Island, Teibele, now Tillie, found a job in a millinery shop feathering hats. She and Mashke almost starved themselves on one meal a day so as to save money to bring their parents and siblings to America, a feat they accomplished in early 1920.

> "My brother was extremely bright, we could tell that early on. My mother, of course, thought he was a genius."
> —Lorraine Wine Pivnick

"Sztabin was in the middle of a war zone," Rabbi Wine said. "All hell had broken loose under German occupation, so it was a good time to get out." The plan to bring the remainder of the family to the United States was frustrated when Tillie's mother was found by Ellis Island officials to have trachoma, and she had to make a return voyage to be cured. Eventually, in 1921, she joined the rest of the family in housing that Tillie and another sister, Fanny, had found on Lenox Avenue in Harlem.

In 1923 Tillie's father visited relatives in Detroit and brought the twenty-six-year-old Tillie with him. While in Detroit at a party, Tillie Israelski met Bill Wine, who, out of his carefully saved earnings as a trouser cutter, had purchased a new two-flat upper-lower brick house at 1961 Clairmount. The following year, Bill and Tillie were married in the Bronx. They subsequently took up residence in the house on Clairmount, where their two children, Lorraine and Sherwin, were born: she in 1925, he in 1928. Tillie was to live on Clairmount until 1949, a few months after Bill's death.

Through the eyes and memory of Lorraine Wine Pivnick—twenty-eight months Sherwin's senior—a picture of the young Sherwin Wine emerges:

> My brother was extremely bright, we could tell that early on. My mother, of course, thought he was a genius. However, Sherwin didn't walk until he was eighteen months old—now, of course, he doesn't stop walking. He walks miles and miles a day, maybe that's why. My mother once took him to some pediatrician over on Second Avenue who blithely observed that Sherwin might be retarded. The joke's on him.
>
> Sherwin was always interested in what was going on. He had plenty of playmates and friends, but he never got in any trouble. But there was one day when he was about nine, and he just disappeared—for hours! When he finally came home, we asked him with some exasperation where he had been. "I walked downtown," he said. Well, downtown is several miles [away].
>
> Sherwin was clearly special. By the time he was nine years old, he had memorized the name of every capital in the world, several lists of kings of various countries, and he could tell you the popu-

lation of every major city in America. He absorbed knowledge like a sponge. There was nobody quite like him.

I never had an argument with my brother except over the use of the one bathroom in the house. Typical, I guess.

Lorraine's husband, Ben Pivnick, recalled his first significant contact with Sherwin. "I had not been raised to be particularly observant and had had a few ideas of my own over the years that could not have had much approval by traditional Jews. The first time I heard Sherwin give a sermon as the young assistant rabbi at Temple Beth El, I thought, 'My, this is different.' Sherwin talked about the God of the Bible as not being very benevolent. Seemed right to me."

Lorraine told of bouncing back and forth from Congregation Shaarey Zedek to Temple Beth El and finally to the Reform congregation Sherwin helped to build in Windsor, Ontario. "But when the Birmingham Temple was formed," she recalled, "we joined."

Ben recalled, "What Sherwin was saying was what I had believed all of my life. Most Jewish kids learned Jewish history in the traditional way. At the Birmingham Temple, we learned the real history of the Jews."

> "At the Birmingham Temple, we learned the real history of the Jews."
> —Ben Pivnick

SCHOOL DAYS

Wine recalled his earliest memories in the house on Clairmount. "The No. 22 street car ran down our street, and I was comforted by its sound. It soothed me to sleep at night. There was a vacant lot next to our house, and one of the first visual memories I have, when I was about four [years old], was of women coming to that lot to pick dandelion greens for food. That would have been at the start of the Depression."

Wine was enrolled in Detroit Public Schools in 1933, entering kindergarten at Crosman Elementary School. Unlike many young children at that time, Sherwin was fortunate to have a father with a secure job, and therefore the family had a dependable home life. He recalled:

> I learned to read and write on my own, and I loved to read the newspapers. I remember reading the headlines about Hitler and what was happening in Europe. I quizzed my parents closely about it. They didn't say much, but we did listen to some of Hitler's speeches that were broadcast on the radio. I remember vividly the first of September 1939, when the Nazis invaded Poland. How right my grandfather had been [in his dire predictions of the fate of Polish Jews]. As we know now, Polish Jewry was basically wiped out. We certainly would have had a near-certain chance to die.
>
> I learned to be a good American from unmarried WASP teachers—secular nuns who ruled their classrooms with despotic authority and could stop would-be mischief with a look. All the principal, one Miss McGregor, had to say was "Stop!" and whatever was afoot stopped immediately. It's not P.C. to say so, but I loved school. I was the smartest kid in class, so the teachers liked me and I liked my teachers. They were my American role models. My hand was always in the air to give answers, and I earned excellent grades. I did not receive them; I earned them. I learned early that you need to please the right audience. The right audience was not my peers but my teachers. Because I did not seek to please my peers, I felt a certain distance from them, although I had friends. But the stupidity of some of my peers helped me understand that they were a fickle audience. Their adulation would have meant nothing to me.
>
> It was about that time that I discovered I loved history. When I was in the third grade I made long charts of royal genealogies and memorized them. Those who asked "What's the use?" I could only pity. The librarian at Crosman locked up the nicer books in a case. There was one of them in particular I wished to read. She

was reluctant to allow me to take it, and we had quite an argument in which I prevailed.

From 1940 to 1943—the height of the war years—Sherwin attended Hutchins Junior High School, where he discovered his abilities to debate and to speak without notes. His fellow students were not, in the main, interested in the war or in other current events. "I debated a girl named Mary Power on the question of the United States' entry into the war," Wine recalled. "I defended it. She said that the only people who wanted the U.S. to get into the war were the Jews. I won the debate."

ABSORBING—AND QUESTIONING—JEWISH TRADITIONS

In those formative years, Sherwin became involved in his father's synagogue, Shaarey Zedek, which began its life as an Orthodox congregation. "I went with my father every Saturday," Sherwin recalled. "I loved and admired my father. I remember his erect posture. We walked down to 14th Street, to Chicago Boulevard, past Sacred Heart Seminary—it always seemed a mystery to me. I couldn't imagine what strange and occult things might be going on in there. It had nothing to do with my world."

Sherwin grew up under the tutelage of two of Detroit's most important rabbis of the twentieth century, Abraham Hershman and, later, Morris Adler. Hershman had led Shaarey Zedek into the Conservative movement and, being a confirmed Zionist, became involved in the controversy over Israel's impending statehood. His chief rabbinical opponent was Leo Franklin at Temple Beth El. Sherwin remembers Hershman as a true scholar, though he was neither pastoral nor a particularly good speaker. His authority, however, was untrammeled by those failings. "Hershman could silence anyone with a look," Wine remembered. "All he had to do was to stop in the middle of his sermon and a row of children or even adults would become immediately silent."

Into Hershman's comfortable world came, in 1938, a young assistant rabbi named Morris Adler, who would succeed the former in 1946 and remain rabbi of the congregation until being assassinated by a deranged gunman during Sabbath services in 1966. "Adler became my teacher," Wine said. "He was oratorical, successful, and very popular. Hershman hated him; but Adler won the day and essentially forced the board to retire Hershman so that he could succeed him." Neither Hershman nor Adler is remembered by Sherwin as engaging in theological talk. Mostly their sermons were topical in nature: secular concerns, national issues, and the like. It was a world of ideas and knowledge with the promise of attention and prominence. It was those aspects of the rabbinate that confirmed Sherwin's early predilection to become a rabbi.

During his adolescent years, Sherwin began to chafe under the ritually observant life. His home was kosher, Shabbat candles were lit, no one even thought of working on Shabbat or on the prescribed holidays. In all, Sherwin recalled, it was a good introduction to traditional Judaism—"thorough enough," he said, "for me to know what was important to being Jewish and what was not."

SUCCESS AT CENTRAL HIGH

Upon entering Central High School in 1943, Sherwin decided that he disliked household chores—anything to do with cooking and cleaning. "They seemed so menial and unproductive to me, but it was unfair not to contribute in some way to the household, so I got a job in the Detroit Public Library at the Farmer Street branch, where I became a clerk in the newspaper room. I worked four nights a week. I would often walk home—several miles—and then start my homework around 10:30 [P.M.] or so." That rhythm would become a lifelong discipline for Sherwin, as to this day he begins his serious reading late into the evening, after a long day's work.

At Central, Sherwin treated himself to four years of Latin, and he was part of the cast of Molière's *Imaginary Invalid* ("I loved the stage," Sherwin said). He continued his oratorical and debate activities, even giving several orations in Latin. In 1945, his last year at Central, Sherwin entered the *Detroit Times*' Hearst-sponsored National History Contest. Sherwin recalled that entrants were required to answer questions orally. During the contest, the topic—the Thomas Jefferson–Alexander Hamilton controversy of the late eighteenth century—was introduced, and on the spot, an essay had to be composed. Not long after, during the one day in his life that Sherwin skipped school, the *Times* called his home to inform him that he was the winner. Sherwin had chosen to absent himself from Central that day to travel to Ann Arbor to make arrangements for his matriculation at the University of Michigan in March 1946. When he arrived home late, he found an anxious family (along with reporters and photographers) waiting for him, much as they had almost nine years earlier when he had disappeared for what turned out to be his long walk downtown.

Sherwin recalled that his family blurted out the news that he had won the national contest, with no remonstrances about having skipped school.

THE UNIVERSITY YEARS

The University of Michigan opened a new world for the eighteen-year-old Wine, as he arrived on a campus filled with GIs. He roomed in Chicago House, part of the West Quadrangle dormitory. After the usual freshman-year curriculum, Wine remembered, "I discovered that I loved philosophy. Logical positivism especially [logical positivism is a twentieth-century philosophical movement holding that all meaningful statements are either analytic or conclusively verifiable, or confirmable by observation or experiment; therefore, metaphysical statements are without meaning]. I had excellent teachers, among whom I remember best Irving Kopi, a logician, Charles Stevenson, and Roy Sellars, who was born in West Branch, Michigan, if you can imagine that. Sellars was then noted for his 1917 publication *Humanistic Religion*."

> It was a world of ideas and knowledge with the promise of attention and prominence—those aspects of the rabbinate confirmed Sherwin's early predilection to become a rabbi.

Wine had a tuition scholarship at the University of Michigan, but he worked to earn money for his room and board. "I was lucky enough to get a job in the architectural library as the evening clerk," he recalled. "I had a lot of time for study." He worked a variety of jobs during his summer breaks: he sold encyclopedias, he sold merchandise at United Shirts, he worked as a camp counselor, and he was a bellhop on the SS *South America*, a cruise ship that plied the Great Lakes during the summer months. "I earned a lot of money in that job," Wine said. "People who take cruises tip well." He also joined forces with tens of thousands of other Detroiters as a laborer in Henry Ford's Dearborn industrial complex. "I worked in the tool crib in the summer of 1950," Wine said. "Carried my lunch like everybody else and got dirty. It was good money, though."

As his undergraduate days neared completion, Wine recalled that he was having "vocational stirrings," but he did not want to leave the university. "I thought I wanted to do something in the world of philosophy, perhaps getting a Ph.D. and teaching." But he felt the pull of his memories of Hershman and Adler and the lure of leadership.

"I liked what rabbis did, the public speaking, the leading of good-sized congregations. Besides, I was interested in my Jewish identity, but no longer ritually observant," Wine said. "I had become a humanist and had 'redefined' God as the embodiment of ethical ideals. Think of the most perfect human being, all that you'd want him to be, and that's what the word 'God' means."

Wine realized that no seminary that prepared and ordained rabbis would accept him as a rabbinical student if he went public with those ideas. "And then there was no way to get to be a rabbi in the Reform tradition, which was the only branch of Judaism I could have tolerated." Wine made the decision to become a rabbi, keeping his views to himself for the time being. In the fall of 1949 Wine made initial contact with Cincinnati, Ohio's Hebrew Union College, where he would eventually matriculate in September 1951.

BECOMING A RABBI

Wine's sojourn at Hebrew Union College was tolerated by him as "a necessary but inconvenient passage." He described it as "an advanced

Hebrew school. It was a congenial place to be a private humanist, and I must say that no one there influenced my thinking. I had made some intellectual decisions about matters of belief. I was a committed humanist, and yet I learned some things from some fairly interesting teachers."

Among them, Wine recalled, was Sheldon Blank, a scholar of the prophets under whose supervision Wine wrote his rabbinic thesis. Of the thesis, which Wine inscribed with appreciation to Blank, the professor wrote, "It has a lucid introduction [and] is a compact study excellently done. It is well organized, thought through [and] presented with admirable clarity. No word is wasted." Blank concluded, "I heartily recommend acceptance of this thesis."

In the thesis, entitled "Traditions Concerning the Early Relationship of Jahweh and Israel in Dateable Prophetic Writings," Wine wrote these provocative and prescient words: "Jahweh deliberately, almost unbelievably, promulgated for Israel a body of laws which he knew to be evil and conducive to death, and not life.... The intention of God seems to have been to so frighten and horrify the nation by the consequences of his new legislation, that, out of fear, Israel would come to recognize that Jahweh, and Jahweh alone, was God. This reference to divine laws given with almost perverse intention finds no parallel in any of the Pentateuchal accounts. It is singular and bizarre, but, above all, shocking."

"Think of the most perfect human being, all that you'd want him to be, and that's what the word 'God' means."

—Sherwin Wine

Reflecting on his thesis some forty years later, Wine said he didn't like the prophets very much. "I don't go for these 'thus saith the Lord' people. I'm flattered, of course, if anyone would consider me a prophet, but certainly not as a mouthpiece for a god. I speak for myself." This line of thinking led Wine into a discourse on the gods, which, he said, "are fascinating to me. My view is that some of them would be interesting as cocktail party guests. Jahweh, though, would be a crashing bore. All that sound and fury." Wine thinks few deities have been successfully marketed. "I would make a fine career development consultant for deities that really want to make it."

Two other Hebrew Union luminaries are remembered by Wine with a mixture of appreciation and contempt. Julius Levy, a scholar of the languages of Babylonian times, was exacting, "an arrogant son of a bitch," Wine said. "He was as Teutonic as they came. He served the Kaiser (Wilhelm) during World War I. He was stunningly brilliant and very abrasive." Israel Bettan, a professor of midrash, "really knew his field. You were sure in his class that you were getting good method and content." As for the rest? "They were quite mediocre."

Wine recalled that the majority of rabbinic students at Hebrew Union in the mid-1950s "would go on to become adequate and very unexciting rabbis in comfortable congregations where boredom would pass for peace and contentment. But there were nine or ten of us who were a faction going in other directions. We were what you might call 'low church,' and took what we needed and let the rest go."

The required fieldwork rabbinic students undertook were adventures for Wine, as he conducted services for small congregations in such unlikely places as Hopkinsville, Kentucky; Jonesboro, Arkansas; and Parkersburg, West Virginia. "Those people were largely merchants, lawyers, and doctors descended from the ante- and postbellum peddler class, which flourished before the rise of [the] modern South."

Even though Wine had the common draft exemption of a theological student, Hebrew Union wanted its graduates to serve stints as military chaplains, and Wine saw it as a duty. By the time Wine had completed his five-year rabbinic degree, the Korean war had been over for three years, and the Vietnam war was only in gestation, not to be fully born until eight or nine years later. "The army didn't want me then, so it would be six months before my induction," Wine recalled. Those six months were spent as associate rabbi at the Reform congregation known as Temple Beth El, then located in Detroit on Woodward Avenue at Gladstone. "Richard

Hertz [Beth El's senior rabbi at the time] called me to ask if I would fill in for him for the summer [of 1956] because he was going to Israel. So I went. After one month, the board invited me to become the associate rabbi with no consultation whatsoever with Hertz. I accepted in part because of concern for my mother, a widow of almost ten years at that time. I was caring for her, and the salary would help. Hertz came back to a fait accompli, which didn't help matters any. And I soon discovered that I was not disposed to be anybody's assistant."

Those six months at Beth El would turn out to be of import to Wine's future as he developed, some seven years later, an entity that became known as Humanistic Judaism. Though he might have thought himself somewhat alone in beginning a final disaffection with the language and concepts of Reform Judaism, some younger members of Beth El were likewise growing impatient with patent, sterile tradition. But Wine's initial stint at Beth El came midway in the quiescent 1950s, still in the Eisenhower years, and the breakout era of the 1960s—helped by the election of a forty-three-year-old president in November 1960—had yet to make itself known. So in January 1957, Sherwin Wine, then twenty-nine years old, became First Lieutenant Sherwin Wine who, as he himself proclaimed, "looked good in uniform."

> "Some of the gods would be interesting as cocktail party guests. Jahweh, though, would be a crashing bore. All that sound and fury."
>
> —Sherwin Wine

THE KOREAN INTERVAL

As the winter of 1957 got into full bore, Wine found himself at Fort Slocum, near New York City, where he obtained his chaplaincy training. "It was there I had my first real introduction to 'the clergy,'" Wine remembered. "And I must say it was a disappointment. I despised the dim intellects and banal ambitions of those people and knew I could never bear to really be considered one of them. I could never be so numbingly conventional." By March, Wine was on his way to Korea, where thousands of U.S. troops were still stationed to enforce the Panmunjom truce so tentatively reached almost four years earlier. "This was my first trip anywhere outside the world of Detroit, Ann Arbor, and Cincinnati," Wine recalled. "I'd never been outside of North America. I was excited to see another part of the world."

Wine's transport had a layover in Oahu, so in the spirit of adventure that would come to mark his extensive travels later in life, he took a taxi ride around Oahu. "I absolutely loved it, but when I came back to the [air] base, my plane had taken off. That, of course, was an offense for which I could have been court-martialed. But when I presented myself contrite before the chief of chaplains, he said to me, 'Well, that wasn't very nice.' Never heard another word about it."

Wine was assigned to the Thirteenth Combat Engineering Battalion of the Seventh Infantry Division. Upon arrival in Seoul, among the first things he saw was a green Quonset hut. "There was smoke pouring out of it, and a Korean woman ran from its door screaming. Inside is this man in a yarmulke wearing no shirt. He is koshering dishes for Passover with white-hot rocks boiling a basin of water. The woman probably thought he was a medicine man." The shirtless yarmulke-topped man turned out to be an Orthodox rabbi-chaplain whose name, Wine recalled, was Norman. "I learned soon that Norman's favorite pastime was to play poker with the GIs and beat them. I told him, 'Norman, I don't think beating the boys at poker is what Jewish mothers think should be happening here.'"

The rabbi-chaplain Wine was sent to relieve "was some guy who had spent most of his tour of duty writing a book. He turned out to be the novelist Chaim Potok," Wine said. "When it was time for us to report to the commanding officer for the official transfer, Potok came out and jumped into the front seat of the Jeep where I had been riding. He looked at me patronizingly and said, 'I out-rank you.' I've always resented buying anything he wrote." No common man himself, Wine recalled really liking the regular army people, admiring their pride in their profession. "But I couldn't abide the whiners and complainers among the draftees."

Wine looks back on his nearly two years in Korea as a lark. "I had an incredibly wonderful time. I had two goals: one, to see every Jewish boy in Korea; and two, to see Korea itself." Thus did the twenty-nine-year-old newly minted first lieutenant set out, in the methodic way that would mark all his future work, to identify where Jewish solders were all along the Korean peninsula and to visit them. "That took me down impossible roads, up mountains in Jeeps that might deliberately have been built without shock absorbers." He knew his business: he obtained from one startled quartermaster after another cases of canned chicken soup for distribution to his charges. "It was inedible," Wine said, "but it was home and therefore welcome."

In ways that would be fleshed out in his later rabbinic career, Wine's work as a chaplain had more to do with Jewish culture than Jewish religion. "The boys came not to pray but to talk—and for the chicken soup. Their Jewish identity was important to them in that strange place. I was a connection." Displaying the otherworldly energy at which anyone who knows him cannot help but marvel, Wine went to great lengths to provide Jewish soldiers with that other cultural staple: kosher salami. "I wrote to the ladies of Beth El and asked for kosher salamis. I went to the quartermaster general and talked him into a massive shipment of salamis. I was the 'Salami King,' and my popularity shot up. Everywhere I went—by helicopter, Jeep, on foot—I was bulging with kosher salamis. On one occasion I was on foot with salamis in both hands. I tripped while jumping a ditch and sustained a broken wrist. I refused to let go [of] the salamis and so landed on my wrist. I was operated on in MASH-like conditions and during the operation, of course, the lights went out."

Displaying the otherworldly energy at which anyone who knows him cannot help but marvel, Wine went to great lengths to provide Jewish soldiers with that cultural staple: kosher salami.

Wine recalled that his main ministerial function was to promote what today might be called character-building. The peer influences and pressures of life in the military upon barely post-adolescent men, living in close quarters in places far from home, present a chaplain with plenty to do. "I didn't do the traditional thing, as you might expect," Wine said. "I did a kind of intellectually based series of lectures at the lowest common denominator, lectures on subjects of interest and concern to the troops. I think some of them became pretty interested in a chaplain who was caring about some of the not-necessarily-religious matters they were caring about. I had appreciative audiences."

Of course, Wine did conduct religious services for Jewish soldiers, and he recalls that they were well-attended. "It was like the chicken soup and the salami," he said, "reminders of the comforts of home. Of course, it helped that such persons of note as Richard Tucker would show up from time to time." Tucker was a renowned Metropolitan Opera tenor at that time. "He came in June of 1958 and was my cantor for a Shabbat service. So the boys had Tucker for the music and Wine for the words. They never had it better, and some of them never would."

First Lieutenant Wine did not hesitate to speak up to his military superiors when he thought it was called for. "Bob Hope and Jayne Mansfield came in Christmas of 1957. The troops were ordered to sit in this unheated outdoor amphitheater while Hope rehearsed his jokes. The guys were freezing. Finally, I insisted that the men be released. They were." Evidently the brass were impressed with Wine, for at the end of his hitch he received an award. "I enjoyed my time as a chaplain and learned a lot about dealing with people who believe you are an authority figure. You can't ever forget or permit them to forget that you are the boss. You do it with a smile and make them like it."

Wine took a thirty-day leave just before his tour of duty was over. "I grew up barely getting away from home. The farthest I ever got was Wyandotte, where we had relatives, and Ann Arbor, where I went to college, and, of course, Cincinnati. So since I was in Asia, I wanted to see all I could in a month." He traveled to Vietnam; Bangkok, Thailand; New Delhi, India; and Hong Kong—none of them for the last time. "That's when I knew I would always have to travel and see all I could. Until then, the idea of Sabbath had not really made sense to me. Then I saw that Sabbath could mean nothing as a day. I wanted a week, a month, to see and absorb and learn." Since Korea, Wine has taken an annual month-long sabbatical—usually in July—and he has traveled to all the continents, save Antartica.

BACK TO BETH EL, AND BEYOND

In November 1958 Rabbi Wine returned to Temple Beth El, where he would remain for the next nineteen months. He recalls growing less and less comfortable with the language and way of Reform Judaism. Besides, he said, "Being an assistant to somebody was not my cup of tea. I am not disposed to it. I couldn't be creative without being in charge." His relationship with Rabbi Hertz was not an easy one. It was during this period that Wine made a decision that would affect the rest of his life and the whole of Detroit-area Jewry.

In the autumn of 1959, a group of Jews in Windsor, Ontario—across the river from Detroit—decided to organize a Reform congregation. Its leaders contacted Detroit's Temple Beth El. Aware of this, Wine contacted them, and soon enough he became their rabbi. Remembered by former congregant Miriam Jerris, now a member of the Birmingham Temple and one of its newer rabbis, Wine "had a magnetic appearance and demeanor. He was young and vibrant with a really wicked sense of humor. I was only eleven when he came, but he taught me right away that we could laugh in synagogue. It was what we now call a 'paradigm shift'; Judaism could be joyful."

"I saw that Sabbath could mean nothing as a day. I wanted a week, a month, to see and absorb and learn."
—Sherwin Wine

Soon enough, with Wine's contagious enthusiasm and energy driving its members, the Windsor synagogue put up its own building; Wine, Jerris recalled, "reproduced the Detroit Temple Beth El with his own twist." It would be another decade before Jerris reconnected with Wine at the Birmingham Temple.

It was during his Windsor sojourn that Wine made the decision to stick with the rabbinate but, at the same time, to do it his own way. "I had a sense that whatever I did, I wanted to do my thing here in the Detroit area. I thought I might pursue doctoral studies at the University of Michigan, but the politics of academe didn't much interest me. Teaching in the long run wouldn't have fit with the intensity with which I work. I wanted my own platform, my own venue," Wine said.

He came to conclude by 1962 that the Reform movement was not for him. "How could I be a rabbi? I didn't believe in God. Could I pretend to believe in God? No." At about this time a couple from the suburban-Detroit community of Oak Park, Sue and Harry Velick, phoned Wine; they asked him to talk to them and others about organizing a temple out of a splinter group from Beth El whose members were disenchanted with Rabbi Hertz's leadership. Sue Velick was taken with the young Wine's charisma and none too happy with what she perceived as Hertz's lack of it. "Hertz wasn't speaking to young people's needs. He was interested more in impressing the outside world. We thought him insincere, and, compared to Sherwin, he [Hertz] was a lackluster speaker," she said.

Her husband Harry said that part of what moved him to leave Beth El was the reality that most of its congregation had moved to the northwestern Detroit suburbs but that the Beth El leadership showed no inclination to follow. "It's when they repaved the parking lot—the straw that broke the whole back—that we decided it was enough."

The Velicks were designated by the splinter group to contact Wine for advice in founding a new community. The group met in the Birmingham home of Lois and Richard Lurie on August 21, 1963. Sue Velick said that, as it turned out, "There were more than just Beth El dropouts there. Some were unaffiliated. Some simply wanted Beth El to move. But a core wanted something new, unaffiliated with Beth El, Hertz, and the old system." The people in the group began by thinking that they wanted a Reform congregation. "We didn't know anything else. When Sherwin finally got involved with us, we were on a new road," Harry Velick recalled. "I had no idea where we were going, but I loved the road. It was a great time, a great time. Very invigorating."

Along for the ride came Lorraine and Ben Pivnick. "We joined the temple in Windsor when Sherwin went there, and when the new thing got going, we became a part of that, too," Lorraine Pivnick said. "And for the first time in [his] life, my husband was at home." "It was what I had believed all my life," Ben Pivnick said, "a welcome awakening."

The core group of what became the Birmingham Temple included Sue and Harry Velick, Doreen and Stuart Velick, Bunny and Merrill Miller, Elaine and Steve Fish, Baily and Gil Franklin, Lisa and Joel Hepner, Marge and Bill Sandy, and Mary Ann and Ted Simon.

These eight families discussed with Rabbi Wine what they wanted to come out of this new organization. All wanted something fresh. Everything at the new organization should be subject to inquiry or question. In contrast to Beth El, where there were simply certain questions that were not asked (and were not answered if asked), the new community would offer information.

At first they had little idea of becoming anything other than a small Reform congregation, one small enough so that every member could be involved in some way. The first service was on September 15, 1963, at the Eagle Elementary School in Farmington Hills, Michigan. It would be another year before the congregation actually got organized. And those in the forefront of the effort were determined to make the new entity a free and open one. Harry Velick remembered of those early discussions: "It was no longer to be what was *geschrieben*"—written by the ancients or some enforced tradition—"it was to be what *we* wrote." A Ritual Committee was put in place to look over the services Wine composed. "Sometimes a single word took on great significance," Sue Velick said, as the committee's members carefully savored their new freedom. Eventually "God" became one of those "single words," and soon enough, the congregation that would become the Birmingham Temple rationalized that word out of its collective vocabulary.

Presently, all Detroit Jewry was by the ears. In their very midst was a rabbi and his fledgling congregation that had eliminated "God" from their Sabbath services. Outrage was the common reaction. Rabbis of more venerable congregations insisted that Wine retract and retreat. The answer was, "Nothing doing." That, of course, put members of the new congregation on the defensive, trying to explain to family, friends, and neighbors a Judaism that was moving beyond God. Not helping matters was a December 1964 article in the *Detroit Free Press* quoting Wine saying that he was an atheist. The wire services picked it up, and the fat was in the fire.

Wine and his new congregants responded with a statement defending their philosophical choices as based on the "empirical method in the discovery of essential truth," hoping, the statement said, "to preserve whatever in Judaism is both rational and humanistic." National television personality Mike Douglas got into the act, as did *Time* magazine. Eventually Episcopal Bishop Richard S. Emrich chimed in; in his regular Sunday column in the *Detroit News* Emrich took issue with Wine for abandoning tradition and causing a ruckus. The controversy lost the congregation its temporary rental arrangement with the Birmingham Masonic Temple. The Masonic Temple evicted the congregation because, as the officials said, "Masons believe in God."

In due course, the congregation purchased land on West Twelve Mile Road between Inkster and Middlebelt in the Detroit suburb of Farmington Hills. The building was completed in 1971 and remains at that site today. In the mid-1990s, the Pivnick Center for Humanistic Judaism was added to the south side of the original building.

THE WORLD DISCOVERS SECULAR HUMANISTIC JUDAISM

Marilyn Rowens, a longtime Sherwin Wine associate, has said, on the basis of her thirty-eight-year acquaintance with him and his philosophy, that Wine's "struggle" to make Secular Humanistic Judaism what it is today "was really his pleasure. He had the breadth of vision to see the disparate parts of what is now called 'secular humanism' and found how it beautifully expressed the traditions of Judaism. You could say he 'invented' it or 'discovered' it, but it's probably more accurate to say that, once he saw it as a piece, he named it."

Though Wine takes a dim view of the Hebrew prophets of the eighth and sixth centuries B.C.E. for their "unbearable kvetching and scolding," his forty-year initiative to realize the potential of secular humanism had made him a prophet himself—if what prophets do is to "name" what their rare gifts of perception and their ability to synthesize disclose to them as truth and reality. His early work with those who became the core of the Birmingham Temple was part of that naming process. It was less a deconstruction of Reform Judaism than it was a judicious assembly of pieces of tradition and innovation; this small group of people tried, through the building of a ritual and social tradition, to see what Wine had been seeing in ever-greater fullness since his days at the University of Michigan and Hebrew Union College. And once the temple was up and going, its activities were reported in the press. Once that happened, the secular humanism being lived out in the early days of the Birmingham Temple caught the attention of the nation and then the world.

It was that 1964 *Detroit Free Press* story about the "atheist rabbi" that began it all, according to Wine. *Time* magazine's February 1965 mention of Wine and his new brand of religion brought him a letter from world-renowned English biologist and humanist Julian Huxley and, in a single month, 300 more letters, of which more than half were favorable. "I answered every letter," Wine said, "even the nasty ones." The temple formed the Committee for Humanistic Judaism and arranged for Wine and others to speak to inquirers. Wine himself was invited, he recalled, to participate in speaking series in major cities across the country. He remembers an engagement in St. Louis, Missouri, to which more than 700 people came. "Some were antagonists, of course," Wine remembered, "heckling and shouting at me." But evidently Wine believed in the adage that there is no such thing as bad publicity.

> "How could I be a rabbi? I didn't believe in God. Could I pretend to believe in God? No."
>
> —Sherwin Wine

"Everywhere I spoke, I got people to sign in, to give us names and addresses so we could begin a national network," Wine said.

The message was spread in other ways, too. John Franklin, who had been one of the original members of the temple, moved to Westport, Connecticut, and soon enough Wine was invited there to speak. Out of that speaking engagement came a new congregation. Franklin was a grandson of one of Detroit's most notable Reform rabbis, Leo Franklin, who headed Temple Beth El for most of the first half of the twentieth century.

In 1967 Wine convened seven rabbis of a more or less like mind to discuss the formation of a national movement. "We met at my sister Lorraine's home in suburban Detroit," Wine recalled, "on Sunday, July 23. That was the day the riot began—about a block from my boyhood home!—and there we were debating about theology, and the city of my birth was burning down!" One of those present on July 23 was Rabbi Dan Friedman, who headed a Reform congregation in the Chicago suburb of Deerfield. Within two years, he had converted it into the third congregation of Humanistic Judaism in America.

With his own Birmingham Temple firmly established and on its way to putting up what would become its permanent headquarters, Wine felt it was time to spread out. In 1969 he organized, in cooperation with the late Robert Marshall, the minister of Birmingham Unitarian Church, a conference on humanistic ethics; it was held on the campus of Oakland University in the Detroit suburb of Rochester Hills. While it was not, Wine said, "a Jewish event," it certainly attracted a good many inquiring Jews to a program that included Joan Baez, Paul Goodman, and Albert Ellis. More than 600 people attended, and so the gospel of secular humanism—Jewish, Christian, and non-sectarian—was being spread. That same year, the three Humanistic Jewish congregations—the Birmingham Temple and the congregations in Westport, Connecticut, and Deerfield, Illinois—came together to found the Society for Humanistic Judaism. And in June 1970, more than 150 delegates came to the society's first meeting, held at what was then known as Stouffer's Inn Northland.

The movement of Secular Humanistic Judaism emerged from the vortex of the Americanization of an enlightened European social Judaism and a Yiddish kind of nationalism that flourished in a free and open country. It was helped along by the presence of the German Jewish Ethical Culture movement that held fast at least until World War II. The extraordinary efforts of Mordecai Kaplan and his Reconstructionist Judaism, in which the forms were maintained as skeletal framework for an entirely different kind of ideological tissue, would collapse from the movement's own philosophical weight.

What Kaplan did not understand that Wine and his followers did was that American Jews were secularized by the very fact of their living in America, in a polyglot culture that, at its best, embraced diversity. The phenomenon of the public school and the philosophically free public square was helping some Jews understand that their Jewishness was a matter of culture rather than religion. Or, as Wine said in his book *Humanistic Judaism*, "Judaism must be affirmed as a cultural and aesthetic framework in which a variety of philosophic outlooks are possible.... Jewish custom and ceremony are an adjustable poetry, capable of embracing a wide spectrum of human values and experiences." Wine could be hard-nosed, too, as in this statement: "There are no 'eternal truths.' Rational people live with temporary judgments and the possibility of surprise."

American Jews were secularized by the very fact of their living in America, in a polyglot culture that, at its best, embraced diversity.

The Secular Humanistic Jewish movement radiates out from the Birmingham Temple to include the International Federation of Secular Humanistic Jews, the Society for Humanistic Judaism, and the International Institute for Secular Humanistic Judaism. A veritable "who's who" of world Jewry testifies to the reach of the movement. To name just a few: Yehuda Bauer, Yaakov Malkin, and Ruth Calderon in Israel; Felix Posen in Britain; Albert Memmi in France; Semyon Avgustevich in Russia; Egon Friedler in Latin America; and David Susskind in Belgium.

Wine summed up his role in the movement this way: "While in the beginning I couldn't envision all that is now, I had no idea that I would not succeed. And it's not as if it's been easy[;] I was not surprised by the hostility I encountered, though I did not cultivate it. In fact, I enjoyed the challenge. There were, of course, surprises along the way. People can be very ambivalent. They respond to the intellectual thing, but tradition hangs over them. They love what you say, but are sometimes unprepared to cross the bridge all the way." Enough people have crossed the bridge that today Secular Humanistic Judaism is a recognized and respected alternative to the more traditional branches of Judaism. It is a movement still in the making, but for as long as memory lasts and history is passed down from one generation to another, Sherwin T. Wine will be known as the one who named the emerging movement and gave it its most public face.

■ ■ ■

DAY-TO-DAY WITH THE RABBI

The old saw concerning the rabbi who slept late cannot in any way be applied to Sherwin Wine, who is an early riser in every time zone. He subsists nicely, he says, on five hours of sleep a night. His nineteen-hour days are tightly packed with work, study, and occasionally even recreation. This is a man with the rare combination of a long, intense attention span and a born restlessness. He can keep two or three secretaries busy to the point of exhaustion.

Here is a typical day:

He arises—going from zero to sixty in about ten seconds—at 5 A.M., having not put head to pillow before midnight. After a brief look at the headlines, he leaves his suburban Detroit condominium for what, except in the weeks nearest the summer solstice, is a brisk pre-dawn walk of several miles. This discipline is unbreakable. By 7 A.M., having showered and dressed, he is at his regular corner table in the dining room of Birmingham's Townsend Hotel where, if uninterrupted, he will spend the next two hours reading the *New York Times* and whatever book is on his mind. He eats a sparing breakfast of bran cereal, fresh fruit, and skim milk, punctuated with several cups of lemon-flavored hot water.

Because he is so well known, Wine may be interrupted by other guests who stop at his table to congratulate him on a recent lecture or public speech he has given. On one morning, a U.S. Congressman and a university president paused to greet him.

By 9 A.M., Wine is on his way to a morning lecture at his Center for New Thinking or to one or another of the groups for whom he regularly speaks, reviews books, or explores topics as wide-ranging as "Great Cities of the World," "Historical Fiction," or "Political Trends in an Election Year." He may drive as far east as the Detroit suburb of Mt. Clemens or as far west as Plymouth, Michigan, to speak. He is never unprepared, though he may have read the book he will review that afternoon over breakfast that morning. His decades of omnivorous reading and encyclopedic knowledge leave him at all times generally prepared to deal with hundreds of topics. Over breakfast, he will have covered one side and part of another of a four-by-six-inch index card with brief notes in his distinctive ink-pen script; such reminders are sufficient to carry him nonstop through an eighty-minute lecture. He will use no lectern and will seldom refer to his note card. He will pace the breadth of the platform back and forth, always in motion, keeping constant eye contact with his rapt audience.

> This is a man with the rare combination of a long, intense attention span and a born restlessness. He can keep two or three secretaries busy to the point of exhaustion.

By noon, after having chatted briefly with well-wishers, he is off to a luncheon engagement with a temple board member, a friend, or an acquaintance—almost always with an agenda to be discussed, a task to be accomplished.

Keeping fit not only by his long, brisk walks but also by eschewing entrees and desserts, he will order a spartan lunch, perhaps a vegetarian sandwich on round pumpernickel. "And this is important," he admonishes the server: "No Russian dressing!" That and several cups of black coffee will sustain him through an animated luncheon conversation and an afternoon of work.

By 2 P.M., he will be at his desk at the temple, reading his mail and responding to it. He will return accumulated calls, take incoming calls, and keep a series of appointments. Each person who receives an allotment of precious minutes of the rabbi's work day will come away with the indelible impression that he or she has had Wine's undivided attention.

On certain days, by 3:30 P.M., Wine is teaching a class of aspiring humanistic rabbis, working his way through historical and literary Judaica. "We [the Secular Humanistic Jewish movement] are training our own rabbis," Wine says. "We can't trust anybody else to do it."

Depending on what awaits him in the coming evening, Wine may return to his office for more appointments—for example, with couples preparing for marriage or with people seeking his advice and counsel—and for the return of the telephone calls that have accumulated throughout the afternoon on stacks of pink memo slips. If his evening plans include a lecture or some other congregational event at the temple, or perhaps a lecture elsewhere, he will repair to a nearby restaurant where he will dine alone, examining a book to be reviewed that night or perusing his notes for a talk.

On some nights, he will meet his partner of twenty-five years, Richard McMains, for a 10 P.M. dinner at a Birmingham restaurant near their home. Returning to the house he left some sixteen hours earlier, Wine will relax momentarily and then go into his study for an hour or two of reading before bed at midnight or later.

This routine plays out nearly seven days a week, varied by an occasional movie or concert with Richard. Saturday evenings and Sunday afternoons are likely to be booked with weddings or bar and bat mitsva events.

Wine says he can't imagine life otherwise. "There is a lot to do," he states, "and I do not get it done by just thinking about it." The fact is that for a man in his mid-seventies, he thrives on his long workdays. Few congregants have ever found him inaccessible. Few groups have found him unwilling to speak to them. Few rational, liberal causes have found him unavailable. He is as ubiquitous as he is brilliant, as visible as he is articulate, as well-informed as he is a pleasure to hear.

Does the rabbi ever vacation? Wine has turned over some duties to his associate rabbis, Tamara Kolton and Adam Chalom, freeing the acknowledged leader and guru of Humanistic Judaism to travel several weekends (and sometimes for longer periods) to other U.S. cities as well as to Europe and Israel to visit congregations and centers of Humanistic Judaism. A lover of travel, Wine probably derives vacation-like pleasures from such sojourns, but he makes it clear that he is working.

Real vacation comes twice a year: one break from the beginning of July through the first week of August and another at year's end. Over many years, Sherwin (and, for the last twenty-five years, Richard) has visited virtually every region of the globe: sight-seeing and investigating, absorbing facts, textures, colors, and moods of peoples, nations, and tongues. He will speak of their travels upon the fabled Silk Road, or to Timbuktu, or to the ancient haunts of Genghis Khan.

Predictably, Wine does not keep his accumulated knowledge and impressions to himself. Where he has been and what he has done during a summer vacation will find its way into his lectures the following autumn and winter. And such talks will not be travelogues, but rather dynamic expositions and penetrating analyses of culture, politics, and economics.

Sherwin has visited virtually every region of the globe: sight-seeing and investigating, absorbing facts, textures, colors, and moods of peoples, nations, and tongues.

The New Year's break may find Sherwin and Richard sampling the theater in London, opera in Verona, café life in Paris, or—Wine's favorite—the finest fruits of the Renaissance in Florence, the place he considers his own cultural fatherland. Ask Richard about these so-called vacations, and he will tell you that the rabbi "works at them the way he does everything else." Wine will rise as early in Florence as he does at home. He will walk twenty miles one day to take in as much as can be seen, and then he will do it all again the next day and the day after. Will he collapse on the flight home? No. He will be preparing for a lecture he will give that very evening when anyone else would be nursing jet lag.

Wine says he is anxious to "do some real writing before I die," and so wants to turn over more and more of the temple's work to Rabbis Kolton and Chalom and other younger rabbis. He says he wants to devote more time to the International Institute for Secular Humanistic Judaism, which will, of course, entail more travel.

Wine once said that ever since he was a child he dreamed of living in a hotel, coming down each morning for breakfast and going on about his business and pleasure until late at night. Some would say he has, at least in a basic sense, fulfilled that dream.

SHERWIN WINE: NEIGHBOR, FRIEND, COUNSELOR, TRAVEL GUIDE

Bill Ernst and his family came to Detroit as Jewish refugees from Germany in 1939. They moved into a rented flat in the 1900 block of Clairmount. Ernst recalled that the neighbors across the way—Bill and Tillie Wine—were considered "royalty" because they owned their home "in among a whole bunch of renters." But what caught Ernst's attention was a boy at the Wine house who was about his own age, eleven years old. "He was an adult already, he was observant and very studious. You'd think other kids would have made fun of him. But nobody did. He was so serious. You knew he would grow up to be something, somebody." Many years later, Ernst became a member of the Birmingham Temple. "Sherwin still amazes me," Ernst said. "He surprises me almost every time I hear him talk. All we saw in those days back on Clairmount came out in the wash. I'm glad we moved in there when we did."

Harriet Maza connected with Wine after he had become the rabbi of the Birmingham Temple. In Wine, Maza found the guru who would be her life's guide. "Everything I felt inside me and couldn't organize in thoughts or words, he articulated so clearly," Maza said. "After hearing Sherwin speak for the first time, I said to myself, 'I've come home.'" She remembers Wine's sessions on ethical dilemmas. He provided no answers to these dilemmas but pushed and prodded participants to arrive at their own conclusions, based not on some ancient code but on what would best resonate with humanistic values. "He sure knew how to press the right buttons on each person," Maza recalled.

Maza said that her parents were atheists from Odessa, and she was raised "as you might imagine. That was all right, but here I was in the 1960s, a recent University of Michigan graduate, lost in Detroit and looking for something to help me express the beliefs I couldn't articulate. Sherwin validated me as I was, and helped me become what I am," Maza said.

As one who became deeply involved in the temple's educational programs, she saw firsthand Wine's effect upon children and youths. "I remember there was this one kid who was about to become [a] bar mitsva. He told Sherwin that he was afraid he would faint when he stood up to speak. Sherwin looked him straight in the eye and said, 'I forbid you to do that.' From anybody else, it would have sounded unfeeling and cruel. From Sherwin, it was just a stage direction, and the young man performed beautifully. Sherwin makes it very clear what expectations he has for you, and no one wants to disappoint him or fail to measure up."

Wine provided no answers to ethical dilemmas but prodded participants to arrive at their own conclusions, based not on some ancient code but on what would best resonate with humanistic values.

Wine's approach to dealing with children was not a "pat-them-on-the-head" patronizing one, Maza recalled. "He was never on the defensive. I remember one of the children's classes lay in wait for him on a question they hoped to stump him on. The question was, 'Why don't you keep kosher?' Sherwin turned it back on them and said, 'What do you mean? I eat healthy foods and in moderation.

What do you mean I don't keep kosher?' He said all that not at all in an angry or defensive way, and he helped the children see what being kosher really means and does for people who pay attention to what they eat."

Suzanne Paul, a Unitarian minister whose husband Charles Paul is a longtime member of the temple, was once Wine's secretary. She speaks of his extraordinary mental acuity and memory. She remembers having lost a letter written in Wine's own hand that she was to type and mail. She feared Wine would be angry with her, "but he simply sat down and, after several days had passed since I misplaced the original, wrote the entire letter over again verbatim." Suzanne and Charles were married by Wine, and they recalled with amusement and pleasure how he defused their angst over their parents' objections to a mixed marriage. "Sherwin merely said to us that our parents' feelings were their problem, not ours, and that we should get on with it," Charles said. "Boy, did that free us up and help us see the way. That's what Sherwin does for people."

Wine would be the first to say that there is no such thing as magic power, and that rabbis or clergy of any kind cannot be said to have such powers. But how would he account for the following incident, which is etched so deeply into the memory of so many longtime temple members? The father of a temple member became gravely ill while visiting family in the Detroit area. He was taken to Henry Ford Hospital, where the consensus among the physicians was that he had little time to live. Wine had heard about the hospitalization but had not been asked to visit; nevertheless, he appeared in the hospital room. His presence was enormously comforting to the man's family. Wine spoke with the sick man, and, according to witnesses, had the same kind of impact on him as he had had on the young man who threatened to faint during his bar mitsva ceremony. The man recovered. How dare he die? His family was amazed and, of course, immensely relieved. The physicians were baffled.

Longtime Wine associate Marilyn Rowens said that Wine has that kind of effect on all kinds of people in all kinds of situations. She recalled many stricken families coming to Wine's study at the temple to plan a funeral. "It isn't five minutes, and we hear laughter from in there as Sherwin gets people to tell the stories that are oftentimes funny as well as endearing. He has that way with people, and when they leave, they are smiling again and ready for what is ahead of them. People just love him for that. He doesn't make light of death, doesn't tell people death doesn't matter. He tells them it *does* matter because life matters. It's all we have. No lovely hereafters."

Rowens told of the many people who wait sometimes weeks, until Wine has returned from a trip or vacation, to have a loved one's funeral. "People want his presence and his way of dealing with it." She said Wine does not hesitate to offer himself for comfort and counsel. "This member's mother was dying in Florida. Sherwin heard about it and called [the member] and said, 'I can be down there by this afternoon. Do you want me to come?' He meant it, and he would have done it in a minute if she would have let him."

It was that kind of charisma that attracted Hank Gluckman to the Birmingham Temple in its early years and has kept him there ever since. "We were going to Temple Israel, and we really didn't like it. They weren't answering the questions we were asking, that most people of our age were asking. When we first heard Sherwin, we realized that we were in the right place at the right time. When [the service] was over, I turned to my wife and said, 'Yeah, this is it.' And we didn't miss a Friday night for ten years. It wasn't that we agreed with Sherwin. He agreed with us. He didn't make us feel like a bunch of dumb kids down at the shul; he spoke to us as equals, and he was speaking to us where we were."

> "Sherwin doesn't make light of death, doesn't tell people death doesn't matter. He tells them it *does* matter because life matters. It's all we have. No lovely hereafters."
> —Marilyn Rowens

As with many among Detroit-area Jews who cast their lot with Wine and the new temple, Gluckman lost friends. "Oh, yeah, it was costly to friendships, especially after Sherwin declared himself an atheist. To most people, atheism and Judaism just don't mix. Then there was the night Sherwin said what we were was humanist[ic] Jews, and he retired the Torah. No one could say 'No' to him. He changed the whole direction of our lives, right to this day. He is approachable, unlike typical clergy. He's one of the family. Sherwin is sunshine." Gluckman was the third president of the temple's board, and nearly forty years later he is as enthusiastic about the movement as ever.

Michael Egren, also a past president of the temple's board, thinks of Wine primarily as a teacher. "I know so much more about the world outside America just because I've listened to Sherwin's lectures over the years and traveled with him," he said. "I remember a trip I went on with him to Paris. He took us to the place where Dreyfus was tried. He made it come alive for us. It was like we were there and, through him, heard the voices of history."

Egren said Wine is indefatigable on trips. "Like the TV detective Colombo, he always wanted us to see 'one more thing.' It's like he's in all those places all his life. He knows Paris and Florence and Brussels and Amsterdam like he grew up in them. And the history! I feel like I know so much I could never have learned in a classroom."

Maza said Wine knows all the "really good places. Toward the end of the afternoon when he can see his group slowing down, he'll say, 'Let's just go down this one more street to see …' whatever, and then he'll say, 'There's a wonderful little pastry shop right there.' It would spur us on, and, of course, there was the pastry shop." Wine calls that method of travel "homework then dessert." "I should only run a travel agency," Wine once said. Many who have traveled with him consider him, as one devotee put it, "a university on the go."

■ ■ ■

JUDAISM BEYOND GOD

In 1985 Sherwin Wine finally got around to a systemization, a synthesis, of the ideas that had been floating about in the emerging Humanistic Judaism movement, ideas the Birmingham Temple had been exploring since its inception. While it is fair to say that Wine articulated and shaped the ideas, it is just as fair to say that they were generated not only by him but by those of his inner circle who found philosophical freedom in what Wine helped them put into words and practice.

Judaism Beyond God is Wine's 289-page manifesto. In its pages the tradition-bent Jew will find everything he abhors and fears most. In it, Wine jettisons God—in particular, Jahweh—for good. In it, Wine calls for and makes possible the rationalization of Judaism and the sweeping away of traditions that no longer have meaning to the contemporary Jew. In it, Wine fully embraces the ambiguity of agnosticism and demonstrates the courage necessary to accept not knowing in the place of unsupportable declarations of faith. In it, Wine sets forth the principles—both theoretical and practical—of Humanistic Judaism.

Disdainful of reverence for the unseen, Wine declared that God "has been retired from active duty ... he remains a helpless spectator, an unemployed deity.... If the gods have nursing homes, he (the god posited by theistic religion) is in one of them" (*Judaism Beyond God*, p. 15). This forced retirement from significance and relevance, Wine wrote, came as the result of the Enlightenment, as the world—or at least Europe and Great Britain—saw the priesthood of religion weakened by scientific understanding of how the world works.

> In the pages of *Judaism Beyond God,* the tradition-bent Jew will find everything he abhors and fears most. In it, Wine jettisons God—in particular, Jahweh—for good.

So, Wine wrote, "Interest in God began to wane ... pious reverence seemed out of date" (p. 21). A rediscovery of the wisdom and philosophies of the ancient Greeks aided and abetted the Enlightenment, gave it flesh and muscle. Wine appropriates that strength for Humanistic Judaism, which allows him to contrast the secular rationalist with the "believer." "For the God-believers, God is real before they look for the evidence. But reason starts with no commitment to conclusions. It allows the facts to judge" (p. 25). Wine makes clear a definite preference for reason over faith because the former relies on experience and its objective analysis while the latter begins, at best, with unfounded assumptions and, at worst, with wishful thinking. "Faith is parochial," Wine wrote. "Each faith rests on its own ancestral bed. You either believe or you do not believe. But reason is universal. Facts ... are not possessed by any tradition" (p. 25). Thus Wine, the rationalist, finds no "facts" that can lead him to a belief in any "god," much less Jahweh, who, Wine has declared, is "an absurdity, and if he did exist, I would have nothing to do with him. Petulant, jealous, ridiculous."

Anyone who has known Wine for very long soon grasps that he has what psychologists call "an authority problem." As he said about working with the late Richard Hertz at Temple Beth El: "I am not disposed to be anyone's assistant." He does not easily, readily, or willingly accept the positions, viewpoints, or demands of another. He wants to make up his own mind. This determination is extended to matters of religion and ethics. Wine correctly sees much of historic religious tradition as authoritarian in nature, a style that almost invariably compensates for a lack of certainty with a priori statements. In Wine's view, commands (or commandments, as they are known in Judaism and Christianity) may proceed from, at worst, a perceived authority's own self-interest or, at best, its groundless assumptions.

"While authoritarianism is concerned with the author of the command," Wine wrote, what he calls "consequentialism deals with the consequences of following [a command].... If it produces good consequences, it is right. If it produces bad consequences, it is wrong" (pp. 40–41). Thus Wine follows—and will encourage others to do so—a pragmatic path in making life decisions both great and small.

In Wine's view, Moses did not ascend some Middle Eastern peak to receive 10, or 613, or any number of so-called commandments. The law that evolved in the maturing of the Jewish people had its origins in hierarchical self-interest or came about through pragmatic evolution according to the needs of the people whose lives became more dependable and secure through the rule and application of the law. The logical extension of this theory of authority has lead Wine to encourage and approve of the elimination of such Jewish liturgical staples as the Torah reading and the Kaddish. Of the Kaddish, Wine wrote, "[It] is no longer a rabbinic tribute to a powerful and just god; it is a collection of Jewish sounds stripped of conceptual meaning" (p. 129). Of Torah and the Bible Wine wrote, "[They] are our most valuable resource ... for the study of early Jewish history." He doesn't care for the methods and the agenda of those who gave us the Bible in its present form, those who decided what to include, what to exclude. "We are not obliged to accept the editors' choice" (p. 143).

Wine recognizes the historical and cultural conditions that have led contemporary Judaism to cling to traditional forms and notions. He wrote, "In the century of racial anti-Semitism and the Holocaust, the survival of the Jewish people is an obsessive issue. Jewish survival demands Jewish activity. Prayer and worship are the most familiar Jewish activities" (p. 129). As Wine tells those couples whose weddings he agrees to perform, "I will use words that I believe make sense and are valid. I will not say things that are to me irrational." So realizing the need and insisting on his integrity, Wine has fostered the development of a Humanistic Jewish ceremonial that fills the need to express Jewishness while being intellectually honest. As he wrote in *Celebration: A Ceremonial and Philosophic Guide for Humanists and Humanistic Jews*, "[*Chutzpa*] has replaced worship and resignation as a guideline to behavior" (p. 16).

> "A successful Judaism needs to be a pluralistic Judaism, in which all Jewish options have their place."
> —Sherwin Wine

Trying not to construct Humanistic Judaism along such rigid lines as he perceives the other branches of Judaism—even Reform—to be constructed, Wine has sought a latitudinarian, inclusive expression of Jewishness that, as he wrote, could be successful. "A successful Judaism needs to be a pluralistic Judaism, in which all Jewish options have their place. [A successful Judaism] does not need to be a mushy pluralism that seeks to avoid confrontation and gloss over differences" (p. 133).

While the Torah is not read as part of services at the Birmingham Temple and is not held in particular reverence, it is studied "as an important historical document" (p. 140). Torah, then, takes its place in the temple's library alongside other literature that illustrates human intellectual evolution. Not able to resist needling, Wine has observed that "while most Jews do not study the Torah, they believe they ought to. Even if they do not understand it, they believe it contains eternal wisdom" (p. 136). His philosophy involves a gentle debunking of the whole Jewish theological and liturgical tradition. No sacred cows for Wine. And he will admit other nonreligious literature into the humanistic canon. "The literature of humanism (Epicurus, Democritus, Comte, Mill, Russell, Dewey, Sartre, Santayana) is part of a Humanistic Judaism, even more than the pious writing of pious Jews who did not defend either reason or human autonomy" (p. 144). In that regard, Wine ridicules the official basis for the celebration of Hanukka—the "miraculous, eight-day lasting of the oil" in the Temple lamps—preferring instead a commemoration of the courage and military genius of the Maccabees.

Wine wants Jews to apply reason and to accept natural explanations for events. In one summary paragraph of his manifesto, he lays out the philosophical basis for Humanistic Judaism, which, he acknowledges, could just as well be called rational Judaism if the word "rational" were not perceived as being cold. "Humanists not only do not believe in biblical creation, they do believe in evolution. They not only do not believe in the efficacy of prayer, they do believe in the power of human effort and responsibility. They not only do not believe in the reality of the supernatural, they do believe in the natural origins of all experience" (p. 228). And so the ground is cleared of all the clutter and underbrush of human attempts to sacralize life through imagination, wishful thinking, and the crafting of irrational assumptions to explain what reason has not yet been able to explain. What one is left with is a world of ambiguity and uncertainty, a world with far more questions than answers, a world that draws one into an agnosticism and an openness to the discovery that one's assumptions may be misinformed and mistaken. It is a world in which Sherwin Wine has flourished and in which he has been an unqualified success. His is certainly one of the longest-running shows of its kind in contemporary religious theater, notwithstanding a recent shift to a more "spiritual" and traditional Judaism, a shift that has made a dent in the membership of the temple. In an ironic twist, a young man in his early forties who had come to the Birmingham Temple for a Sabbath celebration at which his late uncle was being remembered, looked around the building in which he spent part of his youth and said, "This place is important to me. This is where my roots are and where I learned Hebrew and what it means to be Jewish." Asked why he no longer goes to the Birmingham Temple, he said, "My wife and I wanted something more traditional for our children"—quite the opposite of what that man's parents were saying thirty-five years ago when they joined the Birmingham Temple.

As if in answer to that man's inclination, Wine wrote in *Judaism Beyond God*, "Humanistic Jews do not reject the Sabbath. They believe that the Sabbath should be a day for family celebration, personal recreation, and Jewish cultural activities" (p. 230). That most characteristic aspect of post-exilic Judaism thus becomes the line of demarcation between Humanistic Judaism and the earlier and more prominent forms of the tradition. For the man who had left the Birmingham Temple, himself a product of the first generation of Humanistic Judaism, Wine's definition of Sabbath did not finally avail. The formalisms of his parents' and grandparents' traditions were deemed necessary for the rearing of the generation of Jews who will come to maturity in the twenty-first century.

Wine works night and day to win the hearts and minds of such younger Jews. He is impatient with the New Age mentality, which he dismisses as "intolerable," and he strives now to articulate a "secular spirituality" so that Humanistic Judaism is not displaced by the irrationality, sentimentality, and intellectual softness that are features of so-called New Age philosophy and of what some call the "postmodern era."

Wine is not willing to part with the understanding and liberty brought by the Enlightenment, the light by which he has been guided, shaped, and formed as the nemesis of the status quo and of limited thinking. His is a full embrace of the ambiguities of a life lived out under the aegis of reason. It is a life of courage and, as such, a path cut through the underbrush of religious and philosophical nonsense on a course of exploration.

Harry T. Cook is the rector of St. Andrews Church in Clawson, Michigan. He is a graduate of Albion College and Garrett-Evangelical Seminary/Northwestern University. Harry Cook was the ethics and public policy columnist for the *Detroit Free Press* for many years. He is the author of *Christianity Beyond Creeds*, *Sermons of a Devoted Heretic*, and *The Seven Sayings of Jesus*. He is a distinguished lecturer at the Center for New Thinking.

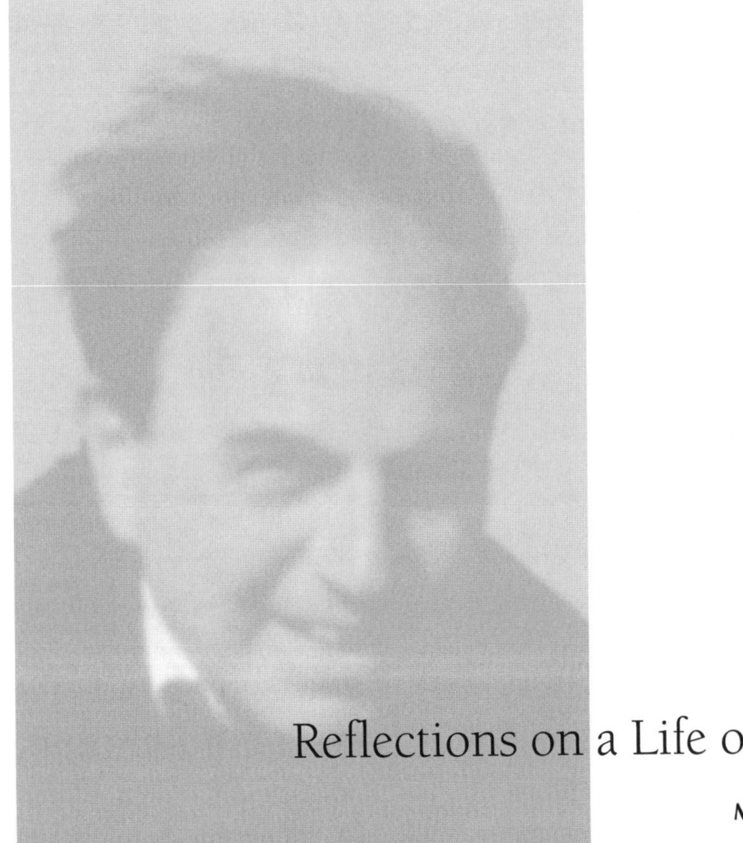

Reflections on a Life of Courage

Marilyn Rowens

Each of us tastes the bitter loneliness of the human condition. To be an individual is to stand apart and sense the separation that makes every person unique. In a soul where instinct has yielded to the challenge of free choice, decision is personal. Neither the tyranny of the species nor the oppression of society can dictate our will without our moment of consent. Birds and flowers conform to their race and offer no resistance. But human beings are plagued by the unpredictable freedom of our conscious mind. Each of us is distinct and different, defined by the path of our *behavior. Within the limits of our possibility we can become what we will to become. Within the boundaries of our talents we can achieve what we choose to achieve. The open possibility of our future is a frightening excitement. We can withdraw in fear and seek to hide from its reality; or we can boldly assume its challenge and bravely confront destiny with the courage of free individuals.*

Sherwin Wine, *Meditation Services for Humanistic Judaism*

When Rabbi Sherwin Wine spoke those words during a Birmingham Temple service in 1976, he was already on a historic journey toward creating a new worldwide religion. *Meditation Services* was in its third printing in 1976 and the building of the Birmingham Temple, completed five years earlier in Farmington Hills, Michigan, was home to more than 400 families.

A people-centered Judaism—a Judaism that embraced Jewish culture, that was a beautiful marriage between Jewish historical literature and modern Jewish thinkers of the Enlightenment—had become a bold adventure for the young rabbi who had been born, in 1928, into a world of tradition in a vibrant Jewish neighborhood in Detroit.

Humanistic Judaism was created by Rabbi Sherwin Wine at the Birmingham Temple, and from that foundation, from that special place, grew and blossomed an awe-inspiring approach to Jewish life that embraced the reality of the human condition and valued and loved the umbilical connection to the Jewish people. In the forty years from 1963—when Rabbi Wine and several families established a new kind of Judaism in Detroit—to 2003, Secular Humanistic Judaism has become a worldwide movement.

A CHILDHOOD IN JEWISH DETROIT

What was it like for a young boy growing up in the late 1930s in the Detroit neighborhood near Clairmount and 12th Streets? That intersection represented the heart of Yiddish language and culture: the Jewish bakery, the

Jewish butcher shop, the delicatessen, and other small-business storefronts were the centers for conversation. Customers and visitors could listen to political arguments, hear stories from the "old country," and learn about socialism, communism, and Zionism, while at the same time absorbing how to become fully Americanized and assimilated into a secular urban world. One summer during that period, Sherwin spent a week at a fresh-air camp sponsored by the Jewish Community Center. His counselors would remember a handsome young boy with thick black hair and bright dark eyes, always curious, reading in his cabin. Already at nine he had memorized all the European monarchs and knew the population of every major city in the United States. At home he listened to the radio. He heard Hitler's speeches; his hero was Franklin Delano Roosevelt. Without question, Jewish culture, political history, and American society were major influences on his emerging worldview.

Sherwin was growing up in a world of Jewish religious orientation, but he was also surrounded by many other philosophical influences. Radical Reform Judaism, brought to the United States by German immigrants, was going through a transition. The Ethical Culture movement was burgeoning. The Eastern European neighbors who argued on the street corners came from backgrounds of socialism and Yiddish nationalism, and they took full advantage of the freedom of expression in America. World-famous rabbi and philosopher Mordecai Kaplan was constructing Reconstructionism and progressive American educator John Dewey was becoming the priest of public education, while the young Sherwin Wine sat in the synagogue.

> From that foundation, from that special place, Humanistic Judaism grew and blossomed as an awe-inspiring approach to Jewish life.

Walking hand in hand with their father, Sherwin and his sister Lorraine went to Shaarey Zedek, a conservative congregation on Chicago Boulevard, every Saturday. Sitting in shul, Sherwin listened to the words of the Torah, sang the songs of his people, and internalized Judaism. He was mesmerized by the new young assistant rabbi, Morris Adler. With his tremendous oratorical presence,

Rabbi Adler had the power and charisma to reach the heart of a young Jewish boy. But the questions emanating from that boy's mind could not be contained. Why? Why? Why? William Wine, Sherwin's father, answered, *Freg nit*—don't ask.

Sherwin's parents came to the United States from Poland. They came to the *goldene medina*, the country where the streets were paved with gold. They came to escape the tyranny of the Russian army and the onset of World War I. They came to a new land to live a life of freedom not unlike the many thousands of immigrants that peopled the Jewish neighborhoods in cities across the United States. Growing up, Sherwin fervently absorbed the many flavors of American life—political thought, religious belief, modern culture—he was exposed to in his neighborhood. Detroit, home of the auto factories, also held for Sherwin the wonder and enlightenment of the public school system, as well as the pain of antisemitism as epitomized by *The Protocols of the Elders of Zion.* A curious nine-year-old started his life's journey early: even at that young age, Sherwin was a keen observer of his neighborhood, his city, his world.

> Each of us is the total of his yesterdays. Layers of experience rise in bold succession to build the personal present out of past performance. While the trauma of life shakes our soul and makes it quiver with each repetition, the heavy hands of strong events mold our minds to their conviction. For we can never escape our memories nor elude the imprints of daily experience. The power of our nostalgia always compromises the purity of our desire and the freedom of our decision.
>
> **Sherwin Wine, *Meditation Services for Humanistic Judaism***

The American public school system was a gift to the first- and second-generation immigrant. The open doors of the public schools proclaimed, Come in to us and become an American. Sherwin Wine loved school. He learned civics, citizenship, and American history. He grew up with Jewish ancestors Abraham, Isaac, and Jacob, but he adopted with a passion Washington, Jefferson, and Lincoln. His Gentile spinster teachers became heroes to Sherwin, and they encouraged him to find intellectual challenges in debate, theater, and poetry. He was a brilliant student both at school and at home. At home he immersed himself in the written word: daily newspapers, library books, textbooks, and encyclopedias. The radio gave him current history. He was aware of the German invasion of Czechoslovakia in 1939. Churchill later became a role model in courage for him, at least in part because, through efforts to provide temporary refuge to Jewish children from Germany and Poland, England became one of the only countries helping the Jews. Even before his bar mitsva, Sherwin was advocating and debating the importance of the United States entering the war.

AN ACADEMIC QUEST

Sherwin's ties to the Jewish people, his roots in that community, always informed his thinking. Although his parents were often silent on subjects he quizzed them about, they shared with him their experiences in the Polish shtetl and the worry of his grandfather that the "Jews would be wiped out." He was fascinated by current events and by what preceded them, and it was only natural that in high school he excelled in history. Central High School, filled as it was in those years with second-generation Jewish immigrants, was a hotbed of ambition and intellectual striving. These children of immigrants were held to the expectation that they would succeed academically: they lived in the United States, the free world, and they had access to universities and career opportunities never even dreamed of by their parents. The adolescents in the old Jewish neighborhood who hung out at the Avalon Theater and Zukins Ice Cream Shop went on to become doctors, lawyers, accountants, scientists, and teachers.

The questions emanating from young Sherwin's mind could not be contained. Why? Why? Sherwin's father answered, *Freg nit*—don't ask.

Sherwin's successful high school years were not without the pain of World War II. The death of Franklin Delano Roosevelt was embedded in his memory. He was still very devoted to his religious connections, but even with his father's continued admonishment, *freg nit*, he did ask, he did question, he did struggle with major philosophical issues, with ethical and moral choices, with who he was and who he wanted to be. It was later, at the University of Michigan, that he put a name to this questioning and discovered his great love for philosophy.

> To live courageously is to live without guarantees, to make decisions without waiting for every fact, to take action without knowing all the consequences. Brave people do not need the illusions of absolute certainty. They will think before acting. But they will never think so much and so long that it is too late to act.
>
> Courage is the refusal to wait for what will never come. It is the willingness to choose when it is time to choose.
>
> **Sherwin Wine, *Celebration***

Sherwin had excellent professors at the University of Michigan, and for a time he considered getting his doctorate in philosophy and staying in the academic world. But his interests went beyond philosophy; he had also discovered in himself a very strong quality of leadership, which he had exhibited in so many ways throughout his high school and college years: helping and advising friends, negotiating problems in the college dorm, discussing with sensitivity and insight people's innermost problems. Sociology and psychology were favorite paths for many of his university peers who felt as he did a need to reach out to the world, to help make it better—the Jewish philosophy of *tikkun olam*, repairing the world. Sherwin's early memories of Rabbi Morris Adler were never far from his consciousness. Adler's charisma, power, and influence over a large congregation stirred Sherwin's questioning mind. Could he also become a rabbi? He had already discovered that he was a humanist, that his connection to his ancestors was unyielding but cultural. He made a decision to attend Hebrew Union College, a seminary for Reform Judaism. Perhaps within the Reform movement he could blend his personal philosophy with a modern Judaism.

A RABBINIC PATH

> Jewish history is four thousand years of Jewish experience. It is the sum total of all the pleasure and pain, triumphs and defeats,

> fulfilled dreams and disappointments which have entered into our memories through centuries of struggle and striving.
>
> The Jewish experience is the experience of change.
>
> **Sherwin Wine, *Celebration***

The decision to attend Hebrew Union College came only after serious deliberation. How could he become a rabbi if he did not believe in God? He considered many careers, thinking perhaps law would be a wise choice. After his father's death in 1948, he reaffirmed his deep connection to his Jewish roots. His loyalty to his father's Judaism, his own love of history, and the memorable impact of Rabbi Morris Adler as a community leader and a role model led him to a career in the Jewish rabbinate.

In 1951 Sherwin entered Hebrew Union College in Cincinnati, leaving his familiar neighborhood in Detroit. By this time, the postwar building boom had begun. Families were moving farther from the core of the city. Folksinger Pete Seeger sang about "little boxes in the ticky tacky" suburbs. Anthropologist Margaret Mead wrote about the phenomenon of the American nuclear family, predicting that it would be short-lived. The nuclear family, made up of a husband, wife, and 2.5 children, peopled all these grassy new neighborhoods. Attending temple or synagogue was socially encouraged, and all the moms and daughters wore their white gloves and hats. The times were definitely traditional and conformist, but Sherwin was a devout humanist studying at a Reform seminary.

The times were definitely traditional and conformist, but Sherwin was a devout humanist studying at a Reform seminary.

A JEWISH CHAPLAIN IN KOREA

Sherwin was at the seminary when another war, the Korean War, began. Hebrew Union encouraged its graduates to serve in the army as chaplains even after the war ended. Sherwin was inducted into the army six months after graduation. In January 1957, at the age of twenty-nine, Rabbi Wine became First Lieutenant Sherwin Wine. At that point, his world travels began, and they have never ceased.

> If Jewish history has any message, it is the demand of human self-reliance. In an indifferent universe there is no help from destiny. Either we assume responsibility for our fate or no one will. A world without divine guarantees and divine justice is a little bit frightening. But it is also the source of human freedom and dignity.
>
> **Sherwin Wine, *Celebration***

When Sherwin joined the military, the Korean War had been over for several years, but numerous U.S. troops were still stationed there in the wake of the armistice. Young Jewish boys away from home welcomed the arrival of a chaplain from a background similar to their own. First Lieutenant Wine, himself new to a very different culture, became a popular Jewish chaplain.

Korea opened Sherwin's mind and heart in so many ways. Serving as chaplain to the young Jewish soldiers reinforced his unique and changing approach to Judaism. Prayer and meditation were not high on the GIs' list of needs. What they welcomed and appreciated in their young Jewish chaplain was his ability to speak directly to their concerns, to listen to their voices, and to appreciate who they were as individuals. His meetings with them—he searched out many GIs in remote areas—were special times for sharing personal issues. He also set up lectures on topics of interest to them, providing intellectual stimulus and a time to share the comfort of their Jewish memories. Their Friday night services were more cultural than religious. Sherwin's distinct leadership style and easy rapport with the troops reached out to the inner needs of these Jewish boys living in a strange land. He enjoyed representing Judaism and trying to make it relevant and meaningful to those soldiers overseas. He was able to provide the young soldiers with a connection to their deepest Jewish roots as well as helping them navigate the uncertainties of the human condition posed by the postwar world they were guarding. Most of all, he shared laughter with them. Sherwin's exceptional sense of humor, expressed not by telling jokes or stories but by listening and laughing with the troops, gave those young men a sense of home and family.

Sherwin's experience as a Jewish chaplain provided the seeds that would one day blossom into a humanistic rabbinate. For Sherwin, Korea was his initiation to the many worlds and cultures he had read about in books and to which he would travel continuously over the next forty years.

> We will not run away from wisdom even though it comes from strange lands and strange people. Our bravery is our dignity. It feeds our strength. If old laws no longer fit, we will revise them. If old postures keep us from moving gracefully, we will find a new way to walk. A free world makes tradition only one of many options. There is more to life than imitation. Our ancestors created. So can we.
>
> **Sherwin Wine, *High Holidays for Humanists***

THE BIRTH OF THE BIRMINGHAM TEMPLE

When his time in the military ended, Rabbi Wine packed away his army uniform and returned to a position as assistant rabbi at Temple Beth El, located at Woodward and Gladstone in Detroit. He enjoyed the opportunity of sharing a large congregation and introducing interesting programs. His sermons, his sense of humor, and his storytelling for children captivated many young families. But the traditional liturgy became increasingly uncomfortable for him. After eighteen months, Sherwin resigned and took a pulpit in Windsor, Ontario, with a new congregation, also called Beth El, which held the promise of developing a more modern Judaism. The Windsor congregation grew under his tutelage. But then he received a call from former Beth El congregants in Detroit, a couple who were disenchanted with Beth El and wanted to meet with him to discuss creating a new suburban-Detroit temple.

Jews in 1963 were moving north of Detroit. Young couples had settled in Oak Park, Huntington Woods, Franklin, Farmington Hills, and Birmingham. When Harry and Suzanne Velick and seven other couples met with Rabbi Wine in 1963, not even Sherwin realized what the future held for them. Eight couples and a rabbi decided to create a new Reform temple. Sherwin met with the core group on Sunday nights, planning the beginning. New people were attracted to the idea, and their numbers grew. On Sunday, September 15, 1963 (Sunday instead of Friday because Sherwin was still committed to the temple in Windsor), a first service was held, and the response was overwhelmingly positive.

It was not until a few months later that the real process of change began. A temple was created, a board of directors was established, and the Ritual Committee, chaired by Rabbi Wine, began to explore what these new members really believed. Meetings were held on Sunday nights throughout the metropolitan Detroit community. More and more people became aware of Rabbi Wine and this new temple. Space was rented in the Birmingham Masonic Temple. Sherwin owned a small Torah that was carried back and forth. And during this initial growth period, the discussions of philosophy, Judaism, and the meaning of God continued after each meeting and after each service until the early hours of the morning.

Was God the ideal in mankind? Was God the angry God of the prophets? Was God the salvation God of the rabbis? Was God the limited God of John Dewey and Mordecai Kaplan? Was God just another name for nature?

> Judaism must be affirmed as a cultural and aesthetic framework in which a variety of philosophic outlooks are possible. Both mystic theism and empirical humanism should feel equally at home. Jewish custom and ceremony are an adjustable poetry, capable of embracing a wide spectrum of human values and experiences.
>
> **Sherwin Wine, *Celebration***

The congregation named itself the Birmingham Temple because the group often met in Birmingham and some members lived there. Rabbi Wine and the Ritual Committee established that the Birmingham Temple believed in Humanistic Judaism, a Judaism that was people-centered rather than God-centered; a Judaism that affirmed that moral and ethical problems were solved from within each individual, not with the assistance of a supernatural force; a Judaism that believed in the strength of ordinary Jewish people to survive a history of persecution.

A line was drawn in the sand between Reform and Humanistic Judaism. The new Humanistic Jewish community wanted to write their own meditations, using words they did not have to reinterpret, words that reflected what they believed. It was an act of courage for Rabbi Wine and the members of his new congregation to make the decision to exclude God-language from their liturgy.

THE GROWTH OF HUMANISTIC JUDAISM

> People give meaning to the universe. If we call to the stars and say "tell us the purpose of life," the stars are silent. If we caress the earth and ask, "what shall we do," the earth gives no reply. If we pursue the wind and plead, "let us know the path we must follow," the wind has no answer.... People give meaning to the universe.
>
> **Sherwin Wine, *Celebration***

Discussions of philosophy, Judaism, and the meaning of God continued after each meeting and after each service until the early hours of the morning.

Almost immediately, the Jewish community was up in arms. On January 29, 1965, *Time* magazine wrote about the "atheist rabbi." Letters of criticism came in from the local community. Letters of support arrived too, not only from the United States but also from around the world. For the most part, however, the local response was one of ostracism. Reform Rabbi Leon Fram wanted Sherwin excommunicated. Some of the Birmingham Temple members left because of hostility from their friends and family, but many others stayed. Sherwin Wine's response was one of defiance.

He was and is a man of strong opinions, and this kind of confrontation energized him. He was determined to grow his community in spite of local Jewish condemnation. Like a locomotive, he forged forward. Some people on the tracks jumped off, but those who became passengers remained for the journey of a lifetime. Sherwin's keen sense of humor was an effective tool not only for him personally, but also for the congregation to use in dealing with disapproval from others.

> Jewish humor is the legacy of the Jewish experience. It did not arise from the Bible or the Talmud. It did not come down from priests, prophets and rabbis. It did not emerge from famous texts and famous writers. Jewish humor is the response of ordinary Jewish people to the extraordinary horrors of Jewish history. In the face of an uncaring and unjust world, we Jews learned to laugh rather than to surrender and die.
>
> **Sherwin Wine, *Celebration***

The Birmingham Temple expanded successfully over the next several years. Enrollment in the Sunday school grew to more than 175 children. Sherwin left Beth El in Windsor, and Birmingham Temple services were held on Friday nights. The first edition of *Meditation Services for Humanistic Judaism* was compiled and published.

In spite of the qualms expressed by tradition-minded Jews, the religious climate in the Detroit metropolitan area was ripe for change. Who were the young people joining the temple? They were second- and third-generation Jews who had benefited from the opportunities of a university education and choice of profession. They were children during World War II and young adults in the 1960s, a time when all authority was questioned. A time of mobility, with people moving from city to city. A time of student rebellion, riots, assassinations. A time to protest the Vietnam War. A time to march for civil rights.

These young parents wanted a new Judaism for their children. They wanted honesty and the values they had absorbed in the secular urban environment in which they lived. They wanted a community of like-minded people who would be their friends and extended family. And so the temple grew to more than 400 families, and the loyal supporters helped to create materials, committees, and the new philosophy of Humanistic Judaism.

Sherwin Wine's sister Lorraine and her husband Ben were loyal supporters from the beginning. Ben and Lorraine Pivnick supported Rabbi Wine emotionally, financially, and even physically, by always being there. They would continue to remain an important part of the Birmingham Temple and the development of the Secular Humanistic Jewish movement.

The congregation, having been expelled from the Masonic Temple building, had to find a new place to meet, and for a time, the meeting site rotated among several different places: the Birmingham Unitarian Church, Eagle Elementary School, High Meadow School, Frost Junior High. Sherwin's mother, Tillie Wine, referred to members as "gypsies," and the idea of a "home of their own" became an important part of Sherwin's vision. In September 1971, services were held in the new building at 28611 West 12 Mile Road, in Farmington Hills, Michigan.

> Young parents wanted a new Judaism for their children. They wanted honesty and the values they had absorbed in their secular urban environment.

> Jewishness is more than a conventional nod to old belief; it is the push of the past and the irresistible attraction of romantic roots. Samson and Samuel, Joshua and Joab may be dim figures of vanished years; but they are also firm links to the chain of our personality. The biography of each of us is not confined to the brief events of our own life; it transcends our time and adds the feel of former years. Since tradition is part of our uniqueness it deserves our wise respect. If it plays the taskmaster and beats us with the whip of conformity, then we shall with justice resist its malice; but

if it acts the teacher and guides us gently to wisdom, we shall embrace it with the tribute of consent.

Sherwin Wine, ***Meditation Services for Humanistic Judaism***

During the early 1970s, a volunteer support group of women contributed tremendously to the rapid growth of the Birmingham Temple. This era was a transitional time in American history concerning the roles of women. The feminist movement was not yet widespread; Betty Freidan was not yet being read in every suburban kitchen. But the women members of the Birmingham Temple became Sunday school teachers, committee chairs, board members, and a dynamic source of creative energy for the development of Humanistic Judaism. Friendships were created, and the temple family grew.

Rabbi Wine's lectures and constant encouragement provided the environment in which the philosophy of Humanistic Judaism flourished. Humanistic Judaism was not created in a vacuum. Jewish history is the history of change. The secularization of America, the influence of the Enlightenment, the impact of Zionism, the questioning of Jewish tradition after World War II and the Holocaust: all led to a need in the Jewish world for a Jewish identity that could blend with a personal philosophy of life. The early years of the temple had less to do with pulling away from God than with pulling together to form a community of "believers" in a humanistic and rational approach to life. The members were a generation of searchers. They had had the opportunity of education and living in a free society. They wanted their children to soar; they wanted to give them wings at a time when having wings meant flying away from tradition toward a universal world of wonder, science, and beauty. Rabbi Wine created meditations, poetry, and ritual to express congregants' deepest human struggles and their attachment to the traditional Jewish world of their youth.

A NATIONAL—AND INTERNATIONAL—MOVEMENT

Rabbi Wine was called upon to lecture all across the country. Responses to his lectures and press coverage resulted in national interest and support.

The next step for the ambitious rabbi was outreach to the general community. Coalitions were formed with other secular Jews, unaffiliated Jews who were not connected to organizations but were motivated to proclaim their Jewish identity with pride. A sense of solidarity with Israel increased for many Jews following the Yom Kippur War, creating a powerful urge to establish a stronger Jewish identity. In its initial years, the Society for Humanistic Judaism—created in 1969 to mobilize communities to celebrate Jewish identity and Jewish culture with a humanistic philosophy—began the serious work of outreach and community-building in other cities.

Sherwin also connected with other like-minded humanist organizations. It was the beginning of the real growth of coalitions of secular groups that had previously operated independently. A list of "alphabet soup" organizations, which have become Sherwin's trademark, began to appear so rapidly that it was hard to define which meeting was being called to order. Rabbi Wine's energy level could easily handle the multitude of meetings. His organizational skills were unparalleled. A first "Conference on Humanism" held at Oakland University in Michigan attracted stellar speakers and numerous participants. It was an exciting time for members of the temple and for so many unaffiliated humanists to come together and discuss and question: What is authentic in life, what is authentic in the human being? This first conference was not only the beginning of a strong philosophy of Humanistic Judaism, but also the nucleus for future connections with the larger world of humanism. Sherwin had the great talent of bringing people together. The list of organizations grew and grew:

- Birmingham Temple (BT)
- Society for Humanistic Judaism (SHJ)
- Association of Humanistic Rabbis (AHR)
- Center for New Thinking (CNT)
- Humanist Institute (HI)
- North American Committee for Humanism (NACH)
- International Association of Humanist Educators Counselors and Leaders (IAHECL)

- TECHILA (formerly Israeli Society for Humanistic Judaism)
- Leadership Conference of Secular and Humanistic Jews (LCSHJ)
- International Federation of Secular Humanistic Jews (IFSHJ)
- International Institute for Secular Humanistic Judaism (IISHJ)
- Voice of Reason (VOR)
- Conference on Liberal Religion (CLR)
- Clergy and Citizens United (CCU)

All of the above organizations began with the very close supervision of Rabbi Wine; as they grew, they became more autonomous but never far from his influence. Simultaneously the Birmingham Temple expanded and became an established and accepted alternative in the Detroit Jewish community.

> The literature of our people is an encyclopedia of many ideas. Some of them sprang from Jewish minds. Some of them were borrowed from the neighbors of our ancestors and the loan forgotten. Our religious tradition has been a matter of give and take.... We are the products of universal wisdom.
>
> **Sherwin Wine,**
> ***Meditation Services for Humanistic Judaism***

Only part of Sherwin's inexhaustible energy has gone into creating organizations and establishing communities. He is also a prolific writer. His articles appear monthly in the Birmingham Temple newsletter, *The Jewish Humanist;* quarterly in the Society for Humanistic Judaism's journal, *Humanistic Judaism;* and twice a year in the International Federation Newsletter, *Hofesh.* He is the author of several books, including *Celebration*, *Judaism Beyond God*, *Humanistic Judaism*, and *Staying Sane in a Crazy World.* He lectures at least three or four times a week locally, he travels across the country to teach seminars several times a year, and he is the core faculty for training rabbis at the International Institute for Secular Humanistic Judaism.

Those who have heard him speak know that Sherwin has a unique lecture style. He is able to present and teach the most difficult subject, somehow making it easy for his audience to understand. He is able to synthesize information and explain ideas in a dramatic and powerful way. This talent has enabled him to stimulate people to cooperate with each other in visionary endeavors, and he empowers others to act on their own to create philosophical connections, communities, and organizations. And this is only his public persona. As a counselor and a friend, he has a special gift. He is able to touch people deeply; he knows which questions to ask and he is an intent listener. He can walk into a room and light it up. His incredible sense of humor generates laughter, but, more important, he possesses the ability to sweep away melancholy.

Sherwin Wine, however, is not a saint. He is often a taskmaster with an exceedingly rigid set of standards for himself and others. He has no patience with wishy-washy endless discussion. He is a man of action who is more than willing to make a decision first and consult later. For forty years, this style has served him well; this style has enabled his visions to become realities. He is a natural leader: to paraphrase the old commercial, When Sherwin speaks, people listen. His congenial arrogance is sometimes abrasive, but it is also a key ingredient in many of his relationships. His peers, his congregants, the couples he counsels and marries, the boards of organizations he has created all give consideration to his ideas and suggestions and decisions he may have already made.

> The early years of the temple had less to do with pulling away from God than with pulling together to form a community of "believers" in a humanistic approach to life.

Sherwin's daily agenda and schedule would be tiring even if divided among three people. Sleep does not seem to be a priority. Weather permitting, Sherwin walks every morning; when he's in New York, he walks across the Brooklyn Bridge. He lectures, attends meetings, and is a sought-after speaker for community groups, clubs, elder hostels, retreats, and college campuses. He may not be totally tireless—occasionally he is caught napping when someone else is the speaker or while sitting in a dark theater during an opera. But when he is speaking in front of an audience, listening intently to others' problems, or helping to solve a critical situation, he is 100 percent involved: supportive, helpful, and inspiring. He believes that "people are their behavior," and he is the prime example of that concept: he is an optimistic friend, a rational counselor, a stimulating and affective teacher, and a loyal shoulder to lean on. Living life well is his daily challenge.

> We are the survivors of two billion years of vital evolution. We are not miniature gods. We are not manufactured puppets. We are not visitors from outer space. We are the proud culmination of an epic of struggle. The earth is our home. We know it intimately. Its plants and animals are our cousins. Like them we have tested the kindness and cruelty of nature. Our brutal setting has made us strong. We have many talents for survival. Our brains, our limbs and our senses cooperate to make us a hardy fighter for life. We are not the heirs of the passive and the resigned. We are the children of action. We are the offspring of the will to live.
>
> **Sherwin Wine, *High Holidays for Humanists***

Over a period of forty years, contacts, friendships, and outreach efforts contributed to the process of creating the movement for Secular Humanistic Judaism. Not long after the Society for Humanistic Judaism was established, three groups—representatives from the Humanistic Jewish congregations in Westport, Connecticut, and Deerfield, Illinois, as well as from the Birmingham Temple—held a first meeting at the Northland Inn in Michigan. The society now boasts more than thirty-nine communities in North America. In 1981 a meeting was held in Israel at Shefayim kibbutz. It was the beginning of cooperation between Israel and the society. The early years of the society with Sherwin directing traffic resulted in many more conferences, the creation of *Humanistic Judaism,* the quarterly journal published by the society, and strong emotional connections between each developing community.

In 1982 Sherwin called a meeting of other Jewish secular organizations as well as the Society for Humanistic Judaism: the Congress of Secular Jewish Organizations, Polizion, Workmen's Circle, the Labor Zionists of America, and Americans for Progressive Israel. That was the beginning of the Leadership Conference of Secular and Humanistic Jews, which marked the first time that so many separate secular groups sat together in one room to proclaim solidarity and to cooperate to create a publication of secular humanistic writing.

In 1985, at a meeting in Jerusalem at the American Colony Hotel, representatives from North America, Israel, and Latin America established the International Institute for Secular Humanistic Judaism. It had become apparent that in order for Secular Humanistic Judaism to have a future and be able to maintain members in a democratic and secular world, leaders would have to be trained. The institute became the educational arm of what was then the beginning of an international movement.

In 1986 representatives from eleven countries came together at the Birmingham Temple, and the International Federation of Secular Humanistic Jews was born. More than 350 people—local, national and international—gathered for the federation's first leadership training seminar and conference. Speakers from France, Latin America, Israel, and North America, whose backgrounds were flavored by the Enlightenment, postwar secularism, Zionism, and the Holocaust, spoke from the heart about a shared philosophy: a Judaism of the twentieth century that embraced the culture, history, roots, and essence of the Jewish people; a Judaism that did not rely on a belief in the supernatural but on reason and the responsibility of human beings to create for themselves and others a life of good deeds and a better world.

Humanistic Judaism relies not on a belief in the supernatural but on reason and the responsibility of human beings to create for themselves and others a life of good deeds.

The Jewish experience is the experience of change.

The power of people is the power of change. Circumstances never stay the same. Culture never stays the same. Judaism was created by Jewish people. It was molded by the Jewish experience. It was flavored by Jewish sadness and Jewish joy.

> Holidays are responses to human events. Ceremonies are celebrations of human development. Music and literature are the expressions of human needs. Life is an evolution, a continuous flow of transformation. And so is culture. When circumstances change, people change. When people change, their laws and customs change.
>
> **Sherwin Wine, *Celebration***

Sherwin Wine is a man of social action. All of the organizations Rabbi Wine created had a focus and purpose. In addition to maintaining coalitions with the humanist world and the secular Jewish cultural world, he also encouraged confrontation in response to injustice and fundamentalist irrationality. A firm believer in separation of church and state, civil rights, individual rights, and personal freedom, Sherwin developed such social action organizations as the Voice of Reason, the Conference on Liberal Religion, and later, Clergy and Citizens United. His ability to recruit outstanding allies and specialists in their fields enabled these organizations to make an impact in the community. His motivation to fix the world had its roots in the traditional Jewish influence of *tikkun olam.*

The 1970s, '80s, and '90s were full of the excitement of the growth of Secular Humanistic Judaism. North American conferences were held, and meetings of the International Federation took place in Brussels, Chicago, Israel, Moscow, Paris, and New York, where, in the fall of 2000, a permanent office of the federation was established.

A PASSION FOR TRAVEL

Rabbi Wine has devoted his life not only to making Humanistic Judaism a viable alternative in the Jewish world, but also to lecturing, teaching, and enriching others. All of the federation conferences have included a lecture series and a personal tour with him through each city. His incredible historical knowledge, his love of travel, and his need to learn about other cultures and people has provided him with yet another trademark: The Sherwin Wine Trip. A yearly fundraiser for the International Institute for Secular

Humanistic Judaism—open to the general public—the Sherwin Wine Trip is the equivalent of a traveling history class and a participatory documentary.

Does Sherwin ever stop? This question has been asked many times by all those who work with him and love him. His energy is endless, his enthusiasm is genuine, and he always makes time to listen to his congregants, his friends, and his critics. But one month of the year belongs to him. Each summer Sherwin and his life partner of twenty-five years, Richard McMains, travel together. The trips have been logged from Turkey to Timbuktu, from India to Japan, from Egypt to Siberia. Sherwin and Richard have traveled the world together. Since his first taste of the wonders of travel during his military service in Korea, Rabbi Wine has absorbed the politics, the culture, the architecture, the history, the pain and struggle, and the heartbeat of people all over the world.

> Societies may undergo revolutions and violent social upheaval; they may experience the overthrow of every existing value and idea. But the explosion is powerless to alter the relentless sequence of spring, summer, fall, winter—birth, puberty, maturity, and death. Nothing is more "eternal" than the seasons. Their continual repetition is an ultimate "security."
>
> **Sherwin Wine, *Humanistic Judaism***

Sherwin's trips have been logged from Turkey to Timbuktu, from India to Japan, from Egypt to Siberia.

THE INTERNATIONAL INSTITUTE FOR SECULAR HUMANISTIC JUDAISM

The International Institute for Secular Humanistic Judaism, established in 1985, became the important educational arm of the movement. The need for communities to have leaders—the key to ensuring a future for Secular Humanistic Judaism—was the motivation for the development of the Leadership Program, designed to train those leaders. New Humanistic communities needed specialists in ceremony and holiday celebration in order to grow.

Established secular groups wanted to make sure that they had educators, spokespersons, and trained leaders to keep secular Jewishness alive. Dedicated volunteers in the institute representing the Society for Humanistic Judaism and the Congress of Secular Jewish Organizations worked diligently and created the Leadership Program, which became the most successful program of the institute. Rabbi Wine was the organizing force and energy that propelled the institute into the twenty-first century.

Again with the generous help of Ben and Lorraine Pivnick, and with matching funds from the Birmingham Temple, an addition to the temple was built to house the Pivnick Center for Humanistic Judaism. The Pivnick Center became the headquarters of the institute, hosting seminars and meetings and housing administration offices and the Milan Library.

Certified leaders, also known as *vegvayzer* or *madrikhim*, were trained and graduated from the institute. They then went out to their communities to reinforce and rekindle the flames of Secular Humanistic Judaism.

In 1990 the Institute initiated a five-year rabbinic program. Classes were held weekly in the institute's Milan Library. Rabbi Wine was the core faculty. Arrangements were made with the University of Michigan to engage guest faculty members from its Judaic Studies department, and the rabbinic program began to take concrete shape.

By October 2001, the International Institute for Secular Humanistic Judaism had ordained four rabbis. By virtue of the acknowledgement and recognition from the United Jewish Communities, three of the rabbis serve on the Detroit Metropolitan Council of Rabbis, and the fourth will be recognized in Washington, D.C.

THE FUTURE FOR RABBI WINE AND FOR HUMANISTIC JUDAISM

The International Federation of Secular Humanistic Jews met for its ninth biennial conference in September 2002. An enthusiastic assembly from Israel, France, Italy, Belgium, Sweden, Ireland, Latin America, England,

Germany, and North America (plus greetings from Russia and Australia)—all interested in building communities—indicated a promising future for Secular Humanistic Judaism.

Sherwin Wine is not the Wizard of Oz. He does not stand behind the curtain and pull levers. He has worked industriously to promote and make available to Jews all over the world a Judaism rooted in personal strength; a people-centered Judaism; a Judaism that embraces Jewish history and literature, culture and ethics; a Judaism that speaks to the needs of a cyberspace world and at the same time loves and recognizes with devoted attachment the wisdom and tradition of ancestors.

> In the twentieth century, the true meaning of Jewish identity has been dramatized. It is no pious call to faith and humility. It is no saccharine invitation to prayer and worship. It is a summons to all that modern humanism stands for. If a people will not assume responsibility for its "fate" and its "destiny," no one else will. If human beings will not take charge of their own happiness, the indifferent forces of the universe may arrange for human suffering. Reason and dignity are not built into the structure of the world. They are difficult human achievements.
>
> **Sherwin Wine, *Judaism Beyond God***

In May 2003 Rabbi Wine was honored with the Humanist of the Year award from the American Humanist Association, an organization that has joined with him in so many of the challenges and accomplishments of the last forty years. His enthusiastic unwavering voice for Judaism and humanism is cause for public appreciation and celebration.

The achievements of Sherwin Wine, summarized in the alphabet soup of organizations he founded, rely on who he is as a man, and as a human being. Sherwin never stopped being a philosophy major. He is a student of ethical behavior, an avid reader who maintains a constant passion for knowledge. The Birmingham Temple library is filled wall to wall with the books he has read and reviewed. His broad and deep knowledge is extraordinary. His lectures include spontaneous map drawings to help him clarify his topics. Rabbi Wine is a great teacher, in large measure because he loves to teach.

In his role as a rabbi, Sherwin meets the needs of his congregants in a very special way. During a hospital call he is able to soothe the family, inspire the patient, and often create a secure moment of healing laughter. Families rely on him to help them with the torturous decision of continuing or ending life support. His empathic presence at a house of mourning validates the family's pain while enabling loved ones to join in a celebration of life. And Sherwin has the ability to empower people, to help them accept responsibility and find motivation to do things they never dreamed they could do. His lectures on themes of biblical history or new scientific theories, politics or psychology, poetry or current social issues have an exceptional way of touching and uplifting his audience.

This does sound like a lot for one person to do, but that's what Sherwin Wine does. Upon his retirement from the Birmingham Temple, he plans to add a few more things to his agenda. To begin with, he will be the full-time dean of the International Institute for Secular Humanistic Judaism. He will increase his involvement with the congregations and communities that make up the Society for Humanistic Judaism. He will travel to off-campus sites to teach institute seminars as well as choreographing the Sherwin Wine Trips. He will maintain his important role in the International Federation of Secular Humanistic Jews. He will continue his walking tours, his lectures, his traveling, his writing, his reading, and his outreach to other people. As long as there are still letters in the alphabet, they will certainly appear in the names of new organizations envisioned and directed by Rabbi Wine.

> Happiness is no distant event which we strive to achieve, some future bliss we suffer to enjoy. It is the sensitive awareness of what is intrinsically valuable in the here and now. It is the special pleasure of helping others, the beauty of friendship, the thrill of running, the excitement of learning, the exaltation in simple striving.

Happiness is not, in reality, the goal of life at all. It is the feeling of aliveness that pervades the pursuit of challenge.

Sherwin Wine, *Sabbath Services*

Marilyn Rowens is the executive director of the International Institute for Secular Humanistic Judaism. She also serves as the Leadership Program director and the Rabbinic Program director. She was the ceremonial director of the Birmingham Temple for twenty years. She is the resident cartoonist for the monthly Birmingham Temple publication, *The Jewish Humanist.* She is also the author of many plays and short stories that reflect the human condition.

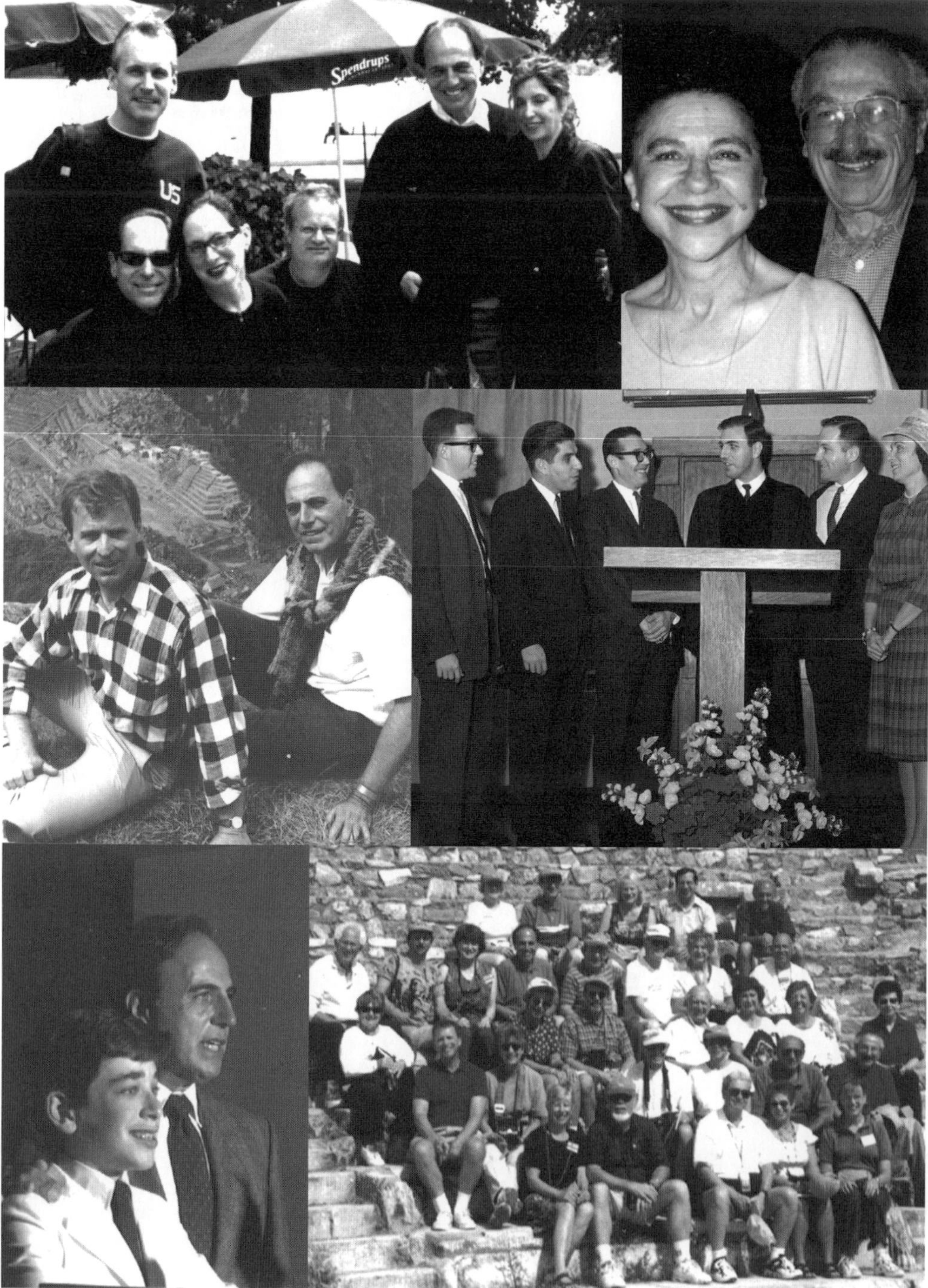
Spendrups
US

tributes

Friendship is like the air we breathe.

We cannot live without it.

We are not designed for loneliness.

We thrive on the opportunity of human response.

If we need to receive the love of others,

we also need to give love.

If we need to feel the concern of others,

we also need to give our care.

To cry alone, to laugh alone,

to think without the challenge of other minds

and other voices is to cease to be human.

Sherwin Wine

Embracing Humanism

Shulamit Aloni

In April 1980 I received a surprising invitation. The synagogue of the Society for Humanistic Judaism asked me to come to Michigan on 3 May, in order to take part in a bat mitsva ceremony—the two girls had chosen me as the subject of their bat mitsva project—and also to receive the congregation's 1980 Leadership Award. The invitation was from Sherwin Wine. I was, of course, greatly flattered, and also greatly intrigued.

Although I was familiar with the various traditional "streams," or denominations, of Judaism in the United States, this was the first time that I had heard of the Humanistic Judaism communal organization. In the Israel of 1980, organized Judaism had a stranglehold on the religious government establishment. It was not yet as aggressive, conservative, and domineering as it has become since the settlers and the fundamentalist Jews began countering attempts by the government to bring about peace (prior to and following Yitzhak Rabin's assassination in 1995), but nevertheless it already had vast, oppressive power. Any reference to a humanistic Judaism gladdened the heart and was very exciting. By 1980, Israel's 1970 Law of Return had already been amended along *halakhic* lines, so that only somebody "born to a Jewish mother or who has converted and is not affiliated with another religion is considered Jewish." From 1977 onwards, when the late Menahem Begin became prime minister, the ultra-Orthodox Agudat Israel party enjoyed great power. A number of edicts were issued in the name of religion, including the ban on El Al flights on Shabbat and during Jewish festivals, as well as the mass exemption from army service of girls as well as yeshiva students, to mention just a few.

In addition, there was the ongoing occupation, which had begun in 1967. By then we were—as we still are—ruling another people. The Gush Emunim settler movement had already overrun the occupied territories and begun to undertake settlement activities, stealing land from the native-born inhabitants and adopting an anti-humanistic attitude towards the indigenous Palestinian populace. By then the settlers' rabbis had begun to relate to the Palestinian natives as "Amalek" against whom genocide must be performed. The former rabbi of Bar-Ilan University, Rabbi Hess—may he rest in peace—and others wrote about this issue. Rabbi Hess said that the Palestinian people are the offspring of Amalek, and hence Israel must follow the biblical command to wage a holy war of extermination against them (Deuteronomy 5:12–19). Turning their backs on the time-honored tradition of loving the stranger (Deuteronomy 10:19), settler rabbis have ruled that the Palestinians are to be treated like the seven nations inhabiting the land promised to Israel, about whom it is said: "Thou shalt utterly destroy them; thou shalt make no covenant with them, nor show mercy unto them" (Deuteronomy 7:2). In other words, nowadays the humanism that is such an essential part of Judaism is to be found in secular circles, and especially in the peace camp.

In the education system (Israel's education minister in 1980 belonged to the National Religious Party), Joshua was held up as an example of positive attributes, while the prophets were sidelined. The emphasis was also laid on Adam-God relationships, with less and less importance being attached to relationships between individuals. This period saw the beginnings of the nationalistic prophetic vision in which the entire Land of Israel was viewed as hallowed ground belonging entirely to the Jews. The more dominant this vision became, the more the Palestinian inhabitants were harassed. Naturally all of this was done in the name of the Glory of Israel and God's command.

In the midst of this state of affairs, I was pleased to hear about the existence of a Humanistic Jewish congregation and eager to learn more about it.

As soon as I arrived and actually met Sherwin Wine and Miriam Jerris, then the society's president, I knew that they were my kind of people. I was so excited when I entered the sanctum itself and saw the word "Adam" in large letters where the Jews normally put the Ten Commandments, with the stress on all their different "thou shalt nots." Since my youth, and in particular since Israel came into being, everything I have done—all my work, my energy, and my efforts—has tried to introduce into people's awareness, into public discourse, and into legislation the basic principles of human rights and freedoms proclaimed in the Universal Declaration of Human Rights of 10 December 1948. I have done so on the radio, in the press, in the Knesset, and in lectures, waging a never-ending struggle against the arbitrariness of the system and of those in power. It is necessary to realize that in Israel, most of the difficulties—and above all the discrimination against minorities, against women, against human liberties in the law and in day-to-day life—have a religious basis. The religious forces in Israel enjoy great political power because, given the country's political structure of coalition governments, neither of the big parties can establish a government without including the small religious parties. The political might of the religious forces can also be traced to the absence of a written constitution in which democratic principles and human rights can be anchored.

> In Israel, most of the difficulties—and above all the discrimination against minorities, against women, against human liberties in the law and in day-to-day life—have a religious basis.

To tell the truth, in Michigan what excited me especially was the sign, the inscription "Adam": this combination of Judaism, being free, being autonomous, and the use of the attribute "Adam," which applies to men and women alike, guaranteeing equality too. This also follows the original Jewish text, which says: "male and female created He them, and blessed them, and called their name Adam, in the day when they were created" (Genesis 5:2).

In the State of Israel, this equality is sadly absent. Even its Basic Law on Human Dignity and Liberty does not have a section guaranteeing full, equal rights to all individuals. The reason is simple: the religious political parties insisted on removing any such guarantee, even though it was certainly present and very prominent in the draft bill. They opposed giving equality to women and minorities, and as usual for the sake of keeping the coalition intact, those who were "willing to compromise" agreed to their demands, citing as justification the need for national "unity." It should be realized that in the Old Testament—which has had such a vast impact on European culture, Jewish and Christian alike, as well as on Muslim culture—at the very beginning, in Genesis, there is manifest equality between man and woman. Created in the image of God, they were both called "Adam": persons, human beings.

In chapter 1, at the very beginning of the Creation, it says (verse 27): "And God created Adam (man) in His own image, in the image of God created He him; male and female created He them." And later in Genesis, in chapter 5, which completes the story of the Creation, the first verse reads:

> This is the book of the generations of Adam. In the day that God created Adam (man), in the likeness of God made He him; male and female created He them, and blessed them, and called their name Adam, in the day when they were created.

So "Adam" applies to all men and women of all peoples, all origins, all colors, and all abilities, since we are all descendants of the original Adam in the Bible. As the sages put it, one human being cannot say to a fellow human being, "My lineage is superior to yours." The way I see it, the concept of

"Adam" contains much of the principle of equality. It also encompasses the principles of liberty, personal autonomy, choice, and responsibility. The text says that God created Adam and Eve in the image of God, and so we need to consider the precise nature of that divine image.

Let us read the text of Genesis 3, verse 22, carefully. After Adam and Eve had committed the original sin, they were punished:

> And the Lord God said: "Behold, the man is become as one of us, to know good and evil; and now, lest he put forth his hand, and take also of the tree of life, and eat, and live for ever." Therefore the Lord God sent him forth from the Garden of Eden.

So our two human beings, "Adam," were not actually expelled from the Garden of Eden for violating the command not to eat from the Tree of Knowledge, an action for which they received the harshest of punishments: man is to eat bread by the sweat of his brow, woman is to give birth in pain and suffering, and the snake is to go on his belly. They were actually expelled from the Garden of Eden because they had become like God, to know good and evil. Psalms (8:6–7) elaborates on this as follows:

> Yet Thou hast made him but little lower than the gods,
> And hast crowned him with glory and honor,
> Thou hast made him to have dominion over the works of Thy
> hands;
> Thou hast put all things under his feet.

Here, then, we have the lords of creation: Adam, man, who is able to distinguish between good and evil, between truth and falsehood, between right and wrong, between what is allowed and what is prohibited; who possesses judgment, the capacity to differentiate, and the capacity to choose; and hence who is responsible for the choices he makes, for his actions and his omissions, for the things he does and the things he fails to do. The sages further endorse this sovereignty on the part of Adam, this autonomy of choice, the capacity to judge and decide: "Everything is in God's hands other than the fear of God" (Tractate *Berachot* 16:72), as well as: "Everything is predetermined but there is freedom of choice" (*Ethics of the Fathers* 3:19). The kabbalists teach that God contracted himself in order to leave room for Adam—man—to investigate, to act, to create, and to make decisions.

Even those who despise the masses, those who establish their own power base, accruing physical and economic might, counting on the ignorance of the masses, on the poor and their fears—even they know that the ability to distinguish between good and evil, between the permitted and the forbidden, is an innate human trait. After all, it would be impossible otherwise to put on trial a thief, a murderer, a traitor, a pimp, let alone anyone "framed" by the authorities or the Church, as Jezebel infamously did to Naboth of Jezreel. But those who crave power, the despots and tyrants of this world, the generals and in particular clerics of all kinds—Catholic, Orthodox, Jewish, and Muslim alike—amass power for themselves, claiming all the while that they are doing so in the name of God: "*Halakha* says ...," "the Koran says ...," "the Pope says...." God's messengers on earth. They all exploit the hidden power and the fears of death and what comes afterwards, emasculating and enfeebling man's desire to be free and think for himself. And always—always!—ostensibly in a spirit of self-sacrifice, so as to redeem man and the world.

Dostoyevsky's *The Brothers Karamazov* has a chapter on the Grand Inquisitor, where (in the Inquisitor's voice) the author explains what a favor the Inquisition is doing to man by rescuing him from the burden of freedom, the burden of deciding about his actions on an independent basis—what a favor it is doing him by demanding his obedience.

The story goes that one day, Christ suddenly appeared on earth. People walked around with a feeling of enlightenment and joy. But then the Grand Inquisitor, hearing about this, issues instructions to arrest the Savior. At night he comes to the prison to visit Christ, saying he must make himself scarce or he too will be burnt at the stake, because he is a disruptive element. This act will allow the Church to continue showering the masses with the "happiness" with which it endows man. True, he says, you gave man freedom, but what use is it to him, his freedom? People do not want freedom, because they do not know how to use it. True, you gave him the ability to make decisions and to distinguish between good and bad, but what use is this to him? He doesn't want to make decisions, because nobody out there is listening. He doesn't understand the world, a place where bad things happen to good people, and the wicked thrive. The poor people, beset with adversity, thirst for comfort and consolation. So we the clergy generously take away his freedom, his authority, his ability to discern, his critical sense, his inquisitiveness, and his curiosity, relieving him of the burden of making up his mind. In turn he receives from the Church secrets, enigmas, miracles, belief in the world to come, which will compensate him for his suffering in this world—as long as he is an obedient believer. The Church even makes it possible for him to sin and then, by making confession, to atone for his trespasses. For what use to man is the freedom that you have given him? the Grand Inquisitor asks the Savior. What will he do with this authority that he has? And so we, the Church, have volunteered to ease his burden and to relieve him of his freedom. We have assumed the burden of authority, responsibility, and decision-making, and so we instruct him how to act in accordance with our decisions, for his own good; we have shown him the way to be faithful and to pray to the Savior.

> The concept of "Adam" contains much of the principle of equality. It also encompasses the principles of liberty, personal autonomy, choice, and responsibility.

History shows that all religious establishments, as well as all autocrats who have made promises of happiness and comfort, have been extremely effective in "relieving" man of his freedom and enfeebling his critical faculties—instead of teaching him knowledge; fostering a lively, inquiring mind; encouraging critical thinking and the ability to make decisions and assume responsibility. What we see all around us is that from childhood onwards, man is taught to obey. The churches and religious heads are fearful of (and at the same time inculcate in others the fear of) any manifestation of criticism, of inquisitiveness, of innovation or a spirit of discovery. At the very beginning of the period of emancipation and the Enlightenment—influencing the Western European Jewish world also, including such figures as Moses Mendelssohn and others—the authoritative figure of German Jewry, the Hatam Sofer, reacted by imposing the strictest prohibition on introducing any innovation to Jewish life outside the Torah.

"Liberating" man from his freedom and emasculating his critical faculties is not a difficult thing to do. All it takes is a little mass psychology, a certain amount of intimidation, and some promises. Add a great deal of demagoguery and forcefulness combined with a good PR job, and success is assured. Rallies with speakers setting passions ablaze, manifestations of power followed by contempt: these are tried-and-tested means of triggering emotional agitation among the masses as well as securing authority. When the individual, a lone figure, is in the midst of a crowd that has been whipped up into a frenzy, he feels strong, this individual, together with the masses roaring such slogans as "death to the Arabs," "Rabin's a traitor," "kill the homosexuals," "death to traitors," "down with Lefties," "drive the atheists out," "long live Rabbi Ovadia," "long live Arik," "long live our mother country," and so on and so forth. In this way an individual in a crowd is able to discharge his passions and frustrations. He feels great strength and empowerment because when he is part of a crowd, he does not need to account for what he says and what he does. We have only to think of Ibsen's *An Enemy of the People*, of Ionesco's *Rhinoceros*, of Orwell's books, including *1984*, and of the "lords," Mussolini, Lenin, and other twentieth-century "heroes."

Finally the Jews have a state: they have power, an army, occupied territories, and somebody to oppress and hate, somebody on whom they can vent all their pent-up historical bitterness, always in the name of God and his promises to the Children of Israel, and with the blessing of the rabbis. And it works.

During the Enlightenment, which swept over Europe in the seventeenth, eighteenth, and nineteenth centuries—that period of reason that brought with it the development of science and research, the United States' Revolutionary War and its Constitution, the French Revolution—philosopher Immanuel Kant, in his 1784 article entitled "What Is Enlightenment," defined the need to become mature, to dare to know, to dare to use one's intelligence and reason, to dare to make decisions. Before him the Jewish philosopher Baruch Spinoza, who made the link between reason, freedom, and peace, who despised prejudices that were entrenched in ignorance and a yearning for tyranny, wrote in his introduction to the *Tractatus Theologico-Politicus* that "those who believe in all kinds of superstitions" discard the paths of reason and pursue foolishness and delusions that they ascribe to divine actions. These people, whose minds have been confused by the superstitions that religion has fed them, reach a stage where "they will fight for their service as if it were their salvation, so that they will consider it a sublime honor and not a disgrace to shed their blood and sacrifice themselves for the arrogance of one man"—something that would not be countenanced in a free, rational community.

Prejudices, as Spinoza points out, reduce "intelligent people to animals, by utterly preventing each man from using his free judgment and distinguishing between good and evil … and, worst of all, those who have nothing but scorn for understanding and reject reason on the grounds that it is harmful by its very nature, are precisely those who are considered to enjoy the divine light."

Immanuel Kant defined the need to become mature, to dare to know, to dare to use one's intelligence and reason, to dare to make decisions.

In conclusion, Spinoza says that every single human being is entitled to be vigilant in safeguarding his freedom, he is entitled to freedom of opinion, and he is allowed to interpret what he believes as he sees fit.

However, he was advancing these arguments during the Enlightenment. By the twentieth century, the blaze of glory of the enlightened spirit had faded, not to say entirely vanished, and fascist and communist regimes alike, proclaiming extreme nationalism and racism, became slaves to the cult of power. Two terrible world wars fostered the propensity towards autocracy and expansion. And as the globe, still terribly mauled by the events and consequences of long-drawn-out conflicts, has tried to establish enlightened democracies, to safeguard human rights, we have witnessed a return to the culture of the masses, to unbridled demagoguery, to the cult of power, to the revival of superstitions, religious rituals, and expansion of the rule of the various churches in Christianity, Judaism, and Islam—rule based on exploitation of fears, feelings of inferiority, and anxieties related to scientific concepts. What is particularly striking is the struggle, both visible and veiled, for authority, wealth, and power between the civil authorities and religion, making use of various forms of enticement in a mix of competition and cooperation, on the grounds of expediency and electoral considerations, paying no heed to the rising tide of nationalist power, which is becoming ever more strident and fundamentalist.

Set against the realities of our contemporary existence, Sherwin Wine's intellectual and independent stance as a proud and open-minded Jew is exemplary. He is a man who has adopted the wonderful principle of enlightenment, of humanism, of man's importance and standing as a source of authority, creativity, morals, and human solidarity. This is man the humanist, who has shaken off the fetters of the rabbis' fossilized and ritualized Jewish religion. This man is firmly rooted in a Judaism of universal values—values that are to be found in all of the Jewish people's main sources, beginning with the account of the Creation, through the narratives of the life of Abraham the Patriarch, to the prophets and modern thinkers. Think only of Abraham, the man who is chosen in order to teach "his children and his household after him to do righteousness and justice" (Genesis 18:19), and who argues with God against collective punishment, asking "shall not the judge of all the earth do justly?" (Genesis 18:25), and "wilt Thou indeed sweep away the righteous with the wicked?" (Genesis 18:23). The prophets scorn ritual and sacrifices, instead demanding law and justice for all, including the stranger, the orphan, and the widow. In a direct line from them we have Baruch Spinoza the thinker and many other humanistic Jews, a line that extends to today.

The Humanistic Judaism movement has expanded, establishing branches in the United States, Canada, and Israel too. Since the 1980s ties have existed between Sherwin Wine's congregation in Michigan and the Israeli congregation. This relationship has developed in Israel into Humanistic Secular Judaism, affiliated with Professor Yaakov Malkin's undertaking of many years' standing. It already has its own magazine and *beit midrash* for study groups. Close ties have also been established with the largest congregation in Brussels, Belgium, which was founded by the family and friends of David and Simone Susskind, as well as with congregations in France, Switzerland, and elsewhere.

In a world where religious and national fundamentalism is on the rise, including in the Christian United States, the Muslim world, and the Jewish world, especially Israel, we believe that people are autonomous, thinking, and intelligent beings. We believe in human rights and freedoms, which each and every individual—man, woman, and child—should enjoy irrespective of origin, religion, or gender. We are proud of the Jewish nature of the congregation founded by our friend Sherwin Wine and of his many writings and publications in which he has laid the foundations for the Humanistic Jewish outlook, and we are delighted to be counted among his friends and partners in this path.

We must not, however, rest on our laurels, because there is a long way to go and much to be done.

Shulamit Aloni is an attorney, teacher, writer, and journalist. She was a member of the Israeli Knesset from 1965 to 1969 and from 1974 until 1997. Originally a member of the Labor Party, Ms. Aloni founded the Ratz Party, Israel's civil rights and peace movement. She served as Minister of Education and Culture and Minister of Communications, Science, and Arts. Ms. Aloni founded the Israel Consumer Council and Bureau of Civil Rights. Her publications include *Children's Rights in Israel* and *Women As Human Beings*, as well as a political autobiography, *I Can Do No Other.*

Sherwin Wine at Seventy-Five: A Half-Century of Achievement

Khoren Arisian

By any professional measure, Sherwin Wine, whom it has been my pleasure and privilege to know for more than thirty-five years, exhibits all the essential earmarks of a prodigy when it comes to religious creativity, institutional organization and extension, oratorical eloquence, and charismatic presence. I was first privy to Sherwin's incomparable grasp of the rabbinic calling when I heard him speak at the annual Assembly of the Unitarian Universalist Association in Miami in June 1965. Many of us realized we were in the presence of a remarkable person, a man in command of a first-rate intellect who marshaled his arguments with ease, urgency, and passion. Sherwin and I became friends that very day, I believe, and have since enjoyed a warm collegial relationship.

Sherwin had already achieved a certain degree of notoriety as a rabbinic rebel of sorts for having founded the first temple of Humanistic Judaism—the Birmingham Temple in Farmington Hills, Michigan—two years before, in 1963. Indeed, if memory serves me correctly, his visage had already graced an issue of *Time* magazine as America's first outspoken atheist rabbi, a designation Sherwin might well have found wanting. Like any founder of a compelling new religious movement, he probably welcomed publicity, although he could hardly influence the direction it would take. His was an unapologetically nontheist approach to religious experience and understanding. Unlike atheism, whose devotees behold theism with more solemn anger than it deserves, nontheism simply ignores that hypothesis altogether. Be that as it may, the mid-sixties in America was the brief heyday of the so-called "death-of-God" theologies. Humanistic Judaism fit right in with the exciting religious ferment of the time such as we have not seen since.

Humanistic Judaism is the fifth wheel, so to speak, after Orthodox, Conservative, Reform, and Reconstructionist versions of Judaism. Any further theological retailing of this remarkable world religion is unlikely, which only highlights the extraordinary radicalism of Felix Adler's creation of Ethical Culture, the spiritual mainspring of which was Emersonian transcendentalism. Ethical Culture is unquestionably America's first—and very likely last—openly agnostic religion. With little patience for ethnic preoccupation, Adler simply woke up one day to realize he had outgrown even Reform Judaism.

If Unitarianism is the last attenuation of Protestant Christianity, then Humanistic Judaism represents the final attenuation of the Judaic religious sphere from which it emanates. Humanistic Judaism's attractiveness in the first instance was directed toward a cultural and secularized Jewish clientele and audience: individuals and families who might enjoy creating a community of ethical aspiration and celebration. Sherwin's is a strictly humanist conception of the Judaic religious tradition, which he interprets as an aspirational expression and a demonstration of secular seeking for life's meanings. Thus Humanistic Judaism is an entirely worldly religious movement.

Ethical Culture does not eschew rituals, yet it cannot be considered a liturgical movement in any common understanding of that term. Humanistic Judaism, on the other hand, exults in secular, commonsensically appealing interpretations of the life cycles through which people move, celebrating holidays and other familiar but humanistically transposed ritualistic observances of Judaic tradition—also adding inspiring secular festivals extolling the legacy of humanism (World Humanist Days) or the lasting imprint of Darwinism (Darwin Day), and the like.

Similar to Adler, Sherwin Wine believes fervently in extending the movement he founded and attentively nurtures. As early as 1969 he created the Society for Humanistic Judaism to serve as a vehicle of national outreach. In 1982 he was a leading force in organizing the North American Committee for Humanism, the singular and lasting achievement of which is the Humanist Institute for the training of humanist leaders; during the first decade of its existence, Sherwin, as NACH president, provided vigorous and timely direction. In 1986 he helped establish the International Federation of Secular Humanistic Jews, a worldwide association of member groups in Mexico, South America, Western Europe, Israel, and elsewhere. He has been instrumental in putting together the Leadership Conference of Secular and Humanistic Jews, the Center for New Thinking, and what used to be called the Conference of Liberal Religion, now somewhat reduced in scope and intermittently continuing under a series of different rubrics.

The mid-sixties in America was the brief heyday of the so-called "death-of-God" theologies. Humanistic Judaism fit right in with the religious ferment of the time.

Sherwin is also the author of a number of full-length books, with perhaps his signature volume being *Judaism Beyond God.* A brief summary of his conception of Humanistic Judaism would include the following:

1. Every Jew enjoys the natural right (herewith the prime importance of the individual) to carve out a distinctive Jewish lifestyle for him- or herself without benefit of supernatural assurance or established traditions.

2. One's life goal is to become self-possessed/autonomous yet be aware of and participate in the sustenance provided by communal bonds—human life is ultimately with people.

3. Personal dignity is attainable and highly desirable but requires that one first conduct oneself as a free being among other free beings.

4. If Jews are to survive as a people, they must seek to reconcile the simultaneously convergent demands of modern science and scientific rationalism with their notion of Jewish loyalty and attention to personal needs.

5. The religious and secular springs of Jewish life are to be seen and appreciated as equally important.

Not surprisingly, if the above set of convictions is to be nourished and developed, a congregational setting is necessary, hence the organizational apparatus of Humanistic Judaism. Ethical Culture, predominantly but not exclusively attractive to Jews, is no less a congregational movement, which, however, eschews all sectarian appurtenances and terminologies of other religions, drawing its inspiration chiefly from the moral domain of human experience and, broadly, from humankind's spiritual legacy.

Creation of the aforementioned Conference of Liberal Religion revealed Sherwin Wine's expansive awareness that liberal religious tendencies inhere in many spiritual and cognate traditions. Here hangs not only a tale, but also a possible road down which nontheistic philosophies and religious movements might care to go. Let me, in view of this thought, change my focus from being a minor memoirist to being a minor *festschrift* contributor. These closing remarks are therefore no less in further tribute to my good and loyal friend and distinguished colleague of many years, Sherwin Wine, reflecting on whose biography and accomplishments causes me to peer a bit into the future in light of the past.

"Liberal religion" is a term that originated in the nineteenth century, an echo of the Enlightenment that continues to be invoked among those movements and denominations that variously have come around to the position that religion need not be the domain of the chained mind; that supernaturalism is inferior to naturalistic earth-oriented spiritualities; that the scientific method and ethos from which liberal religion rises lead best to whatever objectively verifiable truths we humans can acquire; that religion, insofar as it is an offshoot of our social and ethical nature, must address the chief issues of the day in an effort to affect public opinion. None other than Abraham Lincoln once commented that the molders of opinion are far more influential in the long run than the makers of laws.

Involved as I have been professionally all my adult life in the liberal religious ethical humanist sphere of endeavor, I have frequently noticed that liberal religious/humanist leaders often bemoan the fact that they don't have a "narrative" like that of major world religions. I submit that such yearning—namely, the notion that something old and comfortable is missing in one's life—is beside the point. We are not empty wine bottles waiting to be filled. An inspiring, mostly untold saga of liberal religion lies before us, waiting to be seized and shaped from the moral, secular, and religious history of Western culture. There's a whole body of experience in this frame of reference that's often only alluded to in bits and pieces instead of pieced together. Common strands exist, for example, between Ethical Culture and late-nineteenth-century Unitarianism of the Free Religious variety that need to be reassessed and reinvented with the present and future in mind. If history needs to be legitimately re-envisioned and rewritten, say, from a feminist point of view—à la Betty Friedan and hosts of others—it's no less time for the same need to be fulfilled with regard to the entire development of that ever-maligned and bravely noted story we call liberal religion. *This* is our common narrative in which all ethical, nontheist, and humanist enterprises need to be resituated. Liberal religion, in short, is an entirely new spiritual dispensation on the world-historical scene. It is mainstream, not tangential, even if it is not culturally and demographically in the middle.

Liberal religious/humanist leaders often bemoan the fact that they don't have a "narrative" like that of major world religions. I submit that such yearning is beside the point.

Although this modern liberal religious impulse represents an emergence of the late nineteenth century, the need and desire for freedom in religion are of ancient lineage. Witness British monk Pelagius, whom I have long admired: Condemned as a heretic by the Roman Catholic Church in the early fifth century C.E., he courageously denied the denigrating doctrine of original sin and affirmed the ability of human beings to lead ethical lives through exercising their free will. Pelagius maintained that Adam's alleged transgression affected only himself, that he would have died anyway, and that one can live an exemplary and effective life without the need for supernatural grace. Pelagius, whose most prominent opponent was Augustine, was acquitted of heresy at Jerusalem but condemned twice thereafter, by a church council at Carthage and another at Ephesus. He never recanted. A tireless and convinced advocate of human freedom, he asserted the individual's inherent power of free choice and insisted that we are endowed with sufficient reason and free will to make of our existence whatever we choose. We are the determining agents of our own salvation. His high moral character notwithstanding, Pelagius, who died in 420, was posthumously condemned yet again in 431.

What Pelagius embodied was a deeply felt sense of moral agency, an idea that marked much of American religious life and conviction, traditional as well as liberal, in the first half of the nineteenth century. The American Revolution had been a struggle for liberation, freedom being thereafter democracy's watchword, however incomplete its practice. Emerson and Theodore Parker were imbued with the American idea of the free individual and from their respective public perches spoke of it eloquently, far and wide.

These musings bring me to a final reflection concerning Sherwin's career. His influence as an exponent of humanism, Jewish secularity, and the free mind has been notably purveyed through his confident and engaging manner as a public orator, far more so, I'd venture to say, than as an author of books or through printed texts of his brilliantly focused extemporaneous remarks and speeches. Let us remember that reading is in essence a private matter; unless what one is reading is of rousing revolutionary quality, reading in essence goes nowhere as a significant stimulus for the shaping of public opinion. The power of the human voice cannot be gainsaid.

Members of humanist organizations read a lot of humanist literature *in private.* Because many of them are solitary folks at heart—who care little about coming together in groups to *do* anything, who frequently pride themselves on their isolation and their status as non-joiners, who are almost terrified of committing themselves organizationally or monetarily in support of needy causes—their joint effectiveness is practically nil, no matter how many e-mails they may forward from home to an unresponsive White House, complaining rightly, say, of the removal of yet another brick in the wall of separation between church and state. Often too concerned with their own views, sometimes vehemently so, they do little on behalf of their philosophic posterity.

What originally attracted me to Ethical Culture was its historic inclination toward activism and institutional outreach to the public. We are at a critical juncture in American life when, more than ever, we of humanist persuasion need to *go public* with our most deeply felt convictions and enthusiastically seek out our fellow citizens to help spread anew the message of the democratic faith and its permutations. And if we don't know enough about that faith and don't realize how much it is entwined with the liberal religious legacy, let us educate ourselves and others. The Hebrew prophets, be it recalled, were not mere rabble-rousers; more important, they were political realists who spoke in the public square and educated the people. In effect, they were ethical educators. There's an old lesson here to be learned again, and in that regard Sherwin Wine's eminent career is exemplary and telling.

Khoren Arisian is Minister Emeritus of the First Unitarian Society of Minneapolis, where he served from 1979 to 1997. He is currently senior leader of the New York Society for Ethical Culture. Dr. Arisian helped found both the North American Committee for Humanism and the Humanist Institute. He was the associate dean of the Humanist Institute from 1990 to 1996, and he continues to serve on its board of governors. He is a distinguished member of the Humanist Institute faculty.

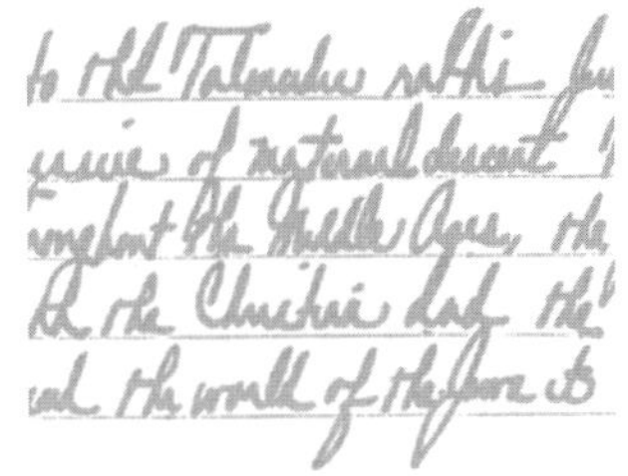

On Religion and Secularism

Yehuda Bauer

It is a pleasure to devote a brief essay to my friend and colleague, Rabbi Sherwin Wine, the first Secular Humanistic rabbi in the United States. We all owe Sherwin a tremendous debt of gratitude, for all he has done for us in the Secular Humanistic Jewish movement worldwide. He has shown that it is possible to establish a living, working community in which a form of Jewish tradition is combined with a nontheistic belief system, in the service of the individual, the family, the community, and the wider people, indeed in the service of humanity, beyond narrow borders. There is no contradiction, Sherwin taught us, between loyalty to and identification with the Jewish people and its fate, and a desire to be part of a universalistic message.

It is that double message that is being attacked today, from a number of quarters. The ugly face of antisemitism has appeared again, in two forms: one, in the Western world, and the other in the Muslim world. In the West, it is not so much a matter of overt attacks on Jews as individuals, or on Jewish institutions, buildings, or cemeteries. Such attacks, which recently reached a high point (especially in France, but also elsewhere), have decreased measurably. Today there is no Western-type government that will tolerate attacks such as these, nor is there any current danger of a government-sponsored antisemitic outbreak in the West. But there is a growth of antisemitic feeling among the chattering classes—media, academia, free professions—reflecting, I think, the emergence of feelings that were contained in a box of latency that is now becoming unlocked. The fact that a French ambassador in Britain referred to Israel as "that shitty little country" at a cocktail party does not reflect on him as much as it does on the fact that he felt absolutely free to utter these highly intellectual sentiments at a party where hundreds of guests were standing around, holding glasses in their well-manicured hands. Also in the United Kingdom, His Grace the Bishop of Guildford has mounted an anti-Israeli hate attack that is spreading in England, an attack that provoked the Archbishop of Canterbury to take countermeasures, including the nomination of a special person to thwart antisemitic propaganda in the Anglican Church.

Much more dangerous than the rising intellectual antisemitism in the West, however, is the spread of radical Islamic antisemitism. One has to emphasize immediately that radical Islam is an abhorrent interpretation of Islam just as the anti-Gentile and chauvinistic attitudes of the ultra-Orthodox represent a repugnant interpretation of Judaism (though it must be admitted that all religions, and not only the monotheistic ones, are prone to be interpreted in an antihumanistic way). Radical Islam is the enemy of what it sees as the decadent West; it explicitly seeks world domination in the name of a utopia that will establish an Islamic rule based on the medieval Muslim religious law, the *shari'a.* Radical Islamists view the Jews as the spearhead of the West and explicitly demand their eradication, unless they meekly submit to Islam as the hardliners interpret it. There are certain parallels between this and the National Socialist and Marxist-Leninist ideologies, though of course there are also very big differences. Both Nazism and Communism were or are quasi-religions, with holy texts that had to be followed literally; both sought world domination and the abolition of binding legal norms; both were radically anti-Jewish, though Nazism of course was much more extreme. Radical Islam is as extreme (so far, only in theory) as Nazi ideology was. It is unpleasant but, in my view, very realistic to regard religion, in all three cases, as legitimizing antihumanistic, antidemocratic, genocidal theories. The fact that Marxism-Leninism was not theistic makes little difference: it had all the characteristics of religious fanaticism. Nazism was explicitly theistic, in its own distorted way.

I am not antireligious. I acknowledge the fact that there were and are religious humanists who interpret their religious beliefs in ways that one should admire. They are our allies in our quest to imbue our society with humanistic values. I also believe in the freedom of all individuals or groups to follow their beliefs as they wish, provided they do not prevent others from following theirs. As a secularist, I favor a radical liberal approach—in other words, not passively waiting for changes to occur in society but proactively furthering these ideas as much as possible.

> There is a growth of antisemitic feeling among the chattering classes—media, academia, free professions—reflecting the emergence of feelings that were contained in a box of latency that is now becoming unlocked.

It must be admitted, however, that uncounted millions of people were murdered not in the name of liberal, democratic, or nonreligious belief systems, but rather in the name of a compassionate and loving God or gods, or of nontheistic religions such as Nazism and Communism. From the mass murder of the Saxons at the hands of Charlemagne, to the Catholic-Protestant wars in Europe in the sixteenth and seventeenth centuries, to the annihilation of Amerindian civilizations in the name of the Cross, to the obliteration of Japanese Christians by the ruling Shinto elite in the early seventeenth century, to the Nazi and Soviet murder campaigns, and any number of other instances before and after, religious beliefs, often but not always theistic, provided the murderous ideologies.

Democracy and liberalism are, we all know, tender shoots that must be carefully tended in order to survive. Until the latter part of the eighteenth century, there were no examples of successful attempts at creating democratic societies. Ancient Greek cities were based on slavery. So was the American South, but the Civil War changed that, at least formally. Women's voting rights were granted in Britain only in 1919, and it is only in the last century that things began to change, even as the whole idea of democratic governance was brutally challenged by Nazi Germany and the Soviet Union. Today one could argue that India is a democracy and that Communist China is slowly, painfully, and very much in zigzags, moving towards democracy. But the Muslim world is ruled by corrupt, authoritarian regimes. It is increasingly endangered by a radicalism that is in principle opposed to human lawmaking, arguing that God is the lawgiver and he has decreed the law in the *shari'a;* hence, all attempts at parliamentary government are heresy and must be abolished. There is some logic in this: if one believes that a God (or gods) rules the world and has pronounced his laws in holy texts, and if there is only one correct interpretation of those texts and God-given laws, and if that interpretation is in the hands of wise men (never women, of course), then indeed no human agency can argue, subtract, or add to such laws without denying God's will. When radical Islam threatens the Jewish people with extinction, calling them apes and swine—there is a wealth of quotations to show that Muslim intellectuals propagate these views—it is part of an attack on Western democracy. A postmodernist argument might say that there is no right or wrong here, that all points of view are legitimate; such an argument would simply play into the hands of those that would put an end to all arguments, including postmodernist ones. I would argue that there is a difference between legitimate dissension within democratic norms and an attack on all norms that do not tally with extremist religious ideologies.

Some liberal and universalist forms of modern religion do help in the solution of problems, when they forego the exclusivist and absolutist claims that have been the usual fare of religious thought. But in too many cases religion is not the solution; it is the problem. Antisemitism is not a marginal issue in the discussion of the dangers to Western democracy—it is, as it always was, the litmus test of liberalism and humanism. At the present, this notion is fairly clearly shown in the international arena. Israel is—again, as after the Zionism-Racism United Nations resolution—the pariah among the nations. It is the only U.N. member that is not part of any regional organization, for it does not belong to Europe and is rejected by Mideastern and Asiatic countries. Quite literally, the majority of resolutions passed in bodies such as the U.N. Human Rights Commission, UNESCO, and others, deal with real or invented wrongs that Israel commits, and such resolutions are passed by staunch defenders of democracy and progress, such as Saudi Arabia, Syria, Libya, Pakistan, Egypt, or Sudan. A peak of genocidal propaganda was reached at the Durban Conference against racism, which was hijacked by Israel's enemies, and where the Israel-Palestinian conflict became the main, sometimes the only, topic of discussion. In the end, this became too much even for the Europeans, and the worst resolutions in this direction were rejected. Just as the individual Jew in the Middle Ages was a pariah among people, and every injustice could be committed against him, so Israel today, as the collective Jew, has become the pariah among the nations. This situation is not only a problem for Israel and the Jewish people; it is, as always with antisemitism, a problem for all of humanity.

Antisemitism is not a marginal issue in the discussion of the dangers to Western democracy—it is, as it always was, the litmus test of liberalism and humanism.

This is not to say that criticism of Israel is equated with antisemitism, or that Israel does not deserve to be criticized on many counts. The Israeli-Palestinian conflict is basically a national conflict between two ethnicities, over a (small) piece of land. Such conflicts can only be settled by compromise, and both sides today are ruled by elites who want victory for their respective side, and who reject compromise. Sharon does not want any compromise: he wants to rule all of historic Palestine and is prepared to grant the Palestinians, who will soon be more numerous than the Jews in the whole area between the Jordan River and the Mediterranean Sea, local autonomy, with no civil rights. Increasing numbers of right-wingers who are even more radical than that want to engage in ethnic cleansing and deport the Palestinians from their homes—and they say it publicly. Most of these radicals are religious Jewish fundamentalists. The difference between them and the radical Muslim variety is simply that they are not powerful enough to endanger Western civilization, or the world; but that is the only difference. The religious texts that would justify mass murder are readily available. On the Palestinian side, it is quite clear that a large majority would love to get rid of all the Jews—"getting rid of" meaning "murder." Arafat and his cohorts see any compromise as temporary, a base from which they would wish to proceed to a total elimination of the Jewish presence in the area. Radical Islamic groups, such as Hamas and Islamic Jihad, argue that there is a religious justification for a policy of annihilation. They do not want a national Palestinian state, but an Islamic one, which would also, incidentally, deny civil rights to Christian Palestinians. The nationalist groups within the Palestinian movement demand what would appear as a compromise. There are, on both sides, those who genuinely wish for a lasting compromise solution, and they constitute strong minorities. They face an uphill struggle, but one that stands a chance. Nothing is predetermined, there are no absolutes. As secular Jews, and as liberals, whatever our opinions may be within the wide range of liberal, conservative, or social-democratic democracy, we are duty-bound to devote ourselves to a struggle for a better and more civilized world, and within that for a Jewish people that will indeed be worthy of the great traditions that we inherited.

Yehuda Bauer is a world-renowned Holocaust scholar. He was born in Prague, Czechoslovakia, and immigrated to Palestine in 1939. He served in the War of Independence and joined Kibbutz Hoval in 1952. He was historical advisor to Claude Lanzmann for the film *Shoah* and to Abba Eban for *Heritage*. He is the academic advisor at Yad Vashem in Jerusalem. His books include *My Brother's Keeper*, *The Holocaust in Historical Perspective*, *Out of the Ashes*, and *A History of the Holocaust*. His most recent book is *Rethinking the Holocaust*.

To Destroy and to Build: The Balance of Creativity and Continuity

Adam Chalom

A TALE OF TWO RABBIS

The first in this tale of two rabbis is Rabbi Moshe ben Maimon (Rambam), a rabbi between two worlds. With one foot, Rambam—also called Maimonides—stood solidly in traditional Judaism, writing a new code of laws, the *Mishneh Torah*, which he hoped would supersede the Talmud.[1] With the other, he stepped into a secular world of learning, seeking out the most advanced science and philosophy of his age, from Arabic medicine and physics to a rediscovered Aristotle. Maimonides wrote a work of Jewish philosophy in Judeo-Arabic, *The Guide of the Perplexed*, which was burned not by the Church, but by rabbinic authorities.[2] Today, however, Rambam is revered as a great Jewish hero.

The second in this tale is a modern rabbi named Sherwin Wine. Wine felt compelled to speak a message of contemporary thought that a Jewish audience may not have appreciated—in his case, philosophical humanism.

And, like Maimonides, he was torn between his attachments to Jewish identity and his personal philosophy. His creation, Humanistic Judaism, is a balancing act between Jewish tradition and the most advanced science and philosophy of his age. At its heart, Humanistic Judaism seeks equilibrium between continuity with Jewish civilization and creative expressions of a new Jewish identity.

THE REJECTION IMPULSE

In the quest for this balance, two actions are at odds: rejection and reclamation. When Humanistic Jews look at their past, they come to an inevitable conclusion: they disagree with most Jewish historical belief. As one example, consider an abridged version of Maimonides's Thirteen Principles of Faith, the "basics" of traditional Judaism:

> I believe with complete faith that the Creator ... creates and guides all creatures.
>
> I believe with complete faith that the Creator ... is unique.
>
> I believe with complete faith that the Creator has no body.
>
> I believe with complete faith that the Creator is first and last.
>
> I believe with complete faith that the Creator, to him alone may one pray.
>
> I believe with complete faith that all the words of the prophets are true.
>
> I believe with complete faith that the prophesy of Moses *Rabbenu* was true.
>
> I believe with complete faith that the entire Torah in our hands now was given to Moses.
>
> I believe with complete faith that this Torah will not be exchanged nor will there be another from the Creator.
>
> I believe with complete faith that the Creator knows all the deeds and thoughts of humanity.
>
> I believe with complete faith that the Creator rewards those who keep his commandments and punishes those who transgress his commandments.

> I believe with complete faith in the coming of the Messiah; even though he delays, still I believe he will come.
>
> I believe with complete faith that there will be a resuscitation of the dead at the time the Creator desires.[3]

For comparison, a summary of Humanistic Judaism from its founder, Rabbi Sherwin Wine:

> The humanistic Jew is an individual ... who believes in the ultimate value of self-respect and in the principles of humanism, community, autonomy, and rationality. He also finds meaning in the celebration of life as expressed through the historic Jewish calendar and seeks to interpret this calendar in a naturalistic way. He perceives that the power he possesses to determine and control his own life is the result of two billion years of evolutionary history. Therefore, his religious feeling reinforces his sense of human dignity.[4]

Clearly, there is a wide gulf of belief between these two formulations. Humanistic Judaism rejects most if not all of Maimonides's principles—no petitional prayer, no divine omniscience, no immutable revelation of the Torah to Moses, and so on.

At its heart, Humanistic Judaism seeks equilibrium between continuity with Jewish civilization and creative expressions of a new Jewish identity.

Humanistic Judaism is not the first movement in Jewish life to face this discontinuity with the past—the Zionist movement addressed similar issues. When the Israeli writer Yonatan Ratosh was asked if Israeli literature were also Jewish literature, he wrote the following:

> The choice is between [a meager and detached] literature and a native, rooted literature, a literature of nationhood—one that will break out of that closely guarded wall and expand historical and territorial horizons; ... one that might ultimately be able to embrace people as a whole, rather than as Jews, members of a cer-

> tain community, and the world as world, rather than as a stage for the generations of the wandering Jew.
>
> But for the sake of this future, for the sake of the reception and development of national values and problems, freedom is necessary, liberation from the framework of Jewish literature and values, from the contents and problems of Judaism.
>
> To put it bluntly: Take the case of an old building. It is impossible to build a newer and better—or, at any rate, more suitable—building in its stead without first clearing away the old. Or, to put it more simply, take the case of a chick in its shell. It has to pierce its shell, to crack it open, to shake it off in order to emerge into the daylight. Failing this, it will be destined to suffocate within.[5]

In other words, the Jewish past may be no more than a discarded shell, a ruin that must be destroyed to build a suitable home for a humanistic identity. Liberation from the authority structures of the traditional past is clearly part of the program of Humanistic Judaism, but Humanistic Judaism has not traveled so far as to absolutely reject "the contents and problems of Judaism."

Let us look to the Jewish experience to see the "rejection impulse" taken to extremes. Here was one radical Jewish response from the late nineteenth century:

> Grand Yom Kippur Ball, with theater. Arranged with the consent of all new rabbis of Liberty. Kol Nidre Night and Day. In the year 5651, after the invention of the Jewish idols, and 1890, after the birth of the false Messiah.... The Kol Nidre will be offered by John Most. Music, dancing, buffet, "Marseillaise," and other hymns against Satan.[6]

Those socialist and anarchist rebels from the shtetl, whose childhood was marked by rigid religious restrictions, declared their freedom from tradition by striving to negate it: eating ham-and-cheese sandwiches on Yom Kippur, smoking on the synagogue steps on Shabbat, and willfully forgetting or mocking all they knew of traditional Judaism. Yet this "in your face" reaction did not ultimately provide a source of future life: if one is an *apikoros*, or heretic, who refuses to teach one's child about a rejected tradition, then the child grows up an *am ha-arets*, or ignoramus, who knows nothing about why their parents are so angry at those other Jews, or what those other Jews do every fall during the Kol Nidre Ball. While stories of such renegades may be emotionally satisfying to Humanistic Jews, the lasting value of such rebellion is about the same as putting one's thumbs in one's ears, sticking out one's tongue, and making the appropriate sounds. Such rebellion is willful discontinuity without enough rooted creativity to compensate. It is creativity at the expense, and to the destruction, of continuity.

THE RECLAMATION PROJECT

If Humanistic Jewish communities call themselves Jewish congregations, and they identify with the Jewish people, then there must be some connection with the Jewish past. Clearly Humanistic Jews will not return to practices and beliefs that do not conform to their philosophical commitments—that, for them, has little dignity. Instead, they must explore the process of reclamation—reclaiming parts of the Jewish past for present use. Hannah Arendt once described the role of the historical critic in similar terms:

> Like a pearl diver who descends to the bottom of the sea, not to excavate the bottom and bring it to light but to pry loose the rich and the strange, the pearls and the coral in the depths, and to carry them to the surface, this thinking delves into the depths of the past—but not in order to resuscitate it the way it was and to contribute to the renewal of extinct ages. What guides [it] is the conviction that although the living is subject to the ruin of time, the process of decay is at the same time a process of crystallization, that in the depth of the sea, into which sinks and is dissolved what once was alive, some things "suffer a sea-change" and survive in new crystallized forms and shapes that remain immune to the

> elements, as though they waited only for the pearl diver who one day will come down to them and bring them up into the world of the living.[7]

Humanistic Jews do not recreate the past. They search the depths for what time has preserved and even improved, and they bring it back to our world to make our lives more beautiful. The wisdom Humanistic Jews seek from the Jewish depths is more complicated than commandments: it involves old articulations of contemporary humane instincts, new ethical dilemmas to consider, the sense of roots and self-knowledge that enables one to stand with confidence and strength. For Humanistic Judaism, the descent into the past confirms Jewish roots, and the contrast between ancient and modern confirms present philosophical commitments.

Humanistic Jews, like the majority of modern Jews, are anything but traditional, but some modern Jews are tempted to pretend that they are. Such claims to traditionalism represent diving for pearls, and drowning. For if contemporary Jews live in an open society, integrated with their surroundings and intimately connected with the peoples among whom they live, even if they strive to feel "traditional," they remain anything but traditional Jews. This problem has afflicted the Reform and Conservative movements as well as Humanistic Judaism. The courage of the initial religious reformers to declare their break with the past in the name of progress and modernity has often given way in later generations to the desire for continuity. So the yarmulke and the tallis have returned to prominence in Reform Judaism. After all, it's hard to claim full continuity in a temple that one drives to on Friday night without at least putting on the costume. Every Yom Kippur, millions of Jews sit in synagogue audiences and celebrate their smooth continuity with the traditional Jewish past, whether or not they fast, or drive home, or wear yarmulkes.

Reform and Conservative Jews have radically changed, but they are generally uncomfortable admitting how open and divergent from the Jewish past they really have become. Finding pearls and pretending that nothing has happened to them—that no time has passed to create the contrast between antique beauty and its current setting—is having your tradition and abandoning it too. The challenge for Humanistic Judaism is to balance a love of the past with a sense of contemporary authority; what is old is not more "Jewish" than what is new. And simply because some practice or text is "traditional" is not sufficient reason to adopt it. For example, there is no drive among Humanistic congregations for a *mehitza*—the screen in an Orthodox synagogue separating the women's section from the main sanctuary—for Shabbat services, though it is clearly "traditionally Jewish." How to find the balance?

HABAD FOR HUMANISTIC JUDAISM

Has Humanistic Judaism built buildings with no foundations, missing opportunities for historical transcendence? Or has it kept what is old to the exclusion of creating something new and meaningful, suffocating in its shell?

The Lubavitch branch of Hasidism has a favorite acronym, *Habad*, for its school of thought. *Habad* comes from *hesed* (love), *bina* (understanding), and *daat* (knowledge). Here, then, are three principles for Humanistic Judaism in relation to its past, formulated into *Habad* for Humanistic Jews.

> Humanistic Jews do not recreate the past. They search the depths for what time has preserved, and they bring it back to our world to make our lives more beautiful.

Hesed: Just as romantic love waxes and wanes, the connection of Humanistic Jews to their past can fluctuate. At times and in places, they feel very Jewish. At other times, they feel very human. They may find a passage in the Talmud that they love. They may run across a biblical verse that they detest. Sometimes joyful and sometimes onerous, the connection to the Jewish past does, however, remain. As with any love, Humanistic Jews must connect with their past on equal footing, knowing what their ancestors believed and celebrating what truly is continuous with their own religion.

Their lives are free-standing buildings of their creation, and all buildings need roots and foundations to survive. And if Humanistic Jews seek special moments of transcendence, to contact some plane of experience beyond their own, the literary and cultural past of the Jewish people may well provide such a connection. Can they not hear the words of the Bible and the Mishna, the voices of Rashi and Maimonides and Mendelssohn, and then add their own, becoming part of a chorus that transcends language, belief, time, and space? If Humanistic Jews love being Jewish, then they must come to terms with a past that is a mixed bag of rejection and inspiration. It turns out that *all* Jews have their cross to bear.

Bina: Understand the past for what it is, not what we wish it to be. Jonah and Job and Maimonides were not Humanistic Jews. Such anachronistic projections would be irresponsible and unethical and would deny the past the dignity of identity. Humanistic Jews *may* discover themes in these stories that they find interesting, or useful, or even inspiring. But the past remains a product of its time and place, even if the words have "undergone a sea-change" to become something beautiful in contemporary eyes. Humanistic Judaism is not only the pearl-diver who seeks beauty from the past; it is also the jeweler who must find the right setting in which the pearl can shine. The ancient rabbis may have been humane, but they were not humanistic. To claim the dignity of saying what we believe and believing what we say, we must have the courage to be grateful for what is received, and, when we feel it is necessary, to change it.

Daat: Knowledge of the past is a prerequisite to evaluating it. An *apikoros* possesses a special dignity that the *am ha-arets* lacks. Ignorance of what Humanistic Jews do not accept is not a virtue. At the same time, self-respecting Humanistic Jews will not allow themselves to be haunted by shtetl ghosts who would have them surrender their liberty to choose how to be Jewish. Judaism has always changed, though more in the past two hundred years than in the previous one thousand. Humanistic Jews have thrown off their shells—they must have the courage to spread their wings and fly where they will. But they cannot pretend that the past never existed, that they sprang like a self-created Adam from the dust of the ground.

Humanistic Judaism, more than any other denomination in contemporary Judaism, directly addresses the dilemma of continuity in the face of the radical discontinuities of accepting modern life. The real challenge is to postpone the practical question of how to be a Humanistic Jew until one explores the more foundational issue: What does it mean to be a Humanist *and* a Jew? To live with a foot in both worlds is the task of the modern Maimonides, and that of the inheritors of Rabbi Sherwin Wine and Humanistic Judaism.

NOTES

1. Regarding the *Mishneh Torah*, the title of "second Torah" indicates some of its author's ambitions.
2. *The Guide of the Perplexed*, in denying the literal truth of the more philosophically awkward passages in the Torah, was heretical for its day.
3. Maimonides's Thirteen Principles of Faith, originally in his commentary on the Mishna (*Sanhedrin* 10), are today part of the weekday Orthodox service; see *The Complete Artscroll Siddur* (Brooklyn, NY: Mesorah Publications, 1984), 178–81.
4. Sherwin Wine, *Humanistic Judaism* (Buffalo, NY: Prometheus Books, 1978), 121.
5. Yonatan Ratosh, in *What Is Jewish Literature?* (Philadelphia: Jewish Publication Society, 1994).
6. Irving Howe, *World of Our Fathers* (New York: Simon & Schuster, 1983), 106.
7. Walter Benjamin, *Illuminations*, ed. Hannah Arendt (New York: Schocken Books, 1968), 50-51.

Adam Chalom is a rabbi at the Birmingham Temple. He is assistant to the dean of the International Institute for Secular Humanistic Judaism. Rabbi Chalom was raised as a Humanistic Jew at the Birmingham Temple and went on to receive a B.A. in Judaic Studies from Yale University, rabbinic ordination from the International Institute for Secular Humanistic Judaism, and an M.A. in Hebrew and Jewish cultural studies from the University of Michigan, where he is completing his doctoral dissertation.

The Courage and Creativity of Sherwin Wine

Joseph Chuman

In the battle between Jewish humanism and Jewish orthodoxy, humanism wins. How can such an audacious claim be made? Humanism trumps orthodoxy because a moment's reflection will yield the insight that Judaism is ultimately what Jews say it is.

The Orthodox maintain that Judaism is what the Torah, the immutable and eternal word of God, says it is. But the higher truth is that, even if the Torah is of divine authorship, human beings interpret the Torah. The word must pass through the filter of the human mind, informed by human experience, and the product of this interpretive process is what we call "Judaism," or "Judaisms," to be more precise. It simply cannot be any other way. Judaism is a human creation, as are all other putatively immutable religious faiths. Humanism has the last word.

It was the great American philosopher William James who compellingly asserted that we do not discover "truth" as much as create it. Truth is what "works" in the sense that a true idea must cohere adequately with our previous fund of knowledge, with prior ideas that we already accept as true. In this sense, truths evolve—slowly to be sure, but they do change, as new, better ideas replace those that no longer work so well any more.

Enter Sherwin Wine. Rabbi Sherwin Wine shares with Mordecai Kaplan alone the illustrious designation of being the founder of a branch of Judaism created by a single individual. In his tireless career, Sherwin has articulated and defended a new foundational philosophy of Judaism. He has given this philosophy organizational structure and has nurtured its institutional solidity. Out of his fertile mind has grown an entire liturgy, totally new, replete with narrative, celebration, and song. He has educated and inspired countless thousands who, like himself, hold dearly to the notion that there is no dignity in affirming what one's heart and mind cannot affirm as true.

In a career that spans more than forty years, Sherwin Wine has brought together in a single person the attributes of a visionary, leader, institution builder, poet, and mensch—all expressed with boundless vigor and confidence. It is one thing to make a contribution here and there. It is another to found a movement. For this, an individual needs powers and talents that transcend the ordinary. Such a person is Sherwin Wine

A moment's digression is necessary with regard to the importance of conscience in the life and work of Sherwin Wine. Together with his love of *Yiddishkeit,* things Jewish, I believe a steadfast commitment to conscience is the second animating force of Sherwin's mission.

A primary commitment to conscience is the foundation on which Sherwin's life's work is built. The implicit assumption of Secular Humanistic Judaism is that any movement worth having, especially a movement committed to ethical values and communal solidarity, and not least Judaism itself, must be based on integrity. I mean by integrity a value that is two-fold: The truths the movement espouses need to cohere with the basic canons of reason and commonsense. At the same time, the mind of each believer needs to be undivided, so that one can profess without contradiction what one believes.

Without this integrity, any movement is gnawed at its center by corrupting contradictions, and the religious quest, if I may indulge that phrase, is undermined at its core.

In this regard Secular Humanistic Judaism stands nobly against prevailing currents of our age. We live in a time of a powerful resurgence of religion that has transformed both Christianity and Judaism in America and beyond. Jews without religion are flocking to the synagogues, and many who had left are returning. But they are not finding in the shuls the faith of their fathers. Riding the crest of the postmodern cult of subjectivity, the religion they find, in its ethos and belief, bears only superficial resemblance to Judaic legacies of the ages. The format may look the same, but the significance has been radically transformed. The cost of the current religious craze is the jettisoning of what was once considered normative and demanding.

Recent surveys investigating the motives of new members of Conservative synagogues, especially among the Baby Boomer generation, yield startling results. When it comes to singing the praises of the Almighty, the new returnees, the *baalei t'sheva*, unable to believe what the liturgy so explicitly connotes, simply make up new meanings, in the privacy of their minds, that suit them better. The blandishments of community and the solace it brings trump belief, and with it thousands of years of religious authority. In order to bridge the gap between the liturgy as it appears, with all its supernatural references born of earlier times, and the beliefs of contemporary worshipers, one simply stretches the words into metaphors they were never meant to be.

> Judaism is a human creation, as are all other putatively immutable religious faiths. Humanism has the last word.

Like Mordecai Kaplan, Sherwin Wine has also reconstructed Judaism, and he has done so radically. But he differs from modern-day enthusiasts in that he has openly, honestly, and forthrightly done so in his public declaration of a new movement. He refuses to invoke theistic language and pretend it means something else. Once again, Sherwin Wine stands on the pillar of integrity and conscience. He refuses to profess what he does not believe. He boldly proclaims that while the Jewish people remain, their religious beliefs have evolved. In the remote past, Jews were idolaters. Since the time of Ezra, they were monotheists. In the modern era, the preponderance of Jews are humanists. The contribution of Sherwin Wine has been to make that humanism explicit and to create a movement to give it form and ensure its continuity.

In the mind of Sherwin Wine, the rationalism of the Enlightenment intersects with the lessons of Jewish history; and for Sherwin, history, not *Halakha*, is the matrix from which Jewish identity emerges. He has written in *Judaism Beyond God:*

> Jewish identity is attached to Jewish memory.... Jewish identity has humanistic values because Jewish experience testifies to the need for reason and dignity. To be Jewish is to feel the indifference and the terror of self-reliance. But given the gifts of destiny, there is no alternative to self-reliance.

The ideological center of Secular Humanistic Judaism is built on the pillars of reason, dignity, and self-reliance, deepened and enriched with an appreciation of Jewish history, culture, and community. It is around these points that Sherwin Wine has ushered in a distinctive Jewish movement fitted for our times.

THE CHALLENGES FACING SECULAR HUMANISTIC JUDAISM

But is it fitted to the future? Wine has staked his Judaism on the truths of the Enlightenment. Although Secular Humanistic Judaism, since its founding forty years ago, has broadened beyond Wine's rationalism to functionally become a big tent providing a home for Jewish secularists, Yiddishists, labor Zionists, and others outside the religious consensus, Wine's philosophy lies at the core and continues to provide the ballast for the movement. It is here that Wine has staked his Judaism and his life's deepest commitments.

But a moment's glance at the Jewish scene in America, and at the religious scene more broadly, will dramatically confirm that Wine's humanism is facing powerful challenges at this time. The resurgence, which witnesses Jews of little or no prior religious allegiance flocking (or flocking back) to the synagogues, is driven by a subjectivism deeply apathetic to the rational categories that comprise the center of Wine's Judaism. An integrity-based yearning to stand within truth is pushed aside in favor of immediate experience that inspires enthusiasm, communal bonds, and emotional uplift.

Such trends are widespread within Judaism and have spread across denominations; indeed they are eroding the denominational boundaries that have defined the varieties of Judaism for more than a century. The trans-denominational Jewish Renewal movement exemplifies this postmodern expressiveness. The Reconstructionist movement has appropriated New-Age indulgences in a manner that would cause its founder, Mordecai Kaplan, whose worldview was explicitly scientific and naturalistic, to turn in his grave. The Lubavitch movement, which at first glance in its ultra-orthodoxy would seem to be immune from contemporary postmodern enthusiasms, instead rides their currents to unabashed heights. Contemporary commercialism and technological wizardry all serve to promote a religious message composed of the rebbe's wisdom served in a hash of New-Age wonder and Buddhist-like spiritualism in order to woo the wayward back to the fold. The classical mode of Reform Judaism, whose *raison d'être* was modernity—its rationality and Enlightenment values—has shifted ceremonially rightward, pulled as is all Judaism by the allure of the Orthodox. All this is sanctified and expressed by the rage for "spirituality" and spiritual experience. But as Wine has wryly observed of the current religious trends characteristic of Reform Judaism, "their food will never be as kosher; their *mikva* never as deep [as the Orthodox]."

> Jews without religion are flocking to the synagogues, and many who had left are returning. But they are not finding in the shuls the faith of their fathers.

Modern Orthodoxy, which is experiencing a triumphalist moment, would seem to avoid the subjectivism that undergirds so much of the religious resurgence. Indeed, for many Orthodox, belief predominates. Yet the Orthodox world is exceedingly pluralistic and its attractions are many. For a segment of Orthodox Jews, the power of community, fear of the perceived corrupting dynamics of the secular world, and even the desire on behalf of many women to escape the sexual predation of the dating scene are strong motives to appropriate the Orthodox lifestyle. Belief, for many, remains a secondary factor, justified, no doubt, by the Judaic mantra that within Judaism, belief is subordinate to behavior.

This has not been Sherwin Wine's approach. Within the contemporary religious whirlwind, Wine proclaims a Judaism and Jewish identity rooted in secular values, reason, dignity, and the hard lessons of Jewish history. His declaration has been militant:

> Humanistic Jews are tired of being timid. They are tired of mergers that do not work. They are fed up with using the theological language of their enemies and never saying clearly what they think and feel. They find no virtue in ambivalence.

Humanistic Judaism emerged on the scene four decades ago in the spirit of rebellion and with a faith securely anchored in modernity. A searing question we need to ask now, which was unforeseen then, is whether times have passed it by. Is Secular Humanistic Judaism merely a product of its times, replaced in our era by the powers of subjectivism, emotionalism, communalism, and the new spirituality? Is it a last gasp of nineteenth-century rationalism on which the sun has set, overcome by the new dawn of the postmodern age? Does the future of Judaism lie in the Enlightenment zeitgeist, humanistic values, and rational thought, or in the enthusiasms sweeping Judaism and the religious world in general? Does Secular Humanistic Judaism hold the promise of success? Assuredly, these issues far transcend the Humanistic Jewish movement. But the value of Humanistic Judaism to these issues enveloping our time is that of a bellwether; through the lens of Humanistic Judaism we will see these issues played out.

THE ENDURING SIGNIFICANCE OF HUMANISTIC JUDAISM

Success can be measured by two broad parameters. The first is popularity and power. The second is grounded in enduring rightness. Indeed, much of human civilization is grouped along these axes. It will always be the case that more people are enthralled by television than by the high arts, yet the high arts are not diminished in their significance because of that. Contemporary visual technologies may attract more users than newspapers, but there will always be a segment of the population that values the written word and the deliberation it evokes. Utilitarian considerations may drive our ethics and social policies, but a sublime appreciation for rights and righteousness is ultimately what gives life meaning. These latter preferences are not merely matters of aesthetics and taste. And that is the cardinal point.

When we shift to the issue at hand, that of worldviews (let's for the moment refer to them as *religious* worldviews), I have little doubt that the appeal of contemporary religion, or religion in general, trumps in popularity the appeal of humanism and secularism on which Wine's movement is based. Freud, in his *Future of an Illusion*, has gone far to explain the broad and pervasive appeal of religion over the dynamics of reason and science. Yet Freud omits from his polemic the mythopoeic structures of the mind to which the religious outlook readily adheres. We are myth-making and storytelling animals, and for the masses of humanity the power of narrative drives out the analytic and discursive dynamics constitutive of a secular and humanistic outlook.

> Within the contemporary religious whirlwind, Wine proclaims a Judaism and Jewish identity rooted in secular values, reason, dignity, and the hard lessons of Jewish history.

The strength of Secular Humanistic Judaism is not to be found in its mass appeal, but in the enduring values it proclaims, values that are necessary for the civilized survival of humankind. The significance of Humanistic Judaism is staked on the faith that the values of humanism, reason, dignity, and the liberal tolerance that grows from them are transhistorical, in a way in which the enthusiasms that drive religion today are not. In short, Humanistic Judaism has saving value not only for Judaism but also, by extension, for what we could construe as the finest fruits of the Western tradition.

We live at a dark moment of ascendant authoritarianism. The forces of parochialism, ethnic particularism, and fundamentalist religion have gripped broad swaths of humanity, both within American society and globally. Combined with political and military power, these forces have turned malignant, ushering in an era of xenophobia, violence, and terrorism.

Within the American context, politics at all levels is propelled by the agenda of the ultraconservative churches, confounding historical trends by allying itself with politicized segments of the Orthodox Jewish community. Our government is veering toward the theocratic as it attempts to destroy the time-honored separation of church and state, the brilliant bulwark that has kept American society relatively free of interreligious strife and that has protectively permitted the Jewish community to flourish as it has historically done nowhere else.

Since the 1967 Arab-Israeli war, the Orthodox Jewish world has been experiencing a period of resurgence and triumphalism. But its headiness has too often led to excess, manifested in the extremes of Jewish fundamentalism and Messianic delusions. It has led to uncompromising and dangerous politics, both in Israel and in the American context. Too often resurgence orthodoxy in this country has led to a separatism, based more on the politics of satisfaction than a requirement of religious law. And ritualism characteristically has replaced ethical mandates as the centerpiece of Jewish life and observance.

In non-Orthodox Judaism, the current waves are too often infused with the desire to spiritually feed the self at the expense of an outer-directed impulse to serve the common good. Storytelling and experiences calibrated to inspire heightened emotions permeate much of synagogue life, but at the expense of the intellectual rigor and learning so characteristic of Judaism. It is disheartening to see contemporary Judaism veering toward anti-intellectualism, while forsaking in so many quarters its prophetic commitments to universal social justice.

The achievement of Sherwin Wine and Secular Humanistic Judaism has been to stand against these currents as they infuse the culture generally and the Jewish world particularly. His movement stands as a beacon sending out a civilizing message that is especially necessary in these times when the dark forces of authoritarianism, illiberalism, and anti-intellectualism so powerfully pervade our religion and politics. And his movement stands also as a crucial redoubt for those who feel the call of its mission and who want to identify with it.

Humanistic Judaism holds a certain ironic place in contemporary Judaism. Here is a movement that declares neither the authority of the Torah, nor the miraculous character of Jewish history, nor even the existence of the God of Israel. Yet, in one particular it stands in a critical and salutary position with regard to all forms of religious Judaism, all the while remaining very Jewish at its core.

It can be compellingly maintained that the most significant and sublime value of Judaism, indeed its defining value, is contained in the injunction prohibiting idolatry. And we can define idolatry as the worshiping of artifacts created by human hands. So much of contemporary Judaism, whether invested in the military power of Israel, the ceremonial preoccupations of orthodoxy, the strength of fundamentalism, or the obsession with institutional forms, partakes of idolatrous values at the expense of more spiritually outreaching and edifying concerns.

Here is a movement that declares neither the authority of the Torah, nor the miraculous character of Jewish history, nor even the existence of the God of Israel.

Humanistic Judaism, which does not worship man but aspires to what human beings and Jews can become at their finest, avoids this most egregious indulgence. By refusing even to give its assent to a transcendent God, lest God become nothing but a tool wielded for material ends and the ends of power, Humanistic Judaism proclaims its commitment to more lasting things. Its allegiance is to those values that above all give life and orient us to a future that remains forever open.

Joseph Chuman is currently the leader of the Ethical Culture Society of Bergen County, New Jersey, where he has served for twenty-eight years. He is visiting professor of religion and human rights at the Graduate School of Arts and Sciences of Columbia University. He teaches at the United Nations University for Peace in Costa Rica. He is a member of the faculty of the International Institute for Secular Humanistic Judaism, and he is on the board of the Humanist Institute and the International Humanist and Ethical Union.

The Road Goes Ever On and On

Harry T. Cook

This collection of essays celebrates the life and work of a true original: Sherwin Theodore Wine. He comes as close to being a polymath as anyone known by any of us. Remarkably intelligent people who have taken in, processed, and retained voluminous amounts of information are, as often as not, antisocial and, frankly, boring. You could not say this of Sherwin Wine, who has found all kinds of interesting ways of sharing his knowledge and analyses with audiences over the years. Wine as rabbi, Wine as teacher, Wine as platform lecturer brings to his vocation as an imparter of information a highly individualistic passion that embraces his listeners/students, turning them on to whatever the topic is: great cities of the world, critical issues of the moment, a controversial book or subject. Being steeped in history, he brings it to life in multiple dimensions.

The other important aspect of Sherwin Wine's lifetime achievement is his clear-eyed worldview. Born, raised, and formed within traditional Judaism—first Orthodox, then Conservative, and later Reform—Rabbi Wine came to what is now called Secular Humanistic Judaism in his late twenties as he began to see through the layers of accretion to what was "the real history of the Jews" (as a later series of lectures would put it) and to what was the relevant and useful core of the Jewish experience. That core was the potential of the human being to become fully human through the formation of belief and opinion by way of observation and rational analysis of the real world and its component parts—not imposed by the priesthood of an unexamined tradition. When all is said and done, that concept will be marked down as Sherwin Wine's greatest contribution to twentieth- and twenty-first-century Jewish life. Equally significant has been his success at leading thousands of other Jews to see what he saw and to embrace that vision with something like his own passion. The key to understanding Sherwin Wine is that he has never stood still and let events and developments go by on parade. He has always been a part of the parade, often enough leading it.

Appropriate, then, is the title given to this essay that celebrates him. It is taken from a song that the late J. R. R. Tolkien gave to his fictional character Bilbo Baggins to sing at the end of his journey as depicted in *The Return of the King:*

> The Road goes ever on and on
> Out from the door where it began.
> Now far ahead the Road has gone,
> Let others follow it who can!

Not only does the traveler move along the road, but the road moves, too. One moves with it and on it simultaneously, or one does not—an interesting perspective. One can step out upon the road, and let it carry one along. Or one can advance even as the road is itself advancing. I offer that image as the operative metaphor of this essay.

It is a fact that Judaism and its younger, irascible sibling known as "Christianity" have, by and large, let the philosophical road go ever on and on without themselves moving along on it—much as one lets an escalator do the work of ascending from the lobby to the mezzanine instead of also taking the steps upward oneself, completing the journey more quickly and efficiently. In fact, one can make the case that classical Judaism and Christianity actually stepped off the road some time ago, with their philosophical development all but arrested as a result.

Judaism, followed by Christianity, long ago settled on theism as its established philosophy of religion, believing, perhaps, that theism represented the acme of perfection, while animism, polytheism, and pantheism represented more primitive, less refined "ism"s. It must be said that theism turns out to be not at all compatible with the general theories of science and nature.

Theism is that philosophical construct that posits an unseen but personally approachable omnipotence/omniscience/omnipresence (PAO3, for short) that is "up there," "out there," or "in there." The PAO3 is believed by theists to be intensely interested in the affairs of human beings, perhaps less interested in other life in the universe. And in those human affairs, theism's PAO3 does not hesitate to intervene. Even though the rain may fall without discrimination on the just and the unjust, a theist's PAO3 is said to be able to make it fall more benignly or malevolently upon either as it wills.

Sherwin Wine has never stood still and let events and developments go by on parade. He has always been a part of the parade, often enough leading it.

Every theism has its holy writ and priestly elite, means by which the nature and will of the PAO3 can be known by mortals. Thus can Osama bin Laden say, "There is but one God, and Muhammad is his only prophet." In the Semitic languages, "prophet" derives from the root *nby*, which in its most unrefined semantic form means "mouthpiece." For Muslims persuaded of bin Laden's analysis, the Koran, as revealed to Muhammad in 610 C.E., conveys PAO3's absolute will that the infidel nation known as the United States must be punished and destroyed along with Israel. It would be one thing if that will were attributed to one among many "gods" because then it is almost inevitable that someone would produce a god who wills the opposite. Then it would be for those gods to duke it out and for the constituency of the losing god to submit to that of the winner. But the PAO3, the "one god" of theism, presents a major conundrum. It cannot want what bin Laden wants for the world at the same time that it wants what Americans want for the world. Moreover, the PAO3 can hardly reveal itself exclusively in the Koran if it has likewise revealed itself in the Torah or in the gospels of "Jesus Judaism"—a term I have coined for proto-Christianity.

Theism worked when the inevitably diverse ethnic and cultural groups on earth were not in communication or competition with one another. Theism worked in the age before empiricism-driven science—through its observations, hypotheses, and theories—yielded its knowledge to modern human beings. Theism made sense at one time. It was where the road had gone and it was the point on that road at which more sophisticated human societies had arrived. It does not work now, not because we do not wish it to work, but because it, in fact, does not work.

So to where has the road gone, and where are we on it? The road, thanks to the aforementioned science, has gone on to a point at which we can say that natural explanations exist for most observable phenomena. And those phenomena for which natural explanations cannot now be found may eventually be explainable as our knowledge of the universe's workings becomes more sophisticated. Therefore, the god of theism, the transcendent PAO3, is no longer helpful in explaining the workings of the natural world. In fact, we might say it is a nuisance.

Must there be something, some concept in its place? Or can we simply say, Goodbye to all that? I'm afraid not, if only because nature abhors a vacuum, and when you have dethroned a god, especially such an entity as the PAO3, something will eventually—or, rather, quickly—jockey in to take its place. History has proven time and again that individual human beings are not trustworthy as god-substitutes. Even granting that religion may have begun with ancestor worship and moved to the point at which kings and emperors were considered gods or at least godlike, it simply does not work to substitute a human being for a god—a real and finite being for an imagined and infinite one.

Meanwhile, it is distressing to observe mainstream twenty-first-century Judaism and Christianity pretending in their theologies and liturgies that the PAO3 actually exists and that people actually believe in Him. *Him.* Plenty of people go through the ritual motions of worship because they have become socio-cultural necessities. Full shuls on Rosh Hashana and Yom Kippur, full churches on Christmas and Easter tell the tale. A huge proportion of those who crowd into those high holy day services end up using language based on concepts that have no meaning in their everyday lives. And plenty of people see no contradiction and no reason to stop going to shul or church, even as they believe in and rely on the sciences and technologies whose understandings *ipso facto* deny the philosophical bases of theistic religion. People keep going and mouthing the largely empty words and phrases because no trustworthy substitute has been found for god.

I will suggest such a substitute, and I will begin by saying that a stable, fundamentally intelligent person cannot regard the plentitude of life and its bafflingly ordered nature without wondering about the cause of that order. One cannot see the images produced by the Hubble Space Telescope and not wonder what the source of those trillions-of-miles-high gas eruptions might be. We see order in the universe—all the way from the startlingly predictable sidereal time to the gestation of a human being—and we see what we take to be chaos, sometimes in monumental proportion, and yet it seems impossible to shrug our shoulders and chalk it up to the issue of molecules bouncing off one another at random.

> The god of theism is no longer helpful in explaining the workings of the natural world. In fact, we might say it is a nuisance.

An inductive pursuit and examination of data in nature leads most people eventually to posit some kind of source and ordering principle in the universe. The poet/philosopher who gave us some 2,700 years ago the famed "P Document," portions of which are scattered among the books of the Pentateuch, envisioned the source of the universe's substance as emerging from a primordial chaos out of which an ordering principle wrought some measure of order. Modern science has been able to grasp that the substance and the order—or ordering principle—seem not to be so arbitrarily divisible. Charles Darwin, among others, helped human beings appreciate the fact that they individually and corporately are part of both the substance and the evolving order—and ordering. A first-century Jew named Saul of Tarsus suggested that human beings were "fellow workers with God," and we might say in a twenty-first-century translation of that sentiment that human beings seem, at their best, to participate with the universe in the ordering of life. While other cultures in other times and places have certainly produced order, the Renaissance of our own European experience of the sixteenth and seventeenth centuries stands out as an example of how human beings can do more than simply react to life—they can master and manage it through art and technology.

Government with the consent of the governed—of the people, by the people, and for the people—may be the best opportunity thus far in the human experience to extend and maintain the kind of dependable order that creates an environment sufficiently secure to provide for advancement of the arts and sciences and, thus, for an enhancing and fulfilling life for all involved. It is within such an enterprise that one acceptable and adequate substitute for god can be found. "God" is simply an imperfect and misleading word for what is best in humanity, what is worth pursuing. The temples of such a god are the concert hall, the lecture auditorium, the art gallery, the laboratory, the corridors of government. The music that is made in them, the information and enlightenment imparted in them, the beauty displayed in them, the experiments carried on in them, the laws defining and establishing standards of human behavior written in them constitute the liturgy of twenty-first-century human beings as, at their best, they share in the ordering of the universe's substance.

We are talking not theism here, but humanism. Humanism invites the human being to consider that he or she partakes in the collective human potential. At the same time, humanists must face up to and acknowledge the individual and collective failures of human beings, failures that have been manifest in what Robert Burns termed "man's inhumanity to man." Conventional theistic religions direct their adherents to undertake complex liturgies of contrition to atone for such inhumanity. Humanism's liturgy—as we have said—is the purposive, egalitarian cultivation of the arts, of law, and of the sciences, which, at *their* best, produce works that seem to be greater than the sum of their parts. Such greatness can satisfy the human need for meaning and fulfillment as well as offering a rational foundation for ethically sound behavior that theistic religions now so ineffectively attempt—and in the end fail—to provide.

That, I think, is where the road has gone. Let others follow it who can.

Harry T. Cook is the rector of St. Andrews Church in Clawson, Michigan. He is a graduate of Albion College and Garrett-Evangelical Seminary/Northwestern University. Harry Cook was the ethics and public policy columnist for the *Detroit Free Press* for many years. He is the author of *Christianity Beyond Creeds*, *Sermons of a Devoted Heretic*, and *The Seven Sayings of Jesus*. He is a distinguished lecturer at the Center for New Thinking.

Celebrating Humanism

Edd Doerr

It is a distinct honor to have been invited to contribute some words of appreciation for the life and work of Sherwin Wine. I write as a friend; as an admirer of his skills and accomplishments; as president of the American Humanist Association; and as president of Americans for Religious Liberty, which Sherwin co-founded (with Ethical Culture leader Edward L. Ericson) more than twenty years ago in response to the upsurge of Religious Right extremism and demagoguery in the United States.

As others will have pointed out, Sherwin is a man of extraordinary learning, ability, energy, charisma, dedication, and empathy. In my three-score-and-some years I have had the pleasure of knowing, meeting, or being acquainted with many admirable people—writers, scientists, attorneys, religious leaders, politicians, activists, and others—but none with Sherwin's combination of gifts, interests, and breadth of accomplishment. He is a mensch and a *macher* like no other.

The seed that Sherwin and Ed Ericson planted more than twenty years ago took root and produced an organization, Americans for Religious Liberty (ARL), which has published some thirty books and eighty quarterly newsletters; put speakers before audiences from coast to coast and on television and radio and in the print media; and participated in litigation before the United States Supreme Court and lower courts. The vision of these two humanist leaders has led to significant contributions to the causes of religion-government separation, religious freedom, and women's rights.

Of particular interest to me as a humanist (a non-Jewish humanist, I might add) are Sherwin's singular contributions simultaneously to Jewish culture and to the worldwide humanist movement. He is at once the organizer and catalyzing voice of the most forward-looking branch (if that metaphor is apt) of Jewish culture and a key leader in the complex multicultural and multinational world of humanism.

Two anecdotes will illustrate what I mean.

In June 2002 my wife and I were privileged to attend bar and bat mitsvas for four young people in the Machar Humanistic Jewish congregation in the Washington, D.C., metropolitan area. At least 300 people were in attendance at a thoroughly humanistic affair that was far more meaningful and inspiring than any bar mitsva we have attended at more traditional congregations. The four young people, three young women and a young man, presented original research papers on such topics as the history of Hadassah and Jewish composers, and then each of them, to our pleasant surprise, performed musical numbers (on flute, violin, and piano) with consummate professionalism. Thanks to the inspiration and organizing ability of Sherwin Wine, something new has been added to our world: thriving, exciting institutions, Humanistic Jewish congregations.

I was struck by the similarity of the Machar bar and bat mitsvas to the civil confirmation my wife and I attended in Oslo, Norway, in May 2001, while we were in that city for a board meeting of the International Humanist and Ethical Union.

Confirmation of fourteen-year-olds in the State (Lutheran) Church has been an integral part of Norwegian culture for centuries. Indeed, it was legally mandated until almost the eve of World War I. Relief from this once state-imposed and later culturally fixed religious indoctrination and ritual came several years after World War II, thanks to the recently formed Norwegian Humanist Association (Human-Etisk Forbund). At the midpoint of the twentieth century, the Norwegian Humanist Association (which today, with over 70,000 members and the right to a proportionate share of public funds with churches, is the largest humanist organization in the world, in both numbers and percentage of the population) began civil confirmations (*borgerlig konfirmrasjon*). These involve several weeks of civic education classes culminating in a civil confirmation ceremony in a city hall. About 16 percent of Norwegian fourteen-year-olds received a civil confirmation in 2001.

The May 2001 civil confirmation, marking the fiftieth anniversary of the ceremonies, was held in the magnificent Oslo city hall. Seventy young men and women—the former in suits and many of the latter in traditional Norwegian dresses—along with an audience of hundreds of relatives and guests (among them International Humanist and Ethical Union [IHEU] board members from a number of countries and a member of the Norwegian royal family, to the annoyance of the country's small Religious Right) were present. The proceedings included an address by a representative of the students and one by Levi Fragell, president of the IHEU and former head of the Human-Etisk Forbund. Fragell's speech was a denunciation of racism, including reference to the skinhead murder a few months earlier of a young man of mixed ethnicity who had had his civil confirmation in that very hall the year before.

> Of particular interest to me as a humanist are Sherwin's singular contributions simultaneously to Jewish culture and to the worldwide humanist movement.

These two very similar, and similarly impressive and inspiring, ceremonies lead me to the following conclusions:

Humanism is a richly diverse life-stance movement with roots in many cultures and traditions that has earned an important place among the world's major life stances (of which most are traditional religions) and that should have increasing influence. Indeed, it is the only life stance fully consistent with a scientific outlook.

Humanistic Judaism, Norwegian Humanism, and the predominantly humanist Unitarian Universalist and Ethical Culture movements in North America all highlight the importance to humanism of community, of organization, of cooperation, of structure, of institutions. And, of course, while a merger of all humanist organizations into one is neither desirable nor practical, increased cooperation is in order.

On the first anniversary of the terrorist attacks of 11 September 2001 in New York, Washington, and Pennsylvania, representatives of several humanist organizations, including Rabbi Binyamin Biber and members of the Machar congregation, gathered at the Jefferson Memorial in Washington for a memorial service. (My small part in the service was singing Lloyd Stone's poetic plea for peace, set to the music of Sibelius's "Finlandia.") This event is an example of the sort of coming together of humanists that holds promise for the future.

Back to our theme: it is Sherwin Wine who has led a focusing of humanist thought in the Jewish tradition. And such works as Sherwin's *Judaism Beyond God* and *Staying Sane in a Crazy World*, together with books such as Renee Kogel and Zev Katz's *Judaism in a Secular Age*, go well beyond being just key contributions to Humanistic Judaism to being significant additions to the literature of world humanism.

If institutions or movements may be said to be the lengthening shadows of particular persons, then Sherwin Wine has cast several very large shadows that, I am confident, will continue to grow in importance and influence.

Edd Doerr is the president of Americans for Religious Liberty, founded in 1981 by Sherwin Wine and Ed Ericson. He is the immediate past president of the American Humanist Association and author, co-author, or editor of more than twenty books. He and his wife Herenia translated into Spanish Rabbi Wine's book *Staying Sane in a Crazy World.* He is a founding board member of the Religious Coalition for Reproductive Choice and the National Committee for Public Education and Religious Liberty. He has lectured widely on religion and government issues in the United States and abroad.

How Sherwin Wine Built the Fifth Branch of Judaism

Ruth Duskin Feldman

A new religious movement starts with a person who has an idea. Reform Judaism started with Moses Mendelssohn, who translated the Bible into German so it would be accessible to the Jews who were coming out of the ghettos and learning the local vernacular. Others, notably Rabbi Isaac Mayer Wise in the United States, organized a movement, drew up platforms, started a rabbinic seminary—Hebrew Union College—and founded the Central Conference of American Rabbis as well as a lay umbrella organization, the Union of American Hebrew Congregations.

Our counterpart to Mendelssohn, Wise, and the other Reformers was one man: Rabbi Sherwin T. Wine, who set out, audaciously, to create a new way to be Jewish. Sherwin has ambition, boundless energy, and *chutzpa;* he is a tireless worker and a charismatic speaker. In addition to his imagination and intellect, he is an organizational genius who knows how to put other people's talents to work—essential for a leader of a movement. But first and foremost, he had a Big Idea.

Sherwin's Big Idea was to create a naturalistic congregational movement relevant to the modern age, with intellectual integrity and teachings consistent with the findings of modern science, history, and archaeology. A Judaism that thinking people could live out every day of the week, and not just on Friday nights or the High Holidays. A Judaism as relevant to adults as to children—perhaps even more so. A Judaism that puts people first. A Judaism based not on belief in God, but on what human beings can do to give meaning and purpose to their lives. He called it Humanistic Judaism.

BEGINNINGS

Given the tumult and intellectual ferment of the '60s, it should hardly have been a shock that a radical Jewish movement would arise, headed by an "ignostic" rabbi. Yet the Jewish establishment and the nation were stunned when, in 1963, the first headlines appeared about a young Reform rabbi who had started a nontheistic congregation, the Birmingham Temple, with eight Detroit-area families. Rabbis from coast to coast denounced this heresy.

Humanistic Judaism, although initially an outgrowth of Reform Judaism, soon proved to be incompatible with Reform, especially as the Reform movement grew more and more conservative in its liturgy and embrace of traditionalism. Sherwin resigned from the Reform rabbinate and set about the ambitious task of creating a new movement, a fifth branch of Judaism. What has happened since then has been a historic journey—and a life-changing experience for those of us privileged enough to have gone along on the ride.

Sherwin Wine has been called "a founder." Here are some of the organizations he has founded: Society for Humanistic Judaism (SHJ), International Federation of Secular Humanistic Jews (IFSHJ), International Institute for Secular Humanistic Judaism (IISHJ), Leadership Conference of Secular and Humanistic Jews (LCSHJ), Association of Humanistic Rabbis (AHR)—and the list goes on. What we Humanistic Jews call "the movement" today consists of this alphabet soup of organizations and a list of members, subscribers, and supporters estimated at 30,000 or more on six continents—all but Antarctica.

First, in 1969, Sherwin and Rabbi Daniel Friedman of Congregation Beth Or in Deerfield, Illinois (a congregation that had converted from Reform to Humanistic), formed the SHJ. The society, which today is the umbrella organization for our national movement, grew slowly at first. By 1979, ten years after its founding, there were only a handful of chapters in such places as Westport, Connecticut; Boston; Los Angeles; Washington, D.C.; and Toronto. Sherwin realized that we needed events to bring people from these far-flung chapters together, to develop solidarity as a movement. So the society held annual meetings, which enabled us to meet Humanistic Jews from other parts of the country, to hear educational speakers, and to compare notes on strategies for growth.

Sherwin also realized that, like an aspiring professor, an aspiring movement must publish or perish. We began publishing curricular and promotional materials, an annual newsletter called *Humanorah*, and a quarterly journal, *Humanistic Judaism*, of which I became creative editor in 1983 with Bonnie Cousens, now the society's executive director, as managing editor. In 1985 we published the first edition of Sherwin's *Judaism Beyond God*, sometimes called the bible of our movement.

> Sherwin's Big Idea was to create a Judaism based not on belief in God, but on what human beings can do to give meaning and purpose to their lives. He called it Humanistic Judaism.

THE PROBLEM OF LOW GROWTH

Still, the movement wasn't growing—hardly at all. Small, incipient communities would emerge, struggle, and die. The SHJ advertised in the *New York Times*, the *New Republic*, the *Humanist*, and the Jewish *Forward.* The ad campaigns drew only modest results. Sherwin had expected hundreds, thousands to flock to our doors. We had built it; why didn't more people come?

We knew the market was out there; it just needed to be told we were here. We knew because of the many times someone who stumbled upon one of our congregations would say, "Where have you been all my life? This is what I've always wanted."

One problem was what seemed like an invisible conspiracy among the Jewish establishment and a skeptical press to deny us exposure as a serious movement—mention in listings of Jewish organizations, participation in all-community programs and rabbinic forums, and the like. After the initial flurry of sensationalized articles, we were virtually ignored. In order to become viable as a movement, we had to be visible. We needed a PR campaign, and we began to put one in place.

We lacked other earmarks of a serious movement. We needed more publications, better-looking ones, and we began to produce them; a basic A-to-Z *Guide to Humanistic Judaism* came out in 1993. We needed to get on the Web, and eventually we did. We needed more professional leaders, both nationally and on the local level, and we needed a plan for developing future rabbinic leadership. We needed money—lots of it—to accomplish our goals. And we needed allies. With Sherwin's foresight and leadership, we began to move in all those directions. But first, the society had to redesign itself.

A NEW AND IMPROVED SHJ

One obstacle to our growth and development as a serious, viable movement was the structure of the society. Originally, it was simply a voluntary association of individuals, with no paid staff. But as new groups emerged, needing help, nurturing, and support, the society, with only individual dues and modest fundraising to depend on, had its hands tied; and many of the emerging groups, despite their initial energy, soon sputtered and died.

Starting an SHJ community takes a major grassroots effort, as well as support from the central office. Unlike the established movements, we don't have a universal prayer book or set of texts, and we can use very little of the material available from standard Jewish sources. So we needed liturgical and educational materials to guide our local communities as they created services and started Sunday schools.

In order to properly service and support our communities and congregations, we had to professionalize. Miriam Jerris, the society's first executive director, was promoted from volunteer to paid (and eventually full-time) status. We expanded the central office, put all our records on computers, and hired secretarial staff. The board took lessons in fundraising. We developed a long-range plan and established working committees.

And finally we came to grips with the other side of the coin. If local communities were going to receive needed services, they had to pay national dues. Under Sherwin's leadership and vision, we transformed the SHJ from a society of individuals into a society of fully affiliated groups. Today the society has about thirty-five affiliates across the continent, ranging from ten families (a Humanistic minyan) to one hundred or more, and new communities emerge each year. We created the position of Community Development Associate to service and visit local communities, along with Rabbi Wine and other leaders. We expanded the board so each community could have representation. We redesigned the *Humanistic Judaism* journal to a more topical format. Today the society has about 2,200 members—still not nearly large enough, but growing—and an annual budget of $356,000.

> Still, the movement was hardly growing at all. Sherwin had expected hundreds, thousands to flock to our doors. We had built it; why didn't more people come?

SHERWIN SEEKS ALLIES

Despite the progress of the first fifteen years, the society was not growing fast enough. To take the next step toward becoming a fifth branch of Judaism, we had to expand our base.

Sherwin looked in several directions. First he reached out to humanistic organizations such as the Unitarian Universalist movement and Ethical Culture. Although these organizations contain large numbers of Jews, they are not explicitly Jewish. Sherwin founded a North American Committee for Humanism (NACH), which established a Humanist Institute for training leaders.

But if Sherwin were to build a Jewish movement, he had to find Jewish allies. For many years there had existed in U.S. and Canadian cities small secular schools, or *shules*, run mostly by Yiddishist, socialist, Bundist, or otherwise left-leaning Jews. Many of these Jews were of East European extraction, steeped in Yiddish language and culture; they wanted to pass on that culture and a sense of Jewish history to their children. Around the time the SHJ was formed, these secularists joined in their own umbrella organization, the Congress of Secular Jewish Organizations (CSJO).

SHJ and CSJO representatives came together for a series of cautious meetings, groping to see whether they could make common cause. Both groups were nontheistic and were engaged in building communities focused on Jewish celebrations and studies. But there were serious differences as well. While SHJ was becoming increasingly professionalized, CSJO was committed to grassroots, volunteer leadership, and it was highly averse to rabbis. Even though most SHJ affiliates did not yet have their own rabbis, several were moving in that direction, and all looked to Rabbi Wine's leadership. Finally, the two organizations made not a *shiddach*, a match, but instead a sort of loose alliance called the Leadership Conference of Secular and Humanistic Jews (LCSHJ). Later, SHJ and CSJO became constituent parts of the North American section of the International Federation of Secular Humanistic Jews, and the Leadership Conference became the certifying professional leadership body for the movement.

THE MOVEMENT GOES INTERNATIONAL

Even with CSJO in the picture, the movement was still a barely noticeable blip on the screen of Jewish life. That began to change as Sherwin turned his sights abroad. Israel, and particularly the kibbutz movement, had been founded by secular Jews, so Sherwin saw it as fertile ground. In 1981 he led a group on a tour of Israel, visiting kibbutzim, searching their records for celebratory materials, and looking for leaders to connect with. The climax of the trip was a conclave with secular Israeli leaders and scholars at Kibbutz

Shefayim, on the coast near Tel Aviv. The outcome was the creation in 1983 of the Israel Association for Secular Humanistic Judaism (IASHJ), with leaders of such stature as Yehuda Bauer, director of the Center for the Study of Antisemitism at Hebrew University and now academic advisor at Yad Vashem; Haim Cohen, retired justice of the Israel Supreme Court; Shulamit Aloni, who served as Minister of Education in the Rabin government; and Zev Katz, a history professor at Tel Aviv University. The Israel Association established study groups and cadrés of lecturers who travel throughout Israel teaching and organizing.

With the Israeli connection in place, and as we increasingly attracted support from such notables as the writer Amos Oz and the late philosopher Isaiah Berlin, Sherwin could begin to think in terms of the giant step to an international movement. It was time to found a training and educational arm. And so the International Institute for Secular Humanistic Judaism (IISHJ) was born. In the years that followed, with Sherwin and the Israeli educator Yaakov Malkin as co-deans, the institute published educational materials in both Hebrew and English, including, among others, the anthology *Judaism in a Secular Age*. The institute also became the vehicle for training rabbis and nonrabbinic leaders.

> With the Israeli connection in place, Sherwin could begin to think in terms of the giant step to an international movement.

Meanwhile, Yehuda, Zev, Sherwin, and others had been making contacts in England and on the European continent. It turned out that there was a community center for secular and humanistic Jews in Brussels, which put out a French-language magazine, *Régards*, with a reputed 15,000 European subscribers. Smaller secular groups were developing in France, London, Italy, Australia, and Mexico.

An international federation was needed to link these national groups. In October 1986, at the Birmingham Temple, the International Federation of Secular Humanistic Jews (IFSHJ) was established, with those in attendance mentally comparing ourselves to the attendees at the historic First World Zionist Conference in Basel nearly 100 years before.

Terminology was an issue. "Secular" had to be in the title of the federation, not only because of our North American association with CSJO, but also because our Israeli and European allies called themselves secular Jews. Humanistic, to them, meant humanitarian. "Secular," in common parlance, meant nonreligious (nontheistic). But the word made some Humanistic Jews uneasy. Many of us thought of our brand of humanism as a religion. A number of articles appeared in our journal, discussing this semantic question and the many meanings of "secular." Then, should we be the Federation of Secular *and* Humanistic Jews or of Secular Humanistic Jews? Both titles had advocates, but the latter won out. Zev Katz, then dean of the institute, insisted that both words—"humanistic" and "secular"—were essential to what we stood for. But there are some today for whom the issue of terminology is still troublesome.

The federation and its growth brought us into intimate contact with Jewish issues in the making and events of historical importance. The second biennial meeting of the federation was held in Brussels in 1988. At that meeting the federation adopted its famous "Who Is a Jew" declaration, at a time when that issue was being fiercely debated in Israel. In a radical departure from tradition, we declared that a Jew is "a person of Jewish descent or any person who declares himself or herself to be a Jew and identifies with the history, ethical values, culture, civilization, community, and fate of the Jewish people."

Sherwin, reasoning that there were millions of Soviet Jews who had been raised on atheism and knew nothing of the Jewish religion, made a trip to the Soviet Union. Zev Katz, who was fluent in Russian, also made contacts there. In 1991, with the USSR in turmoil and Jews coming out of the woodwork—some leaving the country under liberalized emigration rules and others openly forming local Jewish cultural institutions with a watchful eye on the reemergence of antisemitism—the Secular Humanistic Association of the Soviet Union was founded. After the Soviet breakup, the association was renamed the Eurasian Association, with its own educational institute.

In 1994 the International Federation held its biennial meeting in Moscow. There we met Jews, old and young, from such exotic-sounding, faraway places as Kazakhstan and Uzbekistan, many of whom had traveled as long as eighteen hours by slow train to attend the conference, so great was their hunger for Jewish identification. (Once back in the United States, we heard that the historic old university building in which we had held the conference had burned down after we left, possibly the work of antisemites.)

Meetings of the International Federation continue to be held every two years in major cities around the world. Again following Sherwin's vision, in 2000 the federation opened headquarters in New York, a world center of Jewish culture, with Myrna Baron as executive director.

The movement's growth, and the need to train future leaders, required a central headquarters for the IISHJ. Thanks largely to the generosity and devotion of Sherwin's brother-in-law, Ben Pivnick, the Pivnick Center for Humanistic Judaism was opened in 1994 as a wing of the Birmingham Temple.

Just one year earlier, in 1993, the Birmingham Temple had celebrated its thirtieth anniversary, with major laudatory articles in the Detroit press—a far cry from the negative reception that had greeted that institution's founding.

In 1993 the Birmingham Temple celebrated its thirtieth anniversary, with major laudatory articles in the Detroit press—a far cry from the negative reception that had greeted that institution's founding.

THE MOVEMENT PLANS FOR FUTURE LEADERSHIP

Throughout the 1980s, the issue of future leadership for Humanistic congregations was debated. At first, some assumed that our future rabbis would come from the Reform seminary, as in the past. The two earliest prospects, Robert Barr and Rami Shapiro, both ordained at HUC in 1981, had gone through their rabbinic training with the society's financial support and had worked with emerging local communities. But both Barr and

Shapiro went in other directions. Barr, envisioning himself as the leader of a humanist wing in the Reform movement, sought membership in the Union of American Hebrew Congregations but was rejected because of his congregation's godless liturgy. Shapiro moved toward Reconstructionism and then Jewish Renewal. It became clear that we would need to train our own rabbis.

The institute's rabbinic program was established in 1990. To meet immediate leadership needs, Sherwin suggested a new level of clergy—the *madrikh(a)/vegvayzer*—with a shorter period of training. The Leadership Conference adopted procedures for certifying these leaders, as well as teachers and spokespersons, and the institute put in place a program for training them, with university professors and leaders of the movement as instructors. Gradually, with successful fundraising for the institute, the program has grown and diversified its offerings.

In 1993 the institute graduated its first class, certified to lead communities and perform ceremonies. Six years later, the first institute-trained rabbi, Tamara Kolton, who had grown up at the Birmingham Temple, was ordained, with coverage in the *New York Times* and elsewhere. There were tears at the ordination, in Sherwin's eyes and in those of others. Less than fifteen years after the founding of the international movement, it had passed a significant milestone. It would go on beyond its founders.

In 2001 three more rabbis were ordained: Miriam Jerris, SHJ community development associate; Adam Chalom, assistant dean of the institute and a rabbi of the Birmingham Temple; and Ben Biber, rabbi of Machar in Washington, D.C. The movement also has attracted rabbis from other branches of Judaism: Peter Schweitzer, originally from the Reform rabbinate, and David Oler from the Conservative rabbinate. In addition, approximately forty certified *madrikhim/vegvayzer* serve communities all over the United States.

THE COLLOQUIA AND THE QUEST FOR LEGITIMACY

By the time our first rabbis were ordained, Humanistic Judaism at last was becoming recognized as a legitimate, though still relatively small, branch of Judaism. That was no accident. It required strategizing, and again Sherwin was up to the task.

His main tool was involvement in high-visibility religious conferences. In 1993 he and Rabbi Friedman gave a presentation at the Parliament of the World's Religions, along with leaders of non-Jewish humanist groups including the American Humanist Association and Ethical Culture. Our presence there, as well as that of pagan witches and earth goddess worshipers, led to the walkout of the Greek Orthodox delegation. The B'nai Brith Anti-Defamation League also walked out, but their protest was against the presence of Louis Farrakhan.

Next, Sherwin decided that we ourselves would become major conference givers. With the help of a hardworking, dedicated committee, he boldly organized a series of biennial colloquia, held at the Pivnick Center in 1995, 1997, 1999, and 2001, with the fifth scheduled for October 2003, featuring distinguished professors, writers, and thinkers in dialogue with the faculty of our institute. The colloquia have been partly funded by the Detroit Jewish Federation and have been introduced by its president, showing what a force Sherwin's temple has become in the Detroit Jewish community.

> By the time our first rabbis were ordained, Humanistic Judaism at last was becoming recognized as a legitimate, though still relatively small, branch of Judaism.

The stage was set at the 1995 colloquium when keynote speaker Shoshana Cardin, past president of the Conference of Presidents of Major American Organizations, called upon her coreligionists to embrace Secular Humanistic Judaism as one of multiple valid forms of Jewishness. "Unless we begin to redefine who we are, we will lose those who don't see any reason to affiliate with us," she said. "Can we learn to give up turf and give people options?"

Colloquium '99 coincided with Tamara Kolton's ordination. At the end of the weekend, Emmanuel Goldsmith, a professor at Queens College, City

University of New York, and a leading student of Mordecai Kaplan, expressed disappointment with the increasingly theistic direction Reconstructionism has taken and announced that he was joining our movement. While not all of our distinguished guests have become "converts" to our cause, all of our colloquia, as well as other outreach activities, have attracted widespread attention; as a result, a growing number of influential Jewish leaders and thinkers, such as Egon Mayer and Alan Dershowitz, know we exist and have had positive experiences with us.

STANDING ON THE MOUNTAINTOP

Few of us are able to see the full completion of our life's work in our own time. At best, we can stand, like Moses on the mountaintop, and glimpse its fruition. This is where Sherwin stands today. He has built a movement that is still not very large but that has growing visibility, as evidenced by major articles in *Sh'ma*, *Moment*, the *New York Times*, *ORT Reporter*, and others. Further evidence of our new level of legitimacy is our participation since November 1999 in the annual General Assembly of United Jewish Communities.

With greater visibility and acceptance, we can now convincingly claim to be a fifth branch of Judaism. In fact, in a 2000 Jewish population study, the percentage of Jews identifying themselves as Secular Humanists equaled that of Reconstructionists (about 5 percent). Except among diehard traditionalists, we are no longer pariahs.

Humanistic Judaism probably never will be a mass movement. But it can become a significant voice and choice in the Jewish community. That will be the legacy of Sherwin Wine.

Ruth Duskin Feldman is a writer, editor, teacher, and lecturer, and a longtime spokesperson for Humanistic Judaism. She is a graduate of the International Institute for Secular Humanistic Judaism, and she is certified as a *madrikha* (Secular Humanistic Jewish leader). She has been the creative editor of the journal *Humanistic Judaism* since 1983. She has been affiliated with Congregation Beth Or in Deerfield, Illinois, since 1968. Currently she is the congregation's *madrikha*, assisting the rabbi, and she serves on its board of directors.

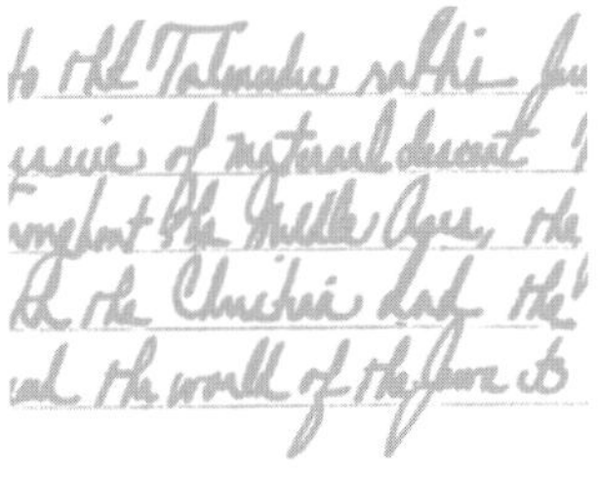

A View through the Courtyard Window; Or, How I Learned Humanistic Judaism by Staring at Sherwin Wine

Helen J. Forman

For sixteen years, it was both my privilege and my challenge to be the executive director of the Birmingham Temple, in Farmington Hills, Michigan. Founded by Rabbi Sherwin T. Wine, the Birmingham Temple is considered to be the flagship of modern Humanistic Judaism. My office and that of Rabbi Wine both had windows that looked out onto a small courtyard; as I looked through my windows, I could see the rather modest, mono-colored, uncluttered room he called his study. Here he would conduct conversations on a straight-backed chair facing his visitors, or he would sit behind his desk, reading, writing, or talking on the phone. It came to me once that if one could remove the electric lights, the telephone, and his fountain pen, Thomas Jefferson could have sat down in that room and felt right at home.

It was here that Rabbi Wine taught me much about life. A good teacher is one who can articulate a philosophy of life, but a great teacher is one who lives as an example of that philosophy in all they do. As the pastoral leader of the Birmingham Temple, he teaches his congregation to live life with courage and hope. He urges them to understand that life is absurd, that the forces of nature are uncaring, that gravity pulls on the saint and the sinner with equal force. He may not have been the first to say, "We are not what we say, but rather we are what we do," but he has always understood that he is looked to as a role model for the philosophy of Humanistic Judaism. Foremost is his clear understanding of the role of a leader. Even regarding his manner of dress, he says, "I wear a suit and tie because someone has to look like the leader."

One day, I sat in his office and we both noticed a small bird that was pecking furiously on his window, seemingly determined to get in. He said, "Helen, what is that bird doing?" I began to say that perhaps it could see its reflection and thought the reflected image was another bird. He thought about this for a moment and said, "No, I think it's my mother, Tillie, who's come back to remind me of something she forgot to tell me." He then laughed uproariously at his own joke and at the memories of his diminutive but steel-minded mother. I thought, Here I am trying to explain bird behavior to someone I consider to be one of the great intellects of our time, and he's slapping the desk in response to his own idea of a joke.

From my office I watched the families come and go, each with the anticipation that the rabbi could ease their way into the next stage of their life. Whether they came in joy for marriage preparations, in fear from the news of a recently diagnosed illness, or in the deep shock of an unanticipated death, each correctly believed that Rabbi Wine would know the right thing to do.

Although a cynic might say that it takes courage to get married, it takes a different kind of courage to tell a couple that perhaps they aren't ready to get married, or that they aren't a good match and should never marry each other. I recall one couple who came to see Rabbi Wine for marriage counseling. They showed up dressed as if they were going to clean out a septic tank. Here's a fashion tip: Don't wear a tank top, cut-offs, and flip-flops when you have an appointment with your clergy. I remember thinking that not only did they not have respect for Rabbi Wine, but they also showed little respect for themselves.

What he said to them was private, but as they left his office, I overheard him say, "I'm sorry that I'm not able to help you, perhaps in the future." I realized that this is a man who, even though he has performed thousands of weddings, has not lost his respect for the ceremony itself. Marriage means something and requires a certain amount of reverence. Even this reverence he tempered with humor, however. He expressed impatience with couples who took years to make a commitment. "I could get to Jupiter before they find themselves," he stage-whispered. And he set limits: "I will only marry the same person three times within my lifetime," he intoned with mock seriousness. Then he laughed, adding, "Especially if they keep marrying the same person."

Anyone who has attended a life-cycle event conducted by Rabbi Wine knows that he does not produce a generic ceremony. How many of us have been to funerals where, at the end, you hardly know the name of the person who died? It could have been anyone and you learned nothing about that person's life. Whether it is a bar or bat mitsva, a wedding, or a funeral, Rabbi Wine produces a mini-biography of the person's life, and he does that by his extraordinary interview techniques. Those gathered for such an event learn not only about the person's early years—where he or she grew up, went to school, lived—but what that person believed in and cared about, and most important, why those things mattered.

Rabbi Wine urges people to understand that life is absurd, that the forces of nature are uncaring, that gravity pulls on the saint and the sinner with equal force.

In the event of a death, Rabbi Wine sits down with a family and skillfully draws out the person's life story. He is able to piece together individual memories and find the common thread that defines the person being remembered. He asks questions such as, What do you remember most about your uncle? Or, What are the stories that your family tells about your brother? By asking such questions, he elicits memories that he weaves together into a tribute to that person's life. A curmudgeon is not converted into a sweetheart; rather, each is presented in a eulogy that captures the essence and preserves the dignity of his or her life. Sherwin taught me that the funeral is the last gift you can give to a person and that the person's philosophy of life should be celebrated at his or her funeral. Those who are life-long secularists should not have theistic ceremonies. If a family member wants to hear the Kaddish, then someone who believes in the words can say them, but Rabbi Wine will not; he feels that it is dishonest to say words one does not believe in. There were times it would have been easier to mumble the words, but he has the courage of his convictions.

It is not unusual to hear laughter coming from Rabbi Wine's study as he listens to the memories that family members relate to him. In his eulogies, an individual's personal quirks and funny mannerisms are presented in a dignified and human way. Did clothes sometimes matter more to Aunt Shirley than they did to most people? Ah yes, but she was also the best dressed at a party and was always neat and stylish. And didn't her daughters learn that people who look good get more respect? Remember how Grandpa gave up trying to remember the names of all his grandchildren and just referred to each one as "that one"? And how each grandchild decided that they were really *the* one, and when they called him on the phone, they would say, "Grandpa, it's me, the one"? Such stories allowed the family members to have a good laugh. Yes, they were sad and would miss their loved one terribly, but at least on this day, at this time, Rabbi Wine gave them the courage to smile.

When sudden death leaves us directionless and lost, Sherwin can become a refuge of rationality and compassion. For example, a man dies suddenly and his wife, adult children, and extended family come in to see the rabbi and prepare for the funeral. The first thing Sherwin does, after expressing his condolences, is to recognize what has happened. The man hasn't passed on, passed over, or gone to a better place. And unless he was suffering, it wasn't meant to be, or for the better.

Rabbi Wine seems to understand that even in the face of death, hope can come as an acceptance of what is real, of what must be, and he can provide the guidance toward a calm, orderly, respectful conclusion. Many times I have observed him as he sat before teary, angry, and often confused people. With his straight back and calm hands, he would lean forward and tell people, through his words and demeanor, that at this time, for this ceremony, things were under control. And if needed, he would hold their hand as they walked into the room for the funeral. When hope was extinguished and one's courage seemed lost, he would be the father, the brother, or the son.

At the Birmingham Temple, bar and bat mitsvas and confirmations are considered to be very important life cycles and opportunities to teach our children the values of Humanistic Judaism. For the mitsva, the child chooses a hero, from either the present or the past, whose life illustrates the qualities that the child admires. For courage, a student might choose Hannah Senesh. For determination, Theodor Herzl. With a tutor, the child studies the person's life and achievements and the values he or she represents, focusing especially on how those values relate to Humanistic Judaism and the child's life. The child then prepares a paper that is presented to the congregation, family, and friends. At age sixteen, the confirmant develops a paper after choosing a moral or ethical issue. As a tutor for many students, I had the opportunity to watch as the inexperienced, nervous students invariably rose to the occasion and delivered a coherent, poised speech.

> Rabbi Wine would repeatedly say to each of the students at the Birmingham Temple, "You are a capable person. You are a strong person."

How did they do this? Where did they get the courage? They were certainly aided by the philosophy instilled in them by our temple school and by Rabbi Wine. He would repeatedly say to each of them, "You are a capable person. You are a strong person. You will have help from other people, but you will be our teacher and we will listen to you." I used to love to watch the parents' faces as their child stood up and delivered an intelligent lecture.

I recall one child who was overly anxious during his rehearsal. The speech was finished and all we needed to do was polish up his delivery. The problem was that each time the child approached the podium, the color would drain from his face, he became visibly sweaty, and he would tell me that he was going to faint. I discussed this with Rabbi Wine, who assured me that he would take care of this at the final rehearsal, which he always attended. It was Rabbi Wine's habit at rehearsals to sit in the very back of the room, to be sure that everyone would be able to hear the speech. As the child grasped the podium in an effort to remain standing, Rabbi Wine stood up and boomed out, "You are forbidden to do that. You can and will give this speech and there will be no fainting." Oh no, I thought to myself, you can't forbid someone to faint. But guess what? The boy got through the rehearsal and from then on, he was much better. He had gained the confidence and the courage to believe that he was a capable person. And this confidence would be carried forward into other ventures of the child's life. Courage can be learned at any age.

During bar and bat mitsvas, keeping modern, extended families straight can be quite a feat. It is not unusual for children to have two or even three sets of parents and eight grandparents. With people living longer, it is not unknown for children to have great-grandparents attend their bar and bat mitsvas. During an interview, Rabbi Wine listens to all the names and only occasionally writes them down. How he keeps them straight has remained a rabbinic mystery, but he has always been able to counsel the proper etiquette for today's extended families.

Rabbi Wine has the ability to define, teach, and imbue his students with the philosophy of Humanistic Judaism. He encourages personal empowerment as exemplified through this statement, from his book *Celebration:* "Courage begins with honesty, the willingness to confront the world as it is and not merely as we want it to be. Courage is the power to make fear our servant and not our master."

Hope is a tricky item. If it is false and baseless, it disappoints and wastes the energy and time we might have spent on appropriate preparation. To be useful, it must be true and possible. How does one distinguish between true and false hope? How does a rabbi know when to say, I believe this will turn out well, or, It's time for us to talk about your funeral? It is always easier to avoid death, but it takes courage to recognize reality.

Sherwin Wine has articulated the philosophy of Humanistic Judaism through the creation of his services, songs, voluminous writings, and personal lifestyle. He knows that it is not enough to tell people that they must rely on themselves or others, but that a rabbi must provide the atmosphere that encourages this kind of personal growth. He knows that most of us will not go out and develop congregations, build buildings, found rabbinic seminaries or international organizations. But we can be part of these things in the presence of a leader who is worth following.

My view through the courtyard window was often profound, frequently funny, sometimes sad, but always clear, kind, and useful. Living a life of courage and hope is an attainable goal made possible by the example of the life of Sherwin Wine.

Helen J. Forman is the immediate past executive director of the Birmingham Temple. In 1973 Helen and her family joined the Birmingham Temple, and she assumed her role as executive director in 1985. She retired from that position in 2001 but remains an important, active participant in the movement of Secular Humanistic Judaism by serving as the secretary of the executive board of the International Institute for Secular Humanistic Judaism and as the chair of the admissions committee.

In Search of a New *Yiddishkeit*

Egon Friedler

It may be difficult to understand nowadays what *Yiddishkeit* was a century ago in America. At the beginning of the twentieth century, America was the largest Jewish cultural center in the world. One million people spoke Yiddish. New York had the most important press in this language. Four newspapers—*Warheit* (nationalist and socialist), *Jewish Morning Journal* (Orthodox and Conservative), *Forwerts* (socialist), *Togblat* (Orthodox and Zionist)—sold together 600,000 copies. Yiddish literature had modest beginnings. It started as part of the press and was thoroughly involved with the social problems of the hard-working immigrant Jews and their social ideals. Morris Rosenfeld (1862–1923) was the poet who expressed best the feelings and hopes of the workers of the famous sweatshops, while Yoash (Shlomo Blumgarten, 1870–1927) gave a more personal, intimate vision of Jewish life in the new country. Yiddish culture became richer and more sophisticated as the community grew. In 1880 there were 250,000 Jews in a nation of 50 million people; forty years later, in a nation of 115 million, there were 4.5 million Jews. Jews had multiplied eighteen times.

But the first decades of the twentieth century were times of poverty and of hard life. Jewish writers and poets were as poor as the public they served. Nobody described this situation better than Irving Howe in his wonderful book, *World of Our Fathers.* With reference to a group of poets who called themselves "Die Yunge" (the young), he wrote: "They dreamed of being pure poets and saw themselves as unrecognized distant cousins to the great Europeans from Pushkin to Rilke. But they were also poverty-stricken immigrant workers: Mani Leib, a shoemaker and for a time a laundryman, Landau at first a house painter, Leivick for many years a paper hanger, Halpern, a jack of all trades. Nothing else underscores so sharply the reason they never could become 'pure poets' in Yiddish. Proletarian aesthetes, Parnassians of the sweatshop—this was the paradox and the glory of 'Die Yunge.'"

However, poets and writers enjoyed the respect and love of their readers. In a fine article on Sholem Aleichem in America in the July/August 2002 issue of *Midstream*—a special issue devoted to Yiddish culture—Oscar Kraines described in these words Sholem Aleichem's death and funeral: "On Saturday morning, May 13, 1916, Sholem Aleichem died of kidney failure, and his hopes of becoming an American citizen and of completing his autobiography ended. For two days, his body lay in his apartment with Jewish writers changing guard. The funeral, on May 15th, arranged by Dr. Judah Magnes, David Pinsky, and others, was one of the biggest ever seen in America. About 100,000 people lined the street from Ohav Tzedeck Synagogue on East 116 Street in Harlem, where Cantor Yosele Rosenblatt chanted the 'El Moleh Rachamim,' to the New York Kehilah on East 21st Street and Second Avenue, where Cantor Rosenblatt again chanted 'El Moleh Rachamim.'" Later, the *Midstream* writer describes a memorial that took place about a month after Sholem Aleichem's death. "On June 17th a memorial was held at Carnegie Hall, with over 2,500 attending. Most of the seats were sold at 10 cents each, and proceeds went to promote Jewish literature. Sholem Asch set the tone: 'He was an apostle of joy, and it was his wish that we be joyful.' Speakers such as Pinsky, Hirschbein, Moshe Nadir, and Avram Raisin recited from Sholem [Aleichem]'s works. Yosele Rosenblatt and his choir sang Yiddish songs and the 'El Moleh Rachamim.'"

Sholem Aleichem only established himself in America in the last years of his life. Other Yiddish writers came to America when they were still young, but they had already won their reputations in Europe: Zalman Schneur, Sholem Asch, Israel Joshua Singer, and Joseph Opatoshu. In later years, when Yiddish was already in a process of decay, the younger brother of Israel Joshua Singer, Isaac Bashevis Singer, thanks to the translation of his works into English, achieved a fame that his brother, who was thought to be a much better writer by the Jewish cultural world, never achieved. The Nobel Prize in 1978 and the fame achieved by Isaac Bashevis Singer were a kind of posthumous homage to a dying culture. Other Yiddish writers felt they were trapped in a dead end. Cynthia Ozick described this situation with outstanding wit and subtlety in her story "Envy; or, Yiddish in America."

Actually, the blooming of Yiddish culture in the United States lasted no more than half a century. For some authors it was between 1900 and 1950. For others, especially those writing for the Yiddish theater, it started earlier and ended earlier. But those who have studied American Jewish history in the first half of the twentieth century agree that Yiddish culture had an extraordinary outburst of creativity. Poets like Abraham Raisin, Moishe Lev Halpern, H. Leivick, Jacov Gladstein, Itzik Manger, and Aharon Zeitlin; fiction writers like Sholem Asch, Joseph Opatoshu, Israel Joshua Singer, Isaac Bashevis Singer, and Chaim Grade; humorists like Moshe Nadir; essayists like Chaim Zhtilovsky, Nachman Sirkin, and Chaim Greenberg; intellectuals and scholars like the literary critic Schmuel Niguer, the historian Jacob Shatzky, and the linguist Max Weinreich, were only the most outstanding and best-known representatives of a large Jewish intelligentsia.

At the beginning of the twentieth century, America was the largest Jewish cultural center in the world. One million people spoke Yiddish.

But as the German Jewish historian Ismar Elbogen wrote: "The Yiddish culture developed an extraordinary vitality, and however it may seem paradoxical, it was a decisive factor for the adaptation to American society. America not only changed their ways of expression but also their ideals and interests. And even more paradoxically, these cultures nurtured in the ghetto became stronger as they were free of its lifestyle. So they could defy openly the synagogue and the *Beit Hamidrash.*"

The Yiddish culture, secular in its spirit and philosophy, gave meaning to the lives of the first Jewish generations in America. But English was the language of the country, and so the Yiddish language was doomed. It had a modest revival when some writers who survived the Holocaust came to America after the war.

In the late 1940s the struggle for the creation of the Jewish state became the center of Jewish life for several years. Yiddish secularism was replaced by Zionist secularism. The creation of the State of Israel had a deep meaning for American Jews. But Zionism could not become a way of life as Yiddish culture had been, for a very simple reason. The dream had become a reality. Whoever wanted to fulfill his Zionist ideal was free to immigrate to Israel. But very few did. American Jews were already deeply integrated in American society, and for the overwhelming majority their only language was English. Indeed, Yiddish did not disappear completely. There are small groups of faithful followers even today. *Forwerts* continues to appear as a weekly, but it is far from the popular and highly influential paper it was during the times of its legendary first editor, Abraham Cahan (1860–1951).

As Jews became richer and more at home in American society and culture, they became, as sociologist Marshall Sklare defined them, "an American group." This status meant, paradoxically, a return to the communal sense given by religion.

Although events like the Six Day War or causes like the struggle for Soviet Jewry could mobilize great numbers of Jews, the deep sense of peoplehood of the first decades of the twentieth century had been lost. The synagogue (of all denominations) was somehow a substitute for the world of *Yiddishkeit* that could not be recovered. Many Jews who did not believe in religion just cared about their own business and quit Jewish organized life. Some of them stopped caring about their Jewishness and did not worry about the identity of their offspring. Others made of their Jewish identity a private affair. But a minority sought a way to keep alive a Jewish secular identity against the stream.

Within this minority there was a young Reform rabbi called Sherwin Wine, who lost his belief in God but not in the Jewish people. After having decided that leading a traditional synagogue was not for him, he sought a way to preserve the rich secular Jewish heritage that had faded away in America. He understood that the America of the *breite Yiddishe massen* (the large Jewish masses) did not exist anymore. To keep secular Jewishness alive, there was no other way than to work modestly and with small groups. So he started in 1963 to organize a small secular community, which was eventually to become the Birmingham Temple. He started from scratch and he succeeded in creating a whole movement, with many branches in the United States, Canada, Israel, Europe, and Australia. Within this movement, he established new patterns of community life, retaining something of an old synagogue for its ceremonial side, but at the same time establishing completely new traditions in their humanistic approach without any theological crutches.

In 1986 Sherwin Wine was one of the leading architects of the International Federation of Secular Humanistic Jews, uniting Jews from all over the world behind Jewish secularism in all its different expressions. In the 1990s Wine was a pioneer in creating a basis for continuity by establishing a program of studies and standards of knowlege for professional leaders, from *madrikhim* to secular rabbis.

There was a young Reform rabbi called Sherwin Wine, who lost his belief in God but not in the Jewish people.

Indeed, all these many accomplishments of Sherwin Wine deserve a detailed and serious study, but here we will deal only with one of his outstanding contributions to Secular Humanistic Judaism: his search for a new *Yiddishkeit*.

As a realistic and strong-minded thinker, Wine understood that Jewish secularism in our time could not be based only on a reverence for the values of the past. It had to be thoroughly related to the present and had to be attuned to the changes of time. If in the past different ideologies were engaged in a bitter fight for the Jewish people, now, half a century after the creation of Israel, the time had come to integrate the work of the leading thinkers writing about different trends in Judaism.

In his most important ideological book, *Judaism Beyond God*, in the chapter devoted to "Alternative Literature," Sherwin Wine describes what a humanistic Jewish literature could be in our time. With an open-minded approach, he accepts as relevant to Secular Humanistic Judaism thinkers and writers of very different schools of thought. He writes: "The writings of Jewish nationalists, whether Yiddishist or Zionist, socialist or capitalist, who rejected supernatural authority and who sought to persuade the Jews to take their own destiny in their own hands, pass the test. I. L. Peretz, Sholem Aleichem, Chaim Zhitlovsky, Ahad Haam, Micah Berdischevsky, Theodor Herzl, Max Nordau, A. D. Gordon, Ber Borochov, Shaul Tchernichovsky, Vladimir Jabotinsky, and Nahum Goldman mocked the pious passivity of the old regime and sought to restore Jewish confidence in human planning and human effort."

This approach opens the door for a new view of the values of the whole range of Jewish experience, for a new approach to Jewish culture and creativity, for Jewish cultural pluralism as a way to build a new sense of belonging. But Sherwin Wine's Jewishness is not based only on a cultural approach. It also deals with a new way to celebrate Jewish holidays and to handle the ceremonies of the Jewish life cycle. It is a way to give a true secular meaning to Jewish life as a totality.

This totality may well be the *Yiddishkeit* of the new century. Sherwin Wine opened a new way. Let us hope that new generations will elaborate and enrich this new Jewishness, which will provide a home for millions of Jews who do not identify themselves with any of the traditional religious conceptions of Judaism.

Egon Friedler, born in Uruguay, is a senior journalist for *Identidad*, the mouthpiece of the Secular Humanistic Jewish group in Uruguay, called Corriente Judia Humanista. He also writes widely on subjects of Jewish interest for several publications in Argentina, Israel, the United States, and England. He has been closely associated with the international movement of Secular Humanistic Judaism since the 1980s and is its best-known spokesperson in Latin America.

Humanistic Judaism: For the Many or the Few?

Daniel Friedman

Our friend Sherwin Wine created Humanistic Judaism forty years ago. It was then and remains today the philosophy of life and of Jewishness that most Jews affirm—whether or not they are aware that this is, in reality, what they are doing. They may "belong" to conventional Conservative or Reform congregations; they may go through the motions of theistic worship and ritual; they may even profess a belief in God; but their operational religion is humanistic. That is, they develop their values and make their decisions by utilizing the wisdom and experience of human beings rather than consulting sacred texts; they conduct their lives without recourse to divine advice. Their life purpose is to maximize their own happiness rather than to serve the wishes of a supernatural authority.

Are they not aware of the contradiction between the theistic Judaism they formally espouse and their actual humanistic convictions? Does it not trouble them that there is a radical incongruity between the prayers they recite and the philosophy of life that actually directs their choices? Why do intelligent, enlightened, sensitive men and women demand so little of their Judaism, of themselves? Why, after forty years, has Humanistic Judaism not become the largest movement in American Jewish life? Why do so few humanistic Jews embrace Humanistic Judaism?

The answer, in my view, is not that they have not yet heard the good news—that there is now available an interpretation and expression of Jewish experience that does not require the compromising of one's convictions. It is not a failure of publicizing and communicating the message of Humanistic Judaism that accounts for its low growth rate. The answer is that most Jews today simply do not care about consistency between belief and behavior and therefore are not interested in what Humanistic Judaism has to offer. Perhaps from their exposure to Judaism as children and subsequently, on the infrequent occasions when they have renewed their exposure, they have learned not to expect from Judaism a rational philosophy of life and an understanding of Jewishness relevant to the world as we know it in the twenty-first century. They have learned not to expect an intellectually challenging and rewarding experience from attending services. These are not the rewards that Jews seek from Judaism.

What do they expect? They expect it to make them *feel* Jewish. They seek an emotional, not intellectual, experience from their "Jewish" activities. Indeed, Jews have come to identify Judaism not with its beliefs, values, concepts, or philosophy, but with what they call "traditions"—that is, with selected rituals, customs, and ceremonies that derive from the Jewish past. Ignoring the theistic beliefs and teachings of *halakhic* Judaism that gave rise to those rituals or traditions, modern Jews seek to identify with what they call their "heritage" by imitating the ritual behavior of *halakhic* Jews. Only in the realm of ritual do most Jews experience, and expect to experience, their Jewishness, and it is only ritual behavior that interests them as Jews. Attending funerals, weddings, bar and bat mitsva celebrations, possibly a service or two annually, and perhaps occasional holiday observances constitute their Judaism, which entails virtually no belief component whatsoever.

A comparison to typical American attitudes toward their secular holidays and ritual observances may be instructive. Thanksgiving dinner, fireworks on the Fourth of July, picnics on Labor Day—it is the ritual, and no longer the principle underlying the observance, that engages most Americans. The story of the Pilgrims or of the signers of the Declaration of Independence may still be told—as may the story of the Exodus on Passover—but it is a perfunctory formality. It is the turkey that is supreme, not the meaning of the holiday for which the turkey has become the symbol.

Still, Americans do take seriously the principles and beliefs on which their country was founded and which continue to inform and inspire its character and its institutions. The Constitution and Declaration of Independence continue to serve as real, not merely symbolic, statements of Americanism. The freedom, equality, and individualism articulated in these documents are essential to American life; they give it its distinctiveness and are understood and genuinely respected—even revered—by Americans of all political persuasions. Whether explicitly or not, it is these values that are celebrated on American holidays.

The Torah and Talmud do not so function in contemporary Jewish life. Indeed, the fundamental principles, values, and teachings contained therein—the ultimate importance of allegiance and obedience to supernatural authority, belief in the Jews as the Chosen People charged with a sacred mission, and faith in divine providence—not only do these ideas not inform the thoughts and decisions of most Jews, they are alien to those thoughts and to the values upon which modern Jews base their decisions.

> Why, after forty years, has Humanistic Judaism not become the largest movement in American Jewish life? Why do so few humanistic Jews embrace Humanistic Judaism?

However, inasmuch as the "Judaism" that most Jews profess as their "faith" is, in fact, barren of belief, it is possible for them to recite blessings and prayers that bear no relationship to their lives or actual values and attitudes—indeed, that contradict their actual values and attitudes—with no sense of the discrepancy. The *words themselves have become ritualized* to the extent that their meaning is ignored as irrelevant.

Absent belief, Judaism is nothing but ceremonials. Accordingly, Jews who wish to demonstrate their Jewishness increasingly request a *ketuba* and the *sheva b'rachot* as part of their wedding ritual, the Kaddish at their funerals, the reading of the Torah at their bar and bat mitsva services. They do not know or care to know the meaning of the words contained therein. Whether those words conform to or violate their convictions is of no concern to them. Judaism is no longer a matter of conviction. Form, not substance, reigns.

It is not surprising, then, that the degree of one's ritual observance is the criterion by which one's religiosity *and one's Jewishness* are judged. Regardless of ideological or theological distinctions among the various expressions of Judaism, the most ritually observant are considered "the Orthodox," the least observant "the Reform," and in the middle are "the Conservative." Furthermore, the most observant practitioners are considered the most religious and the most Jewish. Reform Jews are less religious (and less Jewish) than Conservative Jews. Humanistic Jews are still less religious (and less Jewish). It is no wonder that completely nonobservant Jews wonder whether they are Jewish at all!

Unintentionally, rabbis have encouraged this misunderstanding of Judaism and of Jewishness. Privately acknowledging that many Jews—including not a few rabbis themselves—are no longer believers, publicly they have promoted ritual observance as the essence of Jewish behavior. Never mind what you do not believe; just come to services, light candles, keep kosher, put on tefillin, fast on Yom Kippur. That's what Judaism is all about.

Ironically, this trend toward ritualism is most apparent among the most "liberal" movements. Initially, Reform Judaism opposed "meaningless" rituals and ceremonials performed merely to satisfy traditional requirements. Dietary restrictions were abandoned. The bar mitsva was abolished. Head coverings were jettisoned. Today, it is not uncommon for tallis-garbed Reform Jews to mimic the most Orthodox behavior. After all, if being Jewish is nothing more than performing certain rituals, the more "traditional" the better.

In light of this analysis, it should not be unexpected that when Humanistic Judaism offers a philosophy of life consistent with reason, reality, freedom, individualism, equality, and human dignity—the values on which most modern Jews truly base their lives—their response is indifference. They have learned not to expect substance from Judaism. In its insistence that ritual behavior be consistent with, and expressive of, one's actual beliefs, Humanistic Judaism violates the commonly accepted assumption that beliefs have no connection to ritual. In expecting Jews to take their beliefs seriously and to value their integrity sufficiently to demand consistency between what one says in the synagogue and what one does at home and in the street, Humanistic Judaism falls upon deaf ears.

Today's Jews have given up on Judaism beyond indulging in an occasional ritual. They remain indifferent to Humanistic Judaism, not because they disagree with its philosophy of life or its values, which they in fact embrace, but because they do not look to Judaism as the embodiment of a philosophy of life or of values.

> Never mind what you do not believe; just come to services, light candles, keep kosher, put on tefillin, fast on Yom Kippur. That's what Judaism is all about.

It is unlikely that an epiphany will awaken most of the Jewish people to the merits and joys of Humanistic Judaism. To their loss, they will experience a Judaism of ever-diminishing significance as even its remaining ritual pleasures lose whatever sentimental or nostalgic power they still possess. All the more reason to be grateful to Sherwin Wine's audacity in creating a way of being Jewish that challenges, articulates, and celebrates our deepest convictions. We must be content with the knowledge that the relatively small number of Jews who are attracted to Humanistic Judaism are the unconventional few who prize intellectual integrity above empty ritual, who value honesty more than familiar phrases, and who believe Jewishness is more significant than nostalgic remembrance. Thank you, Sherwin.

This essay is based upon and contains passages from the author's article, "Why Isn't Humanistic Judaism More Popular?" which appeared in Humanistic Judaism *(Summer/Autumn 1995).*

Daniel Friedman is a graduate of Brandeis University and was ordained as a rabbi at the Hebrew Union College. He served for thirty-five years as the rabbi of Congregation Beth Or, a Humanistic temple in Deerfield, Illinois. Currently, he is rabbinic advisor to Kol Hadash Humanistic Congregation in north suburban Chicago. He is the author of *Jews without Judaism: Conversations with an Unconventional Rabbi* (Prometheus Books, 2002) and resides in Lincolnshire, Illinois.

The Birthing of Humanistic Judaism: An Eyewitness Account

Judith A. Goren

Today's international movement known as Secular Humanistic Judaism was born of a union between the traditional structure of Reform Judaism and the philosophical stance of American humanism. The gestation occurred in the mid-1960s, in a series of meetings in various homes in the northwest suburbs of Detroit. The men and women attending these meetings were members of the Ritual Committee of the newly formed Birmingham Temple, originally a Reform Jewish congregation, led by Rabbi Sherwin T. Wine. The sessions were filled with new ideas presented with careful logic by Wine and argued by the group with a passionate response ranging from enthusiasm to incredulousness, from anger to admiration to acceptance. For me, it was a stimulating, compelling time. I rarely missed a meeting.

THE NEW RABBI

One evening my husband and I had friends at our house. Our children, barely school age, were sleeping. One of the women said to all of us, "You have to come hear this new rabbi. He is the smartest person you ever heard speak. We're starting a new congregation, and he's going to be our leader. Come next Friday night." I had not had a religious affiliation growing up, and I wanted to go. I wanted our children to have the training I had missed.

My husband, who had an Orthodox bar mitsva and then left organized religion, said he was not interested. Despite his protests, we went to hear Rabbi Wine. We were hooked. Less than six months after the temple was formed, we became charter members.

THE NAME

The eight couples who initiated the idea of a new Reform temple wanted a smaller, younger, more intimate congregation than the ones available at that time. Some also wanted a place closer to where they lived, in the suburb of Birmingham, Michigan, so they would not have to drive so far. "Birmingham Temple" was to be a temporary name. In actuality, we met in many Detroit suburbs and only briefly in Birmingham. By the time we built our own building in Farmington Hills, we were so well known as the Birmingham Temple that those who argued for keeping the original name won the battle.

THE RITUAL COMMITTEE MEETS

The Ritual Committee was a self-selected group of about fifteen men and women interested in the evolving philosophy of the temple and also in spending as much time as possible in the stimulating presence of our new rabbi. It included attorneys, architects, teachers, writers, doctors, and even the rabbi's sister and brother-in-law who, like Wine, grew up in a Conservative Jewish tradition. As a group, we came from a wide spectrum of Jewish upbringing, ranging from Orthodox to secular.

From the start, Rabbi Wine made it clear that the new congregation should be based not on demographics but on philosophy. The question that Wine posed in our weekly meetings was, How can our services reflect our true beliefs? This entailed many heated discussions about what we actually did believe, a topic most of us had never before been invited to explore. Did we believe that the Torah was literally written by God? Or, rather, that it was a collection of stories written over a period of centuries by human beings? If the latter, why did we put a crown on it and keep it in a special ark on the altar? In fact, did we believe that God was a person who could write books? Or a person at all? If not a person, why did we say prayers that extolled him for being a king? Did these words make any sense to us? How many of us lived our daily lives as if these beliefs were literally true or even meaningful to us?

The old traditions did not get discarded without a lot of heated debate from the committee. Eventually, however, Wine's logic was persuasive. Our services became meditative words on chosen subjects, and the Torah was respectfully stored on a bookshelf.

Wine also introduced us to thoughts about our responsibility as human beings: to ourselves, to one another, to the larger community, and to the world. He encouraged us to think about the qualities that were important to our lives, issues such as honesty, integrity, personal responsibility, courage, and freedom. We were also invited to examine Jewish tradition and to keep the aspects that had real meaning for us. Our true beliefs, Wine said, were reflected in how we lived our lives. Was it realistic to set aside Saturday as a day of rest in this fast-paced secular world? How many of us actually did that? Each Jewish holiday was explored and reinterpreted: was Passover about the killing of first-born Egyptian babies and the parting of the Red Sea? Or was it really about freedom and the renewal of the spring season? Was Yom Kippur only a contest with oneself to fast without fainting? Or was it about forgiveness, about making peace with the important people in one's life? We

Did we believe that the Torah was literally written by God? Or, rather, that it was a collection of stories written over a period of centuries by human beings?

were encouraged to live with integrity by examining the consistency of our behavior, our stated beliefs, and the ritual of our religious services.

Once a week the members of the Ritual Committee sprawled on sofas or perched on folding chairs in someone's family room, munching potato chips and sipping ginger ale while arguing passionately about dogma and personal integrity. We had no idea that we were the planters of seeds for what was later to become an international secular movement.

A PUBLIC SEMINAR ON GOD

The Ritual Committee decided to hold a series of educational evenings, led by Rabbi Wine and open to the public, to educate people about our evolving philosophy. The first topic selected was, "What is our concept of God?" The evening was held in a private home, in a family room designed to hold perhaps forty people. Almost three times that many showed up, sitting on the basement staircase and crowding into hallways. Many definitions were offered, analyzed, and shown by Wine to be illogical.

Wine tried during that evening and in the weeks that followed to reorient people to thinking about God as an ideal of perfection toward which all could strive. However, his redefining did little to change the anthropomorphic concept most people had grown up with. Finally, he grew tired of the fruitless effort. "A word with too many meanings is semantically useless," he insisted. The subject of God was declared to be irrelevant to the goals of honoring Jewish history and ethical values, and to celebrating holidays and life-cycle events as part of the greater Jewish family.

CHANGES AND CONTROVERSY

Within a number of months, many changes were made in the traditional Reform service, most of them relating to the word "God." The Kaddish—the mourner's prayer for the dead, which praises the glory of God—was eliminated. The Sh'ma, regarded by the three traditional branches of

Judaism as the basic credal statement ("Hear, O Israel, the Lord our God, the Lord is One"), was also eliminated. The Union Prayer Book, used by Reform congregations in America, was put in storage, replaced by creative meditation services written by Wine. Sunday school focused on Jewish history and ethics, with little or no mention of the word "God."

None of this happened without tremendous controversy, first within the temple and later within the larger community. In the congregation itself, there was a faction who stood behind Wine in wanting total intellectual consistency. On the other side were the more conservative members, who charged lack of respect for tradition. This aspect of the controversy, while quite vocal, was contained within our own walls.

The labor pains became excruciating when we woke up one Sunday morning to a front-page bombshell in the *Detroit Free Press.* Above a photo of Sherwin Wine was the headline: "Suburban Rabbi: 'I Am an Atheist.'" The story was the result of a semantic misunderstanding between Wine and the religion editor of the paper during a telephone interview. During all of our in-house philosophical discussions, the word "atheist" had seldom, if ever, been used. This turn of events profoundly affected everyone in the temple and stirred up hostility toward us by outsiders.

> The subject of God was declared irrelevant to the goals of honoring Jewish history and ethical values, and to celebrating holidays and life-cycle events as part of the greater Jewish family.

Now all 280 members of the Birmingham Temple were on trial in the court of public opinion, vilified by the Jewish community at large. The building where we had been renting space for services asked us to move. I found that wherever I went, even to the supermarket, someone I barely knew would accost me with, "How can you belong to that temple? Don't you believe in God?" If it was difficult for us as members, I am just now beginning to appreciate how much courage it took for Wine, a thirty-five-year-old pioneer, to be unsupported by his rabbinical colleagues and misunderstood by the community at large. Yet he continued to stand firm with dignity.

The controversy increased when the Detroit story was picked up by *Time* magazine and the *New York Times.* A few couples, some under pressure by their families, left to go elsewhere. Others were drawn to the philosophy and joined us. Despite outside pressure, the congregation grew.

A QUESTION ABOUT HUMANISM

One day, after the atheism controversy broke, but before Wine had ever spoken to us about humanism, I was glancing through the classified ads in the back of *Harper's* magazine and one caught my eye. It said something like this: "If you believe that man is responsible for his own actions, independent of supernatural authority, contact the American Humanist Association." The concept sounded familiar. At the next meeting of our Ritual Committee, I asked Rabbi Wine about it. "Yes, it is similar," he said. "Very much so." It is my memory that it was not long after this brief conversation that Rabbi Wine introduced us to the philosophy of humanism.

NAMING THE PHILOSOPHY

Sometime in 1966, I was invited to attend a meeting about a new publication that was being discussed, a journal to initiate the birth of our new approach to organized Judaism. The journal was to combine ideas from Judaism and humanism. There was a great deal of discussion (as usual) about the name: were we talking about Humanistic Judaism or Jewish Humanism? Which word was the noun, which the modifier? Eventually the solution was to publish a quarterly journal called *Humanistic Judaism* and to also publish a monthly newsletter for our congregation, called *The Jewish Humanist.* To this day, both names and publications stand.

I was an assistant editor for the first four issues of the quarterly journal. The "statement of purpose" declares that the journal is to "provide a forum in which this philosophy can be explored through free discussion and dialogue." The cover design of the first issue is the section from Michelangelo's Sistine Chapel that portrays Adam and God reaching out their hands toward one another. The theme of this issue (June 1967) was, "Can there be a religion in which the concept of God is irrelevant?" The question was addressed in symposium format, with an introductory article by Wine; two other rabbis and a Jewish philosopher responded to his ideas. (As in any good Jewish debate, there were at least six opinions, including some disagreement about the wording of the initial question.)

THE NEW FOCUS

Eventually, the furor settled down and we focused on establishing what we did believe rather than arguing about what we didn't. Discussions about God and the use of related "God-language" were treated as off-limits; they died out or went elsewhere. The Birmingham Temple, under the leadership of Sherwin Wine, grew over the next two or three decades to include more than 400 families. No longer nomads, we built our own building. There was a full program of Sunday school, Hebrew training, bar and bat mitsvas, weddings and baby namings, celebration of Jewish holidays with a humanistic interpretation, Friday night services with Israeli music, and brilliant, stimulating sermons every week by Rabbi Wine. No longer outcasts, we were at last fully included as part of the greater Detroit Jewish community.

No longer outcasts, we were at last fully included as part of the greater Detroit Jewish community.

THE LEGACY CONTINUES

Now, some four decades after its birth, the Birmingham Temple thrives. Three new rabbis serve the congregation and the community. Noted speakers from around the world, addressing topics ranging from world politics to world literature, draw standing-room-only crowds. More than thirty similar Humanistic Jewish congregations, many begun by former Michigan members, have formed in cities across the United States and Canada. In addition, Humanistic Judaism has branched into a North American society (the Society for Humanistic Judaism) and an international federation (the International Federation of Secular Humanistic Jews) with members across Europe, South America, and Israel. Sherwin Wine's early vision of a humanistic alternative within organized Judaism has led to a worldwide movement that is still growing. It all began in someone's living room, and I was privileged to have been a participant.

A PERSONAL NOTE

During my decades of friendship with Sherwin Wine, I have played the roles of learner, supporter, and dissenter. Sherwin has been a teacher, a mentor, and a compassionate listener for me. (The main topic of my dissension had to do with spirituality, a concept that had gone underground with the elimination of "God-language," leaving no words with which to acknowledge the lived experience.) While we often disagreed, I always felt deeply heard and understood.

In recent years, I have begun to appreciate the earlier necessity for Wine to take such a firm stand. Now that Humanistic Judaism is a well-established and respected option in the array of choices, the old rules have softened a bit, and discussion is more open. Recently, the Birmingham Temple was host to a national colloquium on secular spirituality.

More significant to me than intellectual debate, however, have been certain moments such as the celebration of Rabbi Wine's seventieth birthday. When Wine completed his talk, the love in the room was palpable as a thousand people stood as one and broke into spontaneous applause. After many years of questioning, I no longer find a conflict between being a Humanistic Jew and a spiritual human being. I am grateful to Sherwin Wine for his patience while I was figuring that out.

Judith A. Goren, Ph.D., is a humanistic clinical psychologist and the author of three collections of poetry. Her work has appeared in many literary journals and several anthologies. Judith is a longtime member of the Birmingham Temple. She was a contributing editor to *Humanistic Judaism*, the first journal published by the movement, and she is the author of a Sunday school text on the subject of Jews of Eastern Europe.

Celebrating Sherwin T. Wine

Roger E. Greeley

Sherwin and I met in 1980. It was a chance meeting. Immediately, I was struck by his intelligence and his unfailing and remarkable sense of humor. He seemed to enjoy everything he was doing, and his joy was contagious. You could not be around him without being "lifted." His dynamism, his dedication, his unqualified secularism, his inability to dissemble, and his forthright expression of his beliefs stood out from the run-of-the-mill clerics I knew. Euphemisms have no place in his vocabulary. He says what he means and he means what he says. He walks the talk.

Do I have any negatives where he is concerned? Well, to be absolutely truthful, for a time I had one strong reservation about Sherwin. It concerned a rather important and fundamental aspect of his being: his claim that he was, through and through, a Jew. My sister married a Jew, and as a Unitarian minister I was fortunate to attract a number of Jews to the church I served. It was my belief that, based on a rather broad experience with Jews, I was able to determine the authenticity of any Jew's claims to being a Jew. It boiled down to a simple question: "Do you like Henny Youngman?" I remember how crestfallen I was when, in response to that question, Sherwin replied, with a puzzled look on his face, "Who?" Here is a man passing himself off as a rabbi, a born and bred Jew, the founder of the Society for Humanistic Judaism, asking me, a simple goy, "Who, who is Henny Youngman?" This is tantamount to a Catholic priest responding to, "Were you impressed with the conversion of Claire Booth Luce?" with the query, "Who?"

Sherwin's reply taxed my credulity and led me to admire his ability to have fooled thousands into thinking he was a Jew. How utterly preposterous to think that a man who grew up in Detroit, with a TV in his home, during the Ed Sullivan years, had never seen Henny Youngman! Henny's appearances on the Sullivan show were second only to Ed himself. While my faith in Sherwin was deeply shaken by this near-catastrophic revelation, my confidence was gradually restored. The process was really quite simple. After I shared a few dozen "Hennys" with Sherwin, he achieved a state of exhilarated amusement that demonstrated his true Jewishness. No phony, make-believe Jew could react to Henny's non sequiturs as did Sherwin. The more outrageous, cutting, or downright silly the one-liners from Henny, the louder Sherwin's laughter. I was deeply relieved to find that beneath his initial response of "Who is Henny?" there lived a 100 percent bona fide man. He was clearly one of those sometimes called GOPs—"God's Own People."

One of the pleasant professional experiences I have had is when I am privileged to introduce Sherwin to a group unaware of his role in Judaism. I say, "Ladies and gentlemen, I am proud to introduce to you a very dear friend and colleague, Rabbi Sherwin T. Wine. He is the only rabbi I know who gets hate mail from Jews, particularly other rabbis!"

When traveling, I am constantly disappointed when I meet Jews who are not affiliated with any branch of Judaism. I soon discover that their reason for not affiliating is that they have rejected the traditional theological beliefs and cannot sacrifice reason for religiosity. The door has been opened for me to do a promo on Sherwin and his breakthrough creation for all rational Jews, the Society for Humanistic Judaism. It would save time were the organization called the Society for *Secular* Humanistic Judaism, but, regardless, I forge ahead. Usually, when I present the secular aspect of Sherwin's movement, the faint hearts surface. Yet, it was Sherwin's unequivocal "secularism" that first captured my admiration of his work. I continue my discussions with the "fallen away" Jews who are made uneasy by Sherwin's secularism. They insist, "To be a Jew, you *must* believe in God!" My response? To be a Jew is in the blood, the tradition, the culture, the suffering, the sacrifice, and the devotion to scholarship, excellence, and creativity that we often applaud in the arts and other disciplines.

One time Sherwin invited me to do a program I had developed entitled "Eight Rebels with a Cause." Charlie Chaplin was one of the eight. I treated him as a Jew. Following the program one woman came to me and said, "Roger, I loved the program but I think you're wrong on one item. Charlie Chaplin was NOT a Jew." Shaken, I immediately asked Sherwin. He disappeared into his study. Minutes went by before he returned. He said, "Roger, she's right. Chaplin was not a Jew!" He rescued me from total despair by adding, "But he should have been!" We all had a good laugh. How often around Sherwin there is laughter.

To be a Jew is in the blood, the tradition, the culture, the suffering, the sacrifice, and the devotion to scholarship, excellence, and creativity.

There was an international gathering of humanists in Norway. I did not attend. Upon his return, Sherwin and I had our usual monthly lunch. He was my boss in the Humanist Institute. We met monthly for nearly ten years. Every meeting was memorable and a joy. I asked him about the meetings in Norway and specifically about the man whose undying optimism seemed to block out decades of non-achievement in his West Coast humanist offense. I asked Sherwin if the gentleman in question had attended the meetings and asked, "How was he?" Without pause Sherwin replied,

"Oh, as usual, he's happy in failure!" It was sometime before I could continue eating. It was such a perfect description.

This tribute to a genuine hero, leader, and friend would not be complete without my relating Sherwin's all-time favorite Henny one-liner. It seems that Henny agreed to perform at a benefit fundraiser in Las Vegas. A large number of stars would each do his brief shtick. Henny was backstage, awaiting his turn, when he heard, "Henny! You're on!" (As if he was ever "off.") Henny was walking toward the curtain entrance when who should step through but Mickey Rooney, who had just finished performing. As they passed, Henny, looking at Mickey, quipped, "Why Mickey—you've lost height." Say no more.

I was told that in this essay I should "detail what I have done to advance the cause of secular humanism through my career." Not much. Although, through my resurrection of the work of Robert Green Ingersoll, the leading secularist of the nineteenth century, I hope to have moved a few people to discover his incredible legacy. Even though my book, *The Best of Ingersoll,* has sold like "lead-cakes," it has gone through two printings. In addition, I served a Unitarian Church as its sole minister (that's *sole,* not soul) from 1957 to 1985, never missing a Sunday for which I was responsible. We never said a prayer, read from any Bible, engaged in any responsive readings, or sang any Christian hymns. And, to demonstrate our total break from mainstream churches, *we never passed the plate!* During my tenure we went from a Sunday attendance of 30 to well over 160. Our membership went from perhaps 75 (record-keeping was sloppy) to a high of 337. Since my retirement (to go to work for Sherwin, the best boss I ever had), there have been five ministers at People's Church. One was fired, and it resulted in a split in the congregation that has remained in place ever since. Between 1934 and August 1985, the church had just two ministers. My predecessor served twenty-two years and I twenty-eight and a half. It was a half-century of religion without any theology! Unitarian Universalism (we merged in 1961) is a pitifully small movement of 150,000 in the United States. Membership elsewhere is even lower.

The religious right continues to infect mainstream religion, politics, and even public education. I have no idea what specifics would be most effective to overcome or reverse these current trends. They are deeply disturbing, especially where scientific research and innovation are involved. The religious right also threatens women's rights. I have also maintained for years that the gay/lesbian communities ought to get awards for not adding to the population explosion through unwanted, unneeded, unproductive, unregulated human reproduction. We may well breed ourselves into oblivion. Drastic demographic reform is imperative if the species is to survive. Name a major religion that believes we need to "Go forth and *subtract!*" You can't. Right-wing religion as well as the media bombard us with a statistical avalanche on the staggering cost of smoking, overeating, and drugs. Add them all together and they might not begin to equal the problem of overpopulation worldwide and right here in the good old USA.

I cannot say that my ministry has made any significant inroads on the population explosion, racism, the health care delivery system, or the goal of making the United States the leader in enabling the United Nations to be an effective first step towards world federalism. With George "Dubya" and his multimillionaire clones calling the shots, the prospects for genuine internationalism are indeed dim.

> We need to accept the fact that there is no "next life." The real challenge is to make *this* life the sole focus of our rational attention and love.

After having lived almost eight decades, I am not impressed with what the human family has accomplished since the end of World War II. I am not saying that WWII was a total loss—far from it. In addition to bringing an end to the most infamous chapter in the twentieth century, the Holocaust, the conclusion of the war also provided humanity with the chance to start anew. There was never a better opportunity to accept our full responsibility for human destiny and to kiss the supernatural goodbye forever. Humanism began to flourish in the 1950s. Our species, however, has not matured enough to accept the reality of our individual mortality and to devote ourselves to this life. After all, the silence in the graveyard is eternal. We need to accept the fact that there is no "next life." The real challenge is to make *this* life the sole focus of our rational attention and love.

Here is another observation as to why my admiration for Sherwin is so great. Some years ago a "fallen away" Jew died in Detroit. Well known, respected, and successful, he was not affiliated with any organized Jewish experience. Can you guess on whose door the survivors knocked for a memorial service? Sherwin. He agreed to serve. Following the formal service, the family and close friends adjourned to the cemetery. The principal survivor approached Sherwin and said, "We'd like you to say the traditional Kaddish at the grave." Sherwin replied simply, "I don't do that." I learned of this event from my son, a federal magistrate judge in Michigan's Upper Peninsula; he had a good friend who was close to the deceased. My son told me this story, and when he described Sherwin's refusal at the grave, he paused to laugh and added, "You and Sherwin—two peas from the same pod!" I cannot think of a better compliment to me. I have told Sherwin many, many times that in the half-century of my ministry, no colleague has come within a mile of him.

June 2003 marks the month of Sherwin's retirement. I understand that two rabbis are waiting in the wings to *succeed* him. It will take two well-trained rabbis to succeed him. You notice I emphasize "succeed." How often we hear unthinking people say, "So-and-so will REPLACE so-and-so." You *replace* burned-out lightbulbs, broken glasses, your lost car keys; never do we *replace* people. Sherwin's successors are just that; not his replacements. No one could ever replace Sherwin.

I could go on and on about the importance of secularism and the enormous contributions made by Sherwin. Let me finish with a favorite story I wanted to tell at a roast they had a few years back for Sherwin at the Birmingham Temple. I had prepared my remarks and was really looking forward to the evening. The master of ceremonies, however, forgot to call on me. So here is just one of the Hennys I wanted to share at Sherwin's roast.

One time I came into the lovely foyer of the temple. I saw Sherwin. He didn't see me. He was bent over, listening to an elderly, short, grey-haired woman. As I walked behind him, I heard the lady say, "Rabbi, I read your book!" Sherwin replied, "So you're the ONE!"

Sherwin, best wishes for a great new career; my deepest thanks for the twenty-two years we've shared and for being secularism's best role model. And thank you for your friendship!

Roger E. Greeley is Minister Emeritus of People's (Unitarian) Church in Kalamazoo, Michigan. He served the church for twenty-eight and a half years. He received his master's degree in education from Boston University. In 1985 be became the associate dean of the Humanist Institute in New York. Now in retirement, he writes, travels, counsels, and agitates for secularism and separation of church and state.

A Man for All People, Ahead of His Time

Miriam S. Jerris

When I was eleven years old, something happened that changed my life forever. My family was among the founding members of Temple Beth El, the first and only Reform congregation in Windsor, Ontario. The rabbi was a young man from Temple Beth El of Detroit, Sherwin T. Wine. Although I had no way of knowing at the time, Rabbi Wine was to become my mentor, and the man who would help me realize my dream to become a rabbi.

Rabbi Wine served as the rabbi of my congregation until I was fifteen years old, just after my confirmation. He left our congregation in 1964 to serve as the full-time rabbi of a new congregation in suburban Detroit. I discovered something very exciting while Rabbi Wine served as my Reform rabbi: he used humor in his sermons. Rabbi Wine taught me that you can laugh in temple, that congregational Judaism could also be joyous.

After Rabbi Wine left our congregation, I continued studying with the new rabbi. I was very active in the B'nai B'rith Youth Organization (BBYO), serving as the regional Judaism chair. I attended Jewish camps. In 1967, between my freshman and sophomore years of college, I traveled to Israel. My Jewish identity strengthened. As an undergraduate student, I studied both psychology and Near Eastern studies. I discovered my passion for the Hebrew language and for studying things Jewish. By the time I was in my senior year, I knew I wanted to become a rabbi. I wrote to Hebrew Union College, the Reform seminary, and discovered that there were no woman rabbis. What a shock! I was outraged, and then side-tracked. A few months later, I became engaged to be married and my interest in the rabbinate diminished for some time.

In the meantime, a new rabbi arose in Windsor who knew not Rabbi Wine's congregants. When my husband proposed marriage, we both wanted a rabbi we knew to officiate at our wedding. We called Sherwin Wine. A few years later, my brother was tragically killed in an accident, and I needed a spiritual community that would bring me solace without revering a supernatural being. My brother's death terminated the last tenuous connections that I had to a belief in an omnipotent, omniscient, omnipresent deity. I had ceased to accept the idea of a conscious god. However, I had not lost my love for Jewish history, language, or literature—the culture and the experience of the Jewish people.

In seeking a Jewish community, I discovered that Rabbi Wine and the Birmingham Temple were articulating a human-centered, culturally focused Jewish experience. They were advancing a philosophy, a new Jewish denomination called Humanistic Judaism. It was a great "A-ha" moment for me to hear this philosophy explicated. This organization was expressing exactly what I believed. I not only found a philosophy consistent with my worldview, I discovered a community that helped heal my loss realistically and authentically. Rabbi Wine taught me that while I may not be able to rely on a personal god for help, I could depend on my own strength.

In a short time, I became very interested in the philosophy and in the temple. I wanted to participate, and I told Rabbi Wine that I yearned for a significant and meaningful involvement. Now, that is all you ever need to tell Sherwin Wine, and you have a job. My "little" job, which was helping to mail out the journal of the Society for Humanistic Judaism (SHJ), became my life's work. Eventually, I became the first executive director of the SHJ and Sherwin's companion in creating the now-famous alphabet soup: the many organizations of the humanist and the Secular Humanistic Judaism movements. Sherwin Wine taught me to be an organizational activist.

We humans typically involve ourselves in projects that support our emotional needs or tendencies. The philosophy of Humanistic Judaism suits my personality. It supports my desire to be just a little bit outrageous, rebellious, different, outspoken, and unconventional. Humanistic Judaism encourages us to laugh at the absurdity of the world around us and at ourselves. It nurtures creativity. It honors the wisdom of many traditions. Humanistic Judaism is a religion that allows Jews to live in the modern world with consistency between personal beliefs and behavior.

As a young person, I was always uncomfortable with the attitude of my family and other Jews toward those not born Jewish. I was never at ease with the kind of isolation or chauvinism that those attitudes naturally created. I was Jewish and enjoyed being Jewish, but I also enjoyed the world outside of Judaism—a world that did not divide everyone into either Jewish or non-Jewish categories.

> Rabbi Wine taught me that you can laugh in temple, that congregational Judaism could also be joyous.

I especially appreciated the universalism that was part of Humanistic Judaism. I enjoyed learning about philosophical and organizational humanism. One of the organizations Rabbi Wine helped to create was the Humanist Institute, a training program for humanist leaders. I joined the first class and applied to the American Humanist Association to become a humanist counselor, which was clergy for the organization. This position enabled me to officiate legally at wedding ceremonies, and Rabbi Wine began to refer to me weddings for which he was unavailable. Rabbi Wine taught me to find wisdom in many traditions.

I had found my niche and my passion. I absolutely loved working with couples and creating meaningful ceremonies. Most of the weddings in which I participated were intermarriages, and I found that the families were intensely grateful that we were willing and able to provide a Jewish presence at these weddings that consisted of one Jewish partner and one non-Jewish, non-conversionary partner. The level of appreciation fueled my love for the work. Rabbi Wine taught me to live my passion.

I have devoted the past eighteen years of my life to working with intermarried families, developing creative and meaningful ceremonies, and counseling couples and their parents. My business card now reads, "Rabbi Miriam S. Jerris, Ph.D., Intermarriage Specialist." I do not think any of those titles, qualifications, or degrees would surround my name were it not for Rabbi Sherwin Wine. He has been my guiding philosophical mentor for most of my life. His moral commitment to providing a Jewish presence for couples intermarrying long before it was publicly acceptable is an example I am proud to emulate. Sherwin taught me to follow my convictions.

Sherwin has presented three concepts in the field of Jewish-Gentile intermarriage that revolutionize the way we approach intermarriage. First, he differentiates between intercultural and interfaith marriage. The *Guide to Humanistic Judaism* describes this concept as follows:

> Humanistic Judaism distinguishes between an interfaith and an intercultural marriage or relationship. An interfaith marriage consists of one Jewish partner and one non-Jewish partner, either or both of whom are attached to their theistic traditions. This means that the partners have different beliefs. An intercultural marriage consists of one Jewish partner and one non-Jewish partner who share a similar worldview but who enjoy and participate in the cultural aspects of their differing backgrounds.[1]

Those of us involved in Secular Humanistic Judaism who officiate at intermarriages have discovered that many of the couples with whom we work are intercultural couples. These couples share a philosophy of life. Their differences are rooted in their varying upbringings rather than in the way they currently live their spiritual lives. They are confused about how to raise a family. Once they understand the distinctions between interfaith and intercultural differences, they are not as confused or frightened about their future.

Furthermore, Sherwin distinguishes between primary and secondary family identity. The family can choose a primary identity, either cultural or religious, without rejecting the secondary identity that exists in that family. If the family chooses a primary Jewish identity, there is no reason why the family cannot celebrate Christmas and other Christian-based holidays with the family members who share a Christian background, whether that background is primarily religious or cultural. Discovering that your spouse does not have to abandon his or her own identity is a source of great relief and comfort to both partners in a marriage.

Sherwin treats people as individuals, not labels. He communicates to his couples this idea, which is very liberating. It helps them focus on "who" they are marrying, not "what" they are marrying. This notion promotes inclusion, not exclusion. This philosophy supports the dignity of both partners in a marriage as well as their families. I sometimes find that I am the only advocate for the non-Jewish partner. Sherwin has taught me that all partners in an intermarriage relationship, not just the Jewish partner, are entitled to be treated with dignity.

> Rabbi Wine's moral commitment to providing a Jewish presence for couples intermarrying long before it was publicly acceptable is an example I am proud to emulate.

Sherwin also models courage. He provided support for intermarried couples and their families when it was unacceptable to do so. In those early days, people attending a wedding would ask him how he could contribute to the demise of Judaism. The couples may have been grateful, but many of the guests and even some of the family members were outraged. And that sentiment does not begin to describe the attitudes of some members of the rabbinate. He describes the hostility he experienced:

> Well, it [negative response from the community] happened frequently in the '60s and '70s before the rabbis and everybody starting doing them [intermarriages]. I remember about three Hadassah meetings and a couple board meetings where they wanted me to talk about intermarriage, and the audience was very hostile, very hostile. Then, it would happen sometimes at weddings. I would get hostility from the parents of the Jewish groom or bride. That was back in the '60s. On the one hand, they were glad a rabbi was there. On the other hand, [they wondered] why are you doing this? Why are you doing an intermarriage?[2]

Rabbi Wine became something of a pariah in some rabbinic circles, but he did not let it deter him. He explained, "I know that many of them [rabbis] were disturbed about what I did, whether it was about God or intermarriage. But I did not arrange to spend very much time with them. I did not want to. Their opinion of me was not important. So, I was strangely liberated from that."[3] He never wavered. He knew that what he was doing was morally correct. But it was not popular. Sherwin taught me to face rejection and disdain with courage and dignity.

Working with intermarried couples provided the foundation for my academic work. My master's thesis, *Celebrating Differences*, explored this question: How do people from different religious and cultural backgrounds describe the experience of being intermarried? My doctoral dissertation built on that work and explored the Jewish clergy experience as I examined the question, How do Jewish clergy perceive and describe the experience of providing pastoral support for intermarriage?

Sherwin describes how he approaches intermarriage best in his own words as he lays out the four principles he follows in working with intermarrying couples:

> First, I always deal with people as individuals first. That is my way. That is what I do with my counseling. I always try to say to them, "I am not talking to two labels. I am talking to two people." I find that to be very, very important because once they can release themselves to some degree from the label, then they can deal more realistically with what needs to be done.
>
> The second principle is that both parties will be treated [equally]. So, nobody can schlep somebody in here and tell me, "I want her converted." The equality part is very important.
>
> The third is nobody will ever make me say what I do not believe. There are limits to what I am prepared to do to serve them. Some people say, "All I am asking you to do is say this little prayer." I cannot do that.
>
> The fourth principle is I always make them feel good about their choice of marriage partner, because they love each other and the thing they have been receiving is all this hostility towards them.[4]

Sherwin models courage, providing support for intermarried couples and their families when it was unacceptable to do so.

Regarding my relationship with Sherwin Wine, it is not possible for me to separate the personal from the professional. He was my rabbi at my bat mitsva and at my confirmation. He officiated at my marriages—both of them. He has been by my side in times of loss. He named both my babies and celebrated my children's bat and bar mitsvas and their confirmations. He presided over my rabbinic ordination. Recently, he officiated at my daughter's wedding ceremony.

It is an extreme pleasure to offer this tribute in honor of Rabbi Sherwin T. Wine. He has made an invaluable contribution to the Jewish world in expressing and modeling his work with intermarriage. Many thousands of Jewish women and men have stayed connected to the Jewish community because he and the clergy of the Secular Humanistic Jewish movement have supported them and celebrated with them. He is and has been a powerful force in my life and in the lives of countless others.

NOTES

1. *Guide to Humanistic Judaism* [special issue], *Humanistic Judaism* 21, nos. 3–4 (1993) 36.
2. Miriam S. Jerris, "The Silent Minority: Jewish Clergy Who Provide Support for Intermarriage" (Ph.D. diss., The Union Institute, 2001), abstract in *Dissertation Abstracts International*, 62/10 (2002): 106.
3. Ibid., 109.
4. Ibid., 119–20.

Miriam S. Jerris, Ph.D., is a rabbi and the community development associate of the Society for Humanistic Judaism. She was ordained as a rabbi in 2001 by the International Institute for Secular Humanistic Judaism. She is the co-owner of the Wedding Connection, a ceremonial and wedding planning company. For more than thirty years she has been instrumental in developing Humanistic Judaism, and she serves on the faculty of the institute.

A Celebration of Rabbi Wine

Tamara Kolton

What does it mean to have a person in your life who is at once rabbi, at once hero, at once mentor, father, colleague, friend? What impact could be made by such a figure? How could he transform your life, push you to exceed what you thought was possible, and ultimately give you a place in the world where you could create your own dreams while dreaming the dreams of others? How is it that a very little girl would find such a person in a temple with a very big rabbi? She would give him her heart. He would receive it with grace. And she would grow under his care in the temple that Sherwin built.

In the temple that Sherwin built there is a word. The word is declared in Hebrew: "Adam!" It holds the power of his philosophy of life, the way he sees the world. It is a word that speaks of the earth, not heaven. It is a word that is busy reconciling the limitations of being human with all the possibilities for greatness. Like the calling from a great and mighty shofar, it declares the experience of the Jewish people. Written in fountain pen, a (Jewish) trinity of ideas has been delivered to the people.

"If the Jewish experience is anything, it is testimony to the fact that God isn't going to show up."

Rabbi Wine tells a crowd that has gathered at the Birmingham Temple for Shabbat, "God has the best job. He gets all the credit and no blame. If I were to be the CEO of a company and run it like God runs the universe, most likely I would be fired!"

In the temple that Sherwin built, people know that if there is hell on earth, it has been created by people. And if there is to be heaven on earth, people will create that too. Ultimately, whatever we do as human beings, along with the natural world, creates the reality of our lives. If God were held responsible and put on trial for his behavior, he would be found guilty of treason. He would be found guilty of conspiring to destroy the world that he was said to have created.

After the Holocaust, praying to a personal God lacks dignity. It is an exercise in humiliation. It is the abdication of the very power that makes life worthwhile, the power of real hands and real hearts. Prayers are useless unless they are attached to action. Let us pray with behavior and not words. Let mothers stroke the faces of small children, husbands embrace the bodies of loving wives, friends listen to each other with open minds and open hearts, governments seek reconciliation, people lead their lives with purpose and joy, and let dignity shine throughout the land.

In the temple that Sherwin built there is strength. The strength began with the rabbi but now flows easily between the people. Sometimes joyous and loving people come to the temple to deliver strength, leaving it behind with open and generous hearts. And then people in need come and borrow their strength, like a good library book to be returned at a future time.

"Potential wasted is potential betrayed."

In the temple that Sherwin built, the people know that one question stands above all others: "How can I leave the world better off for having lived in it during my lifetime?" They turn this question over and over again in their mouths like cinnamon candy, sucking out all of its juice and letting it melt into the essence of who they are.

Yet, the people also know that answering the question is only the first step. Action must follow awareness. The expression of potential must become daily work, the Sh'ma of existence. We must declare, "In the morning when you wake up and in the evening when you lie down, say to yourself, 'How can I leave the world better off for having lived in it during my lifetime?' Place these words between your eyes, upon the doorposts of your home, say them when you lay down at night and when you rise up in the morning."

"The joy of life is in the climbing."

In the temple that Sherwin built, people understand that the waiting station is very crowded. There are people waiting for all kinds of things to be paid out by the universe in a grand IOU. You will see people leaning against columns in business suits waiting to make enough money to retire. You will see people waiting for their children to grow up in order to appreciate them. There are some people that spend so much time at the waiting station of life, it begins to appear that they live there. Indeed a person can spend an entire lifetime waiting for the results of their effort to make themselves happy and change the circumstances of their lives.

> In the Birmingham Temple, the people know that one question stands above all others: "How can I leave the world better off for having lived in it during my lifetime?"

Rabbi Wine declares, "Clear out the waiting station!"

Fulfillment in life is to be found in the good work of the here and now. There is no grand payoff when it is over. The payoff is in the joy of your feet and hands working together today. Your work in life is to discover how to use your abilities towards meaningful work. Your work in life is to uncover your purpose. Once you do this, you will have no need for the waiting station. You will realize each day that the joy of life is in the effort you put forth on the way to achieving results. It is not the view from the mountain peak that is worthwhile, it is the thrill of conquering the mountain in small and certain steps.

■ ■ ■

Once upon a time there was a little girl in a temple with a very big rabbi. The very big rabbi taught the little girl her lessons. Around a big square table, she joined other children to learn from her rabbi. Sometimes he would teach her Hebrew letters and sometimes he would teach her about Bertrand Russell. But her best lessons were learned in his study, sitting chair to chair. And although the little girl never grew much in height, there in her rabbi's study her spirit grew tall. Sitting there with her very tall rabbi, she sometimes felt as tall as a mountain. At night the big rabbi would leave the temple and go home to those he loved, and the little girl would go home too. But in the daytime they lived together, singing together, laughing together, and developing courage together. Courage was her best lesson with her rabbi. How do you feel the fear and do it anyway? How do you take charge of your life? How do you learn to not let doubt stop you?

Finally, in the temple that Sherwin built, it is time to say thank you. Thank you for creating a new world of ideas. Thank you for defining a new path for Jewish life. Thank you for being my mentor, father, colleague, and friend. My light is in me. And in you.

Tamara Kolton, Ph.D., is a rabbi and the school director at the Birmingham Temple. She has a bachelor's degree from Hebrew University in Jerusalem. She has a master's degree in clinical psychology and a Ph.D. in Humanistic and Jewish Studies. Rabbi Kolton was the first rabbi to be ordained by the International Institute for Secular Humanistic Judaism, in October 1999.

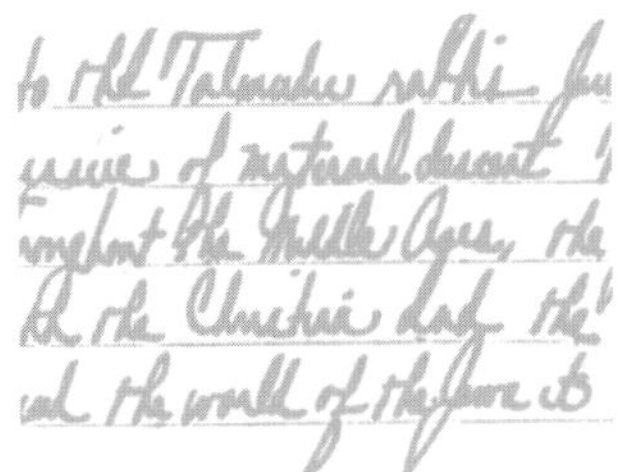

The Secular Synagogue as the Continuation of the Revolution in Judaism and World Culture

Yaakov Malkin

SHERWIN WINE'S PIONEERING PROJECT

In the 1960s, Sherwin Wine, the first secular rabbi, established something that had no precedent in Judaism—a secular synagogue and a burgeoning secular humanist movement in North America, as well as in many other countries. Adjacent to the first secular synagogue in Farmington Hills, Michigan, he founded a school for secular educators and rabbis; the graduates of this school build and run new secular communities. This project for establishing and leading synagogues for the largest stream of Judaism today is the continuation of a 2,300-year tradition, and it answers the need currently felt by secular Jews who want to be active within a cultural community framework.

As a result of the twentieth century's accelerated urbanization process, most communities in the West disbanded, their members becoming passive elements in the television and mass communications audience. This process increased people's spiritual crises and their yearning to belong to a community that would recognize them as individuals, and in which they could actively influence and participate in cultural life and the education of their children.

Despite the social scientists' predictions, national awareness and affiliation to ethnic groups increased, and the need to identify with a definite national group for the purpose of engaging in community cultural activities became more acute. In the West, Jews and non-Jews alike began to search out and join communities promising spiritual activities—Buddhism, mysticism, or those of a semi-religious nature.

Sherwin Wine's unique response and innovation lay in the creation of a secular humanist answer to this spiritual and social demand.

The secular synagogue phenomenon is as yet quite small relative to the number of synagogues that exist in the other, religious streams of Judaism. However, the more educators and rabbis who graduate from its school and take on leadership positions in secular congregations, the greater the likelihood that the phenomenon will grow as a movement, which will change the face of secular Judaism in the future. As Margaret Mead wrote: "Never doubt that a small group of thoughtful, committed citizens can change the world. Indeed, it's the only thing that ever has."

THE CULTURAL COMMUNITY REVOLUTION

The present-day phenomenon of secular synagogues continues a tradition that is at least 2,300 years old. It probably began during the Hellenistic period, when the first synagogues were founded in Mesopotamia by exiles from Israel and Judea. In the Byzantine period, Jews established synagogues in *Eretz Yisrael*, Babylonia, North Africa, and southern Europe. The synagogue quickly became a revolutionary element in religious history, spreading to Christian and Muslim societies and culture.

"Synagogue" means place of meeting or assembly. In many respects, the synagogue stands in contrast to the temples and altars that were the ritual centers of all the world's ancient religions:

- Instead of the sacrifices that were at the heart of temple activity, synagogues, later followed by churches and mosques, functioned as centers for study, prayer, and the perusal of classical literature of each culture.
- Instead of the temple as the House of God, synagogues acted as human community centers.
- Instead of temples, which were part of the hierarchical system of religious, urban, national, or priestly government, synagogues took on the role of independent centers. They were subordinate only to the synagogue's communal leaders. There were often a number of synagogues on the same street.
- Instead of the priests who were appointed by the king or religious authority to manage temples, synagogues were run by their founders, or community leaders and rabbis employed by the latter.

PLURALISM AND MULTIPLE TASKS

As a result of this revolutionary innovation in religious cultural life, cultural communities arose, changed, split, or clashed. They replaced tribal communities or family clans.

> Sherwin Wine, the first secular rabbi, established something that had no precedent in Judaism—a secular synagogue and a burgeoning secular humanist movement.

The increase in independent cultural communities encouraged pluralism in Jewish culture. Communities joined or split off from the various streams of Judaism. Synagogue independence fulfilled a central function both in strengthening Jewish religious and cultural pluralism and in reinforcing a national unity based on the lack of cultural uniformity. In every city or country, Jews could choose a synagogue the members of which believed in one or another stream of Judaism, such as Karaites, Rabbinical, and Judeo-Christian. In the medieval period, there were believers in philosophical rationalism or kabbalistic mysticism.

Following the Renaissance and the Enlightenment, Jews joined a variety of communities—Hasidic or Mitnaged, Maskilim or Reformers. And in our day, Jews can choose among Secular Humanistic, Reform, Conservative, Reconstructionist, Orthodox, Modern Orthodox, New Age, kabbalist, and so forth.

The Rabbi (the great teacher), does not function in the synagogue like the priest in the Temple. He has no defined role in religious ritual (such as the cantor has, for example) and neither belongs to a priestly family nor has priestly status. Individuals become rabbis by virtue of their expertise in the stream of Judaism to which they are ordained, much like a Ph.D. in the academic world.

A rabbi fulfills a variety of functions in service of the community and the individuals within it. These range from lecturer and teacher, judge and consultant, to organizer of prayers and educational activities. A rabbi also officiates at weddings and funerals, comforts mourners, provides spiritual succor to the ill, and so forth.

Synagogues as community cultural centers also created a variety of new roles to satisfy community members' needs: schools for children and study groups for adults; a meeting and celebratory venue for family events and national holidays; a source for interest-free loans; a court for community members; a center for individual life-cycle ceremonies; a prayer center (with its own developing literature); a hospitality center for members from other communities; purification pools for women and men; a pulpit for rabbis' sermons or for community members' speeches at bar and bat mitsva celebrations; and a venue for itinerant preachers (*magidim*), who would visit different synagogues to spread their ideas and interpretations. These pulpits were used by Jewish preachers and scholars from Rabbi Akiva and Paul in the Byzantine era, to the Magid of Minsk, to the participants at the biennial colloquium at the secular synagogue in Farmington Hills, Michigan.

LACK OF UNIFORMITY AND NATIONAL UNITY

The multiplicity of streams to which synagogues belong has not diminished the Jewishness of any of them. Jews belonging to the cultural community of a synagogue identified and were identified as Jews by their environment because of their membership there.

Through the synagogue's activities, its members became aware of the communal nature of all Jewish national consciousness:

- Consciousness of the Jewish people's common history, of *Eretz Yisrael* as the Jewish people's ancestral homeland, of Hebrew as its national tongue, and of the Jewish languages spoken by communities in different parts of the world.
- Consciousness of the Bible as the national and classical literature of Jewish culture and the *only* common denominator for all the streams in Judaism.
- Consciousness of Shabbat and of the historical festivals of the Jewish people and their biblical background.

For approximately two thousand years, synagogues belonged to the various religious streams of Judaism. In the twentieth century, when the majority of Jews became secular, the first secular cultural communities appeared. In Israel they took the form of kibbutzim. In the Diaspora they were an adjunct to secular schools such as the Shalom Aleichem and Y. L. Peretz Schools, and they also found expression in the secular Jewish movements for Yiddish culture of Europe and America.

Sherwin Wine's contribution to secular Judaism is thus inestimable.

The above-mentioned cultural communities began to disintegrate in the second half of the twentieth century because they lacked an organizational structure—a physical center such as a congregational hall or synagogue. They also did not prepare or employ paid professionals who had been educated in the great tradition of Judaism as culture, and who would have been knowledgeable about secular Judaism and its rich works. Such professionals would have been capable of organizing and initiating a continuous variety of communal activities, as well as being available to devote all their time to running the synagogue and the community.

The secular synagogue project of the Secular Humanistic Jewish movement, the headquarters of which are in Michigan—and which also has branches in other Diaspora countries as well as in Israel—is active in remedying this serious lack of active secular Jewish cultural communities. For this purpose, traditional communal activities are also undergoing renewal in the majority stream of Judaism. Such activities include re-evaluation of Jewish sources, the reincarnation of the Bible as literature, and the historical testimony of social and cultural situations.

Sherwin Wine's contribution to secular Judaism is thus inestimable.

Yaakov Malkin, Ph.D., is a professor of Aesthetics and Rhetoric at Tel Aviv University. He is the founder and academic director of Meitar College of Pluralistic Judaism. He is the founder and director of the first Culture Community Centers in Israel: Beit Rothchild and Beit Hagefen, the Arab-Jewish Center in Haifa. He has written more than eleven books on literature and theater. His books on secular Judaism include *Judaism As Culture* and *What Do Secular Jews Believe.*

Reflections on Humanism As a Bifurcated Tradition

Ronald Modras

"Is Saul also among the prophets?" That ancient proverb from Israel's origins (1 Samuel 10,12) came to my mind when I first began thinking about this essay. "Is Ron Modras also among the Humanistic Jews?" Or, to frame the question less biblically, what's a nice, churchgoing, Roman Catholic professor of theology like me doing in a book like this? The answer is simple: I'm here because I try to teach my students the values of humanism. And because for more than thirty years Sherwin Wine has been a close and dear friend, and I am pleased to write an essay for this *festschrift* in his honor.

But even that simple answer requires unpacking. I am not Jewish. (Although, as a Polish American with a very ethnic mother, I often muse that one does not need to be Jewish to have a Jewish mother.) And I am not a secular humanist, in the sense of one who has given up on the meaningfulness of God-talk. But I do consider myself a Christian humanist, or, to use another, broader term I prefer, a "spiritual humanist." And I find that, despite differences in our thinking, there is much that I admire in Sherwin Wine and much in his philosophy and values that I share. I cherish him not only as a friend but as a kindred spirit.

Back in the mid-1970s, while visiting at the home of some of the Birmingham Temple's charter members, I was asked about my friendship with Sherwin, about what we could possibly have in common. Surely, I was told, you would feel closer to a Southern Baptist than to a Humanistic Jew. Why, I asked, would you think that? Because you and the Baptists both believe in Jesus, was the answer. To which I replied, So what? There are more than a few Christians—including clergy—who would have answered similarly. Which is to say, I am neither idiosyncratic nor exceptional but rather representative of many Christians in my admiration and affection for Rabbi Wine.

Readers of these essays who know Rabbi Wine only in the context of the Birmingham Temple and the Humanistic Judaism movement may be unaware of the wide circle of non-Jewish friends and admirers he has. Beyond that, his rational good sense, wide-ranging scholarship, generosity with time, and years of experience cause him to be sought after for counsel and advice. In other words, he is a valued resource to more than the members of the Jewish community. Why that is so warrants reflection.

What is there about Rabbi Wine that draws non-Jewish friends and admirers to him, including Christians who sincerely profess faith in God, go to church, and pray regularly? I would suggest that it is his humanism, but understood more broadly than within its purely secular contours. Humanism is an ambiguous word with a long, sometimes contentious history. But it represents a tradition rooted in the Renaissance that both secular and spiritual humanists share. Jewish and Christian humanists belong to a common, albeit bifurcated, tradition.

HUMANIST ORIGINS

The humanist tradition and the Renaissance both began—as one pundit put it—when the fourteenth-century Italian poet Petrarch put down his Latin translation of Aristotle and picked up a book of Cicero. Although we ordinarily think of the Renaissance in terms of its achievements in art and architecture, it started off as a revival of appreciation for the literary classics of ancient Rome and Greece. The Italian academics who coined the word *Rinascimento*, or "Renaissance," had little regard for the Middle Ages. Both terms—"Middle Ages" and "Renaissance"—betray the bias of fifteenth-century Italians who wanted to distinguish their own more creative times from the centuries after the fall of Rome, during which Italy, compared to northern Europe, had been a cultural backwater. These scholarly Italians were not philosophers or theologians. Their interests were pre-Christian Latin literature, the city of Rome, and the ideal of republican virtue.

Borrowing a phrase from Cicero, the professors and students of these subjects called their discipline the *studia humanitatis*—what today we call the humanities—in contradistinction to theology, the study of divinity. Just as their colleagues in canon law or the arts were called *canonisti* or *artisti*, the student slang of Italy's universities dubbed the practitioners of the humanities *umanisti*. Soon enough their high regard for the literary form of the Latin classics extended to those works' contents. Humanists began to turn to and quote classical authors for the insight and value of their ideas.

What is there about Rabbi Wine that draws non-Jewish friends and admirers to him, including Christians who sincerely profess faith in God, go to church, and pray regularly?

The humanist movement gradually developed into a revolt against the pedagogy and debased Latin of "scholasticism," the medieval system of education. The humanist aversion to scholasticism is the main reason why the movement came to be misread as crypto-atheist or pagan. Recent scholarship finds that practically all the Renaissance humanists were genuinely Christian and that loose morals in their day were no more pervasive than in any other age.

Still, in comparison to the narrower, explicitly religious discourse of the Middle Ages, a return to the pagan classics provided humanists with alternative and competing topics of interest and consideration. Some humanists chose not to engage themselves with religious issues; others had a genuine concern for religion and the Church and brought their humanist training to bear on theology. And when these religiously oriented humanists—most notably Erasmus—called for a return to the classics, they included in their appeal the Jewish and Christian scriptures, as well as the Talmud and Kabbala.

SECULAR HUMANISM

At this point the reader may well ask, what does any of this have to do with Humanistic Judaism? Rabbi Wine quite legitimately draws the defining characteristics of Humanistic Judaism from the eighteenth-century British freethinkers and French *philosophes* who made up what came to be called the Enlightenment. The religious wars that followed the Reformation and the imposing achievements of scientific reason (Copernicus, Galileo, Newton) gave ample grounds for Enlightenment philosophers to forgo interest in contentious religious doctrines. They preferred to concentrate on matters human and empirical. Alexander Pope summed up the attitude of the age famously: "Presume not God to scan; the proper study of Mankind is Man."

Those in England who did give thought to religion gave rise to Deism, which rejected revealed religion in the name of reason and "natural theology." From first polite and then undisguised indifference to religion, there followed the hostile contempt exemplified by Diderot, Hume, and Voltaire. In Germany, Immanuel Kant put an end to natural theology with his critique of rational attempts to prove the existence of God or an afterlife. He also formulated what became the classical definition of "Enlightenment" as emancipation from religious authorities who would presume to shackle human reason ("the end of humankind's self-imposed infancy").

Needless to say, the concept of humanism has wandered far beyond the fifteenth-century Italian taste for classical literature. (As voracious a reader as he is, I don't believe Sherwin has cultivated a partiality for Cicero.) But classicism, the first and foremost characteristic of Renaissance humanists, led to other defining traits as well, traits that constitute a common ground between Humanistic Judaism and Christian or, more broadly, *spiritual* humanism. These are what attract Christian and other religious humanists to Rabbi Wine. There is something of the Renaissance in him.

COMMON GROUND

If there is one simple statement that encapsulates the essence of humanism as I try to live it and teach it to my students, it is a dictum by the Roman playwright Terence: "I consider nothing human to be foreign to me" (*humani nil alienum a me puto*). Renaissance humanists cited wisdom wherever they found it—in the Bible and Church authors but also in Plato, Horace, even Muhammad. This practice gave rise to the Renaissance idea that truth is universal; it can be found anywhere. It can exist beyond any particular religious or ethnic group, ideology, or school of thought. Indeed, the coexistence of wisdom and error requires us to recognize and integrate every element of truth we find, wherever we come across it.

> Renaissance humanists cited wisdom wherever they found it—in the Bible and Church authors but also in Plato, Horace, even Muhammad.

May I say that one of the things I admire most in Sherwin is his profound interest in people, even the most humble and uneducated. And his curiosity is fathomless, whether he is visiting Shinto shrines and Hindu temples or interviewing Buddhist monks and African shamans, always with the deepest respect (quite unlike televangelist Jimmy Swaggart, who once described walking out of a Hindu temple as escaping from a place inhabited by demons). For Sherwin, nothing human is foreign or alien. And for spiritual humanists as well, religious symbols, artifacts, and rituals are human, the human response to mystical or religious experiences.

Studying classical authors like Cicero and Seneca, who were orators and statesmen, led the Renaissance humanists to value an active life characterized by civic virtue. They did not flee the world or reject responsibility for the here and now, quite sure that happiness in the hereafter did not preclude what Cicero called the "art of living happily and well." That Ciceronian ideal did not mean living comfortably so much as virtuously, both as a public and private person, as a member of society and as an individual.

Class differences in fifteenth-century Italy, though undoubtedly real, were not as sharp as those elsewhere in Europe, which may explain why the Italian Renaissance gave birth to a heightened sense of human dignity. The Middle Ages had a fundamentally negative view of human nature. Under the influence of Saint Augustine, medieval culture regarded humankind as a fallen race, exiled from paradise. Humanists had no illusions about the human capacity for vice. They saw it all around them in Renaissance Rome and the city-states of Italy. And one need only read Machiavelli or study the faces in Michelangelo's *Last Judgment* to appreciate that the Renaissance could be just as pessimistic about human nature as Saint Augustine was. But, despite widespread immorality, the humanists were dogged in their conviction that, thanks to our freedom and responsibility, we human beings hold an exalted place in the universe.

Human dignity, self-respect, autonomy, civic duty, a sense of responsibility to the community—all of these Renaissance humanist ideals and values recur regularly in Rabbi Wine's speaking and writing. There too one encounters his call to a universality that transcends ethnocentrism, his "nothing human is foreign to me." And, like Rabbi Wine, I try to espouse and impart these humanist values and ideals to the students in my theology classes as an alternative to religious fundamentalism.

COMMON ADVERSARIES

One doesn't need a degree in social analysis to notice that formerly sharp boundary lines separating Christian churches from one another are blurring in comparison to the widening gaps within them. Catholics and Protestants who acknowledge the existence of truth and spiritual riches in other churches and traditions often have more in common with each other than with their co-religionists who do not, who see only darkness and damnation beyond their particular communities. The latter, those who have nothing to learn or gain from outside their narrow circles, who make exclusive claims for their interpretations of their scriptures and religious authorities, have come to be called fundamentalists.

But how should I describe Christians or other believers who are willing to accept truth, beauty, goodness, grace wherever they find it, including outside their own circles? Should I call them liberal? Progressive? Those terms are mired in historical and political ambiguities. Modernist? Ecumenical? Those words refer to inner-Christian movements. The same gaps that separate co-religionists within the Christian churches are present within other religious traditions as well, as Jewish, Muslim, and Hindu fundamentalist violence has made evident in recent years. What is the alternative to fundamentalist religion? How can one best describe not only Christians but Muslims, Jews, and other religious persons willing to respect and learn from one another? I would suggest that historical usage affords us no better word than "humanist."

In its widest sense, humanism describes those attitudes and beliefs that attach central importance to the human person and human values. This expanded meaning allows the term to be applied to a variety of disparate persons and groups. But it has not become so broad as to lose all meaning and usefulness. It may require adjectives to qualify it, but the term cannot be applied indiscriminately. Any ideology that divides the human race into "us" and "them" cannot be called humanistic. Any belief system that makes exclusive claims to privileges based on being chosen or destined cannot be called humanistic. Antisemitism, ethnocentrism, homophobia, chauvinism: none of them can be called humanistic.

Any ideology that divides the human race into "us" and "them" cannot be called humanistic.

Humanism is the antithesis and alternative to fundamentalism. It is irreconcilable with racist, nationalist, sexist, religious, or cultural claims of superiority or self-sufficiency. We have witnessed in recent years an extraordinary alliance between Jewish religious fundamentalists and Protestant evangelical fundamentalists, both of whom take a messianic or apocalyptic view of Zionism. Both groups regard the likes of us as apostate Jews and Christians, destined to be "left behind." Like it or not, the disdain of common foes is another characteristic that we share.

But isn't there a fissure between spiritual and secular humanists greater than any shared traits or common ground? I am referring here to religious faith and the use of God-talk. At least as Rabbi Wine has described the issue, I am not so sure. Humanistic Judaism rejects the biblical image of Jahweh as a heavenly father-figure who threatens, punishes, and pulls strings. It also rejects concepts like "holy" and "sacred" as leading to ideas of authorities, texts, and symbols claiming to be above rational scrutiny and criticism.

The word "God" is no longer hopelessly and inevitably tied to a Jewish version of Zeus. Feminist thinkers, Jewish and Christian alike, are rethinking the patriarchal origins of their traditions and reassessing the meaning of the word. That examination has pragmatic implications. The patriarchal texts and symbols that are being protected by their respective patriarchal Jewish and Christian authorities are also coming under critical scrutiny. There is a feminist and therefore by definition a humanist revolution going on in religious circles today. In theology classes like mine, no less than in Rabbi Wine's, students are taught to question authority, even the most hallowed.

If I have focused on Rabbi Wine more than other authors in this volume have, it is because, as an outsider, I know *him* better than I do Humanistic Judaism as a movement. But I rather see him like the monk of whom others would say, If all the rule books in the monastery were destroyed, just follow him around, observe him, and you will know what the books said. If Sherwin will forgive the analogy (and, given his good humor, I know he will), he has that kind of integrity. A "voice of reason" who teaches people the art of "staying sane in a crazy world," he embodies Humanistic Judaism at its best. You don't have to be a Secular Jewish Humanist to see him as a kindred spirit.

Ronald Modras is a professor of theological studies at Saint Louis University. He received his doctorate at the University of Tuebingen, in Germany. He received the College Theology Society's Book Award for *The Catholic Church and Antisemitism: Poland 1933–1939*. He is an Annenberg Research Fellow and a recipient of the St. Louis American Jewish Committee's Micah Award.

A Vision of a Religious Humanistic Jewish Congregational Movement

David Oler

When I first met Sherwin Wine in the autumn of 1999, little did I know the impact that he was to have on my life as a Jew and on the direction of my career as a rabbi. That fortuitous meeting led to the culmination of a changing direction in my religious life and opened up new and exciting opportunities for spiritual fulfillment. A great thinker is one whose ideas stimulate others to be creative and productive. Sherwin has influenced many in this way, and I am grateful to be among those who have been influenced, or shall I say liberated, by Sherwin's concept of Humanistic Judaism.

It is therefore a privilege, and I am indeed humbled by this opportunity, to honor Sherwin and his career as a courageous leader in the Jewish community. I am reminded of a book I once read having to do with emotional growth and pastoral psychology, entitled *Taking on the Gods.* That is certainly something that Sherwin has done in a formidable way throughout the past forty years. I, and the community that I serve—Congregation Beth Or in

Deerfield, Illinois—look forward to Sherwin's continuing insightful and productive leadership of our movement for many years to come.

I remember asking Sherwin at our first meeting, "If humanistic, then why Judaism?" He answered that even with a humanistic outlook: "It is important to be grounded in a particular tradition." In this essay I shall present what I believe to be the most profound rationale for being grounded in Judaism, namely, for the resources it provides on the path of religious humanism.

To the extent that Humanistic Judaism is a congregation-based movement, I am convinced that it should be identified with religious humanism rather than with secular humanism. In my view, a secular Jewish cultural identity does not provide for religious development and, because of its emphasis on ethnicity, is contradictory to the essence of humanism. I am talking about the distinction between identification with a particular culture or nationality because it is familiar and comfortable, and the quest for spiritual transformation, which Ken Wilber has identified as the ultimate goal of religion. A secular cultural identification for its own sake is particularistic, can be narrow and even chauvinistic, and is antithetical to a humanistic universalism. As humanists, we in particular should not want to fall into the trap of aggrandizing Jewish identity for its own sake. Just think of the message of exclusivity that is subtly conveyed to others when we emphasize a secular Jewish cultural identity! As humanists we need to ask ourselves what real purpose there is in limiting ourselves in this way. Would not a more universalistic outlook be more consistent with a humanistic perspective?

The purpose of our existence as a humanistic religious movement should be to provide for our members, regardless of their cultural background, opportunities for spiritual growth focused primarily on character development. In regarding spirituality in this humanistic context, we are in good company. The Dalai Lama, the leader of Tibetan Buddhism, has written: "Spirituality I take to be concerned with those qualities of the human spirit—such as love and compassion, patience, tolerance, forgiveness, contentment, a sense of responsibility, a sense of harmony—which bring happiness to both self and others." He goes on to say: "There is no reason why the individual should not develop them, even to a high degree, without recourse to any metaphysical belief system."

An important aspect of our ideology is the absence of theistic dogma. Our liturgy, therefore, makes no reference to divinity. However, our membership at Beth Or, as elsewhere in the movement, is ideologically eclectic. We want to foster an atmosphere where a broad spectrum of people who grapple with what they do or do not believe feel respected, welcome, and therefore comfortable in our congregations. Our members hold divergent views on a variety of topics and find meaning in many different ways. Couples often differ in their ideological outlook, and individuals' perspectives are dynamic over time.

Pluralism and respect for diversity are essential ingredients of a humanistic approach. We are truly a liberal religious community to the extent that we do not require our members to adhere to a particular ideology, only that they respect freedom of religious belief and our commitment to a nontheistic liturgy. We need to avoid being perceived as orthodox or dogmatic in espousing an atheistic perspective. It is too easy to define our religious ideology by what we do *not* believe. It is more productive to define ourselves by what we need to become.

> It is too easy to define our religious ideology by what we do *not* believe. It is more productive to define ourselves by what we need to become.

As humanists, we welcome whatever resources can contribute to our growth, regardless of origin, as long as they are not in conflict with our ideology. However, as a Jewish congregation-based movement, we use primarily Jewish sources and observances to pursue our goal of spiritual or character development. An interesting term for us to ponder, as a humanistic religious community, is the word "humane." In Judaism the highest ideal is the related term *hesed*, most often translated as "loving-kindness." Our religious quest, like that of other religious denominations and other branches of Judaism, should be to become as humane, as compassionate, and as motivated by loving-kindness as possible. The eighteenth-century philosopher Immanuel Kant observed that religion's purpose is to furnish symbols and communities that foster morality. In a discussion of forms of ritual observance, the Midrash declares that these "precepts were given only for the purpose of refining people"—that is, helping them on their path to morality. Our uniqueness as religious humanists is that we are not distracted from this goal by other, dogmatic, requirements.

As Humanistic Jews fostering religious life, our movement needs to have a strong commitment to social action. We can encourage spiritual development among our membership by establishing programs through which they can help others. This priority of focus can distinguish our movement. We do not advocate a vertical religious outlook. But we must advocate a horizontal one. We do not feel obligated by Jewish teachings concerning responsibilities toward the divine, but that should not in any way result in a diminution of our moral responsibilities toward other people, as taught within Judaism and in other religions. A third dimension is the intrapersonal. Any responsible religious environment provides opportunities that foster introspective growth on a continual basis as part of what it means to belong to a religious community.

A story that subtly addresses all three dimensions is that of Garfinkle, the Humanistic Jew, who always went to the traditional *minyan*, the daily prayer service, at the synagogue. His friends challenged him: "You don't believe in god; why do you go to the *minyan*?" Garfinkle answered: "Cohen is my friend, and he is a believer. Cohen goes to the synagogue to talk to god, and I go to talk to Cohen."

Many of us have conceived of ourselves as not being religious because of our inability to relate to traditional teachings and observances. However, to be religious in our liberal humanistic context is not to be distracted by the search for divine approval, but to be devoted to a search for meaning and character development, the highest spiritual task of all. I envision our congregations as providing opportunities to foster such spiritual development in our people's lives. We need to study Jewish sources, such as the Torah and other religious and general Jewish literature, not as the word of god, but because they contain humanistic ideals and values, emanating from the entire course of Jewish history, that can help to shape our character development.

We need to become more related to the larger Jewish community, and we also need to foster a sense of community feeling within our congregations, based not so much on ethnicity as on a bonding that comes from shared values and aspirations. It is these shared goals of spiritual growth and character development that can enable us to build living communities in the form of congregations committed to Humanistic Judaism. Religion teaches about love. What is a humanistic congregation supposed to be about if not love for one another and for those who need us in the larger community?

Recently, I shared with my congregants my vision for the religious education of our children. I trust these ideas apply equally well to other congregations in our movement:

> The mission of our religious school is to impart information and to engage students in spiritual development through values clarification and opportunities for social action. The school's curriculum and activities should parallel the ideological outlook of the congregation, providing substantive learning opportunities in the context of a commitment to our religious approach to Humanistic Judaism. As a Humanistic Jewish congregation, our "ultimate concern"—a term coined by the preeminent twentieth-century liberal theologian Paul Tillich as a way to reinterpret or reframe religious faith in contemporary, more naturalistic terms—is humanization, by which I mean development toward a more humane way of being in the world. While grounded in Judaism, our outlook is pluralistic, both within Judaism and beyond it. For our

What is a humanistic congregation supposed to be about if not love for one another and for those who need us in the larger community?

children, our teachings, stories, and celebrations should lead to a strengthened identity, which in turn fosters their humanization.

With the priority of our school's fostering a warm atmosphere for the children and a desire to emphasize interpersonal respect and kindness among them, I specifically envision an integrated curriculum throughout all the school grades, which would emphasize the teaching of humanistic values. Such a curriculum could be built on these three pillars:

- History, ancient through modern, including the Holocaust, Israel, and the American experience.
- Jewish thought and practices: the beliefs, practices, customs, ceremonies, liturgies, and holidays of Judaism, with emphasis on their rationale from the perspective of Humanistic Judaism. Biblical, rabbinic, and modern literary sources that convey humanistic ideas and ideals.
- Introduction to Hebrew: reading readiness in early grades; beginning sound and word recognition for middle and upper grades, as a basis for bar/bat mitsva preparation and for values clarification, with Hebrew learning emphasizing such terms as *tzedaka* (charity, justice), *emet* (truth), *ahava* (love), *derech eretz* (respect), *shalom* (peace), and *hesed* (loving-kindness).

Similarly, Rabbi Wine, in describing his priorities for our communities, writes that they should emphasize "the celebration of Jewish holidays, the teaching of Jewish languages, the study of Jewish history and literature, the presentation of a humanistic philosophy of life derived from the Jewish experience, and the mobilization for social action." I am in complete agreement and have sought to articulate the underlying rationale and focus for these activities, namely, humanization or character development. I believe that the articulation and actualization of Humanistic Judaism as a religion focused on humanization and character development holds the most promise for the future.

In our religious schools, the curriculum needs to be centered on character development and values clarification, using primarily humanistic resources from Jewish tradition. The children need to learn a humanistic outlook that includes respect for diversity, but they also need to be sufficiently conversant with Jewish tradition that they can function effectively and securely in the larger Jewish community. They can then, if they so choose, espouse the perspective of Humanistic Judaism, but from a context of knowledge and informed choice. Most important is an emphasis on behavioral interaction with fellow students that is reflective of such humanistic character traits as kindness, respect, and consideration for the feelings of others.

Rabbi Abraham Joshua Heschel, an important twentieth-century philosopher, wrote: "Let the youth of today remember that there is a meaning beyond absurdity. Let them be sure that every deed counts, that every word has power, and that we all can do our share to redeem the world in spite of all the absurdities and all the frustrations and all the disappointments. Let them remember to build a life as if it were a work of art."

I envision people being attracted to our congregations because of our emphasis on the priorities of character development, values clarification, spiritual growth, and the deepening of inner life for their children as for themselves. Many people these days are searching for more meaning in their lives. They want to foster their spiritual dimension, but they find notions of supernaturalism and traditional observance difficult to embrace. We need to continue to provide a rational, naturalistic ideology for the religiously liberal spirituality seeker. We must also commit ourselves individually and collectively to a humanistic spiritual life that includes introspective contemplation, study of religious resources, and community service. There are many kindred spirits to join with us if we are able to invite them into communities of spirituality seekers who are traveling on a road toward self-actualization and spiritual transformation.

David Oler, Ph.D., is the rabbi of Congregation Beth Or in Deerfield, Illinois, and the president of the Association of Humanistic Rabbis. He is a graduate of

McGill University and was ordained by the Rabbinical Seminary of Canada. He received the Doctor of Ministry degree from Andover Newton Theological School. He is also a licensed clinical psychologist, having earned his Ph.D. from the University of Maryland.

Rabbi Sherwin T. Wine: A Diamond

Charles R. Paul

In 1955 scientists discovered the means to manufacture a small number of crystals that exhibited many of the same characteristics as diamonds. By subjecting pure graphite to huge pressures, which generated temperatures of more than 5,000 degrees Fahrenheit, these scientists created something overnight in their laboratories that nature took hundreds of thousands of years to accomplish.

At approximately the same time, the recently ordained Rabbi Sherwin T. Wine began to take the first tentative steps into a pressurized cauldron from which he would ultimately emerge as a bright, clear, shining diamond the likes of which no one had seen before. By his seventy-fifth birthday, Rabbi Wine had collected the light of a new form of Judaism and reflected its brilliance back to every corner of the world where Jews live.

The late 1950s and early 1960s were years of enormous change, as American and European Jews shook off the horrors of World War II and began rebuilding a nearly demolished culture. Israel became a reality. Reform

Jews worked hard to redirect the strident anti-Hebrew rules of their turn-of-the-century forebears to a more traditional style. All the while, American society was slowly slipping into the malaise brought on by the Vietnam War. Everyone was questioning everything. Old values and old leaders seemed to lose their luster. What were once held as sacrosanct became curiosities worth investigating. Science—responsible for synthetic diamonds, as well as atomic bombs and rocket ships—was on the rise everywhere.

From this tumultuous environment stepped Sherwin Wine. Clearly brilliant, undeniably charming, obviously well-educated, dramatic, and handsome, wearing the mantle of an ordained Reform rabbi, he managed to infuriate the established Jewish world with a strength that he carries with him even today. The enormous pressures put on this man created a diamond so unique, so fascinating, so attractive that he has been the constant focus of attention nearly his entire life. Those envious of his mental acumen, people threatened by the questions he asks—and worse, by the answers he provides—are quick to become enraged without fully understanding why. Others, and the number is legion, who have been touched by his warmth, his insight, his leadership and direction stand in admiration and appreciation for the refracted light he has shone on them.

It is fitting that the basic chant of Humanistic Judaism is based on the concept of light. "Where is my light?" the poem written by Sherwin Wine asks rhetorically. "My light is in me and in you." This light, this source of inner strength and hope for thousands, originates in Rabbi Wine. Unlike other charismatic leaders who cultivate frothing followers who believe in the infallibility of their hero, Rabbi Wine casts aside unreasoning adoration and turns that emotional force back onto his admirers. He gives freely of his strengths and his abilities to everyone and anyone who asks for them. The rewards he keeps for himself work to make his own inner light, the whitest heart of the diamond, even stronger and more beautiful.

On the outside, Sherwin Wine is as multifaceted as a gem. No matter which side of the diamond you peer into, there is an uncanny depth of knowledge that is sometimes startling. Many observers, accustomed to seeing just one facet of him, are shocked when they glimpse a new side. Others who have spent decades at his side know better but are still sometimes left shaking their heads when yet another aspect of this enormously complex man is revealed. It's not as if he were secretive, hiding parts of his life from the world. Under the intense glare of passionate eyes, some filled with distaste and some filled with love, little has been left uncovered. Yet if your only interaction with him is in a classroom, or at a wedding celebration, or at Rosh Hashana services, it may seem as if you are squinting across a dark room at a lustrous gem.

Perhaps one of the most intriguing aspects of diamonds is that as precious and rare as they are, they are accessible in one shape or another to just about anyone. You can buy diamonds at the most exclusive shops on the fanciest avenues, and you can buy them from mass-merchandisers with very little fanfare. Throughout his life Sherwin has never forgotten his mass-merchandiser beginnings, even while exhibiting a comfort level and self-confidence in the company of top religious, social, academic, and business leaders from all over the world. He is as comfortable talking with waitresses and cab drivers as he is with heads of states and internationally recognized poets.

> Rabbi Wine collected the light of a new form of Judaism and reflected its brilliance back to every corner of the world where Jews live.

The apocryphal stories of Rabbi Wine's intellect are endless. At the very center of these stories is his ability to unravel complex social, political, or cultural situations, and to explain them in the most understandable terms. Speaking in a clear, concise style with a booming voice requiring no amplification, he leaves listeners with a better grasp of the issue at hand, and in awe of the ease with which he outlined his thoughts. Often speaking extemporaneously or, at most, referring to salmon-colored index cards bearing cryptic, handwritten notes, Rabbi Wine can talk with authority on a whole encyclopedia of subjects. This is no parlor trick, no photographic memory sleight of hand. It is a reflection of an endlessly inquisitive mind that has spent more than seven decades in constant training.

Those who think they fully understand Rabbi Wine, who think they know him completely, are mistaken. His oldest childhood friends, contemporaries who were with him through the Detroit public school days, still nod in amazement as they remember his youth. Even then, his vast thirst for knowledge, his ability not merely to read books on all topics but to inhale them, to absorb them at an alarming pace, was staggering. This pace has continued throughout his life.

Many people who see just one facet of Sherwin Wine often attempt to pigeonhole him as one thing or another. This tendency is often a result of their being overwhelmed or threatened or challenged by him. He's been accused of being a charismatic because of the power he holds over people. Others consider him a troublemaker for questioning old establishments. Some think of him only as a brilliant college professor and catch his lectures on cable TV or at the nearby Unitarian Universalist church.

One facet of Rabbi Wine is particularly compelling, however. That is his kindness, his genuine care for the well-being of everyone with whom he comes in contact. Beyond all the reading, all the lecturing, all the organizing of international federations, all the world traveling, Sherwin Wine is exceptional in his ability to reach out in kindness to other people. This sort of attention is somewhat understandable when directed at members of his congregation or longtime friends. But the times he has turned to strangers with a gesture of help, a kind word, a sincere smile of concern, these instances are countless. They are brief, fleeting moments in life.

The name "Humanistic Judaism" is in the appropriate word order. The movement is intentionally not called "Jewish Humanism." Humanistic Judaism puts an emphasis on human power first, then interprets it through a Jewish filter. This name, too, is a reflection of the central being, the central light of Sherwin Wine. His primary focus is on people. He is at his most joyous not when reading books or writing essays, but when he is face to face with one person in a meaningful conversation. He is at his apex with an audience not simply because he is an unabashed showman, but because of the strength and energy he extracts from the interaction.

Life is not a game to Rabbi Wine, although he has gone through life laughing at every turn. To him life is an endlessly rotating series of prospective encounters with people. For those who encounter him, for a moment or for a lifetime, the sense of his caring is palpable. When he turns to look at someone, it is not with a practiced, false face most often seen on actors and politicians. What you find with Rabbi Wine is simply a person, pausing for whatever time is required in order to join with you in life. He is genuine, sincere, gracious.

Upon reflection after an encounter with Rabbi Wine, people often find that the words he has spoken, the suggestions he has proposed, are simply what they already knew to be right. This is perhaps his most endearing quality. The same power he uses to unravel Gordian knots of confusion over world events he applies to individuals and their personal frustrations. Rarely will he lecture people while helping to resolve a personal crisis. Rather, he guides people to discover their own solutions. This help comes wrapped in authentic sincerity, much to the surprise of many who are exposed to it for the first time. There is no judgmental attitude. There is no sense of dismissal from a man too busy to pay attention to the personal problems of others. There is just his boundless well of reasonable advice. It's each person's decision how to respond.

> One facet of Rabbi Wine is particularly compelling: his kindness, his genuine care for the well-being of everyone with whom he comes in contact.

Jewelers can often identify the age of a diamond by how it is cut. In much the same way, Sherwin Wine can be described as being old-fashioned and enormously valuable. He knows no nostalgia, though his proclivities for Franklin Delano Roosevelt and scratchy old black and white movies are often exposed. A forward-thinking man who focuses on the future by controlling the present, he surrounds himself with old-fashioned ways. Modern office conveniences like computers and copiers are foreign objects to him. (A potential crisis was averted by a dedicated assistant who discovered the last of a supply of his fountain pen ink cartridges that are no longer being manufactured.) Although fully aware of and more than willing to take advantage of the benefits of modern contrivances, he chooses to remain apart. This old-fashioned style is part of his charm. At seventy-five years of age, Rabbi Wine's behavior is always that of a gentleman, polite under all circumstances.

So how does one respond to him? It's rare for a person to be ambivalent toward Rabbi Wine. His ability to force people to accept the consequences for their behavior is threatening to some and energizing to others. His articulate questioning of old traditions coupled with his creative responses to normally sacred themes are at once outrageous and thought-provoking. Often, people must make a conscious decision to accept him and participate in his life or to turn away.

For those of us who made the decision to be with him, we know it was the best choice. The energy we have drawn from him, the life lessons we have learned, the unfettered joy of laughing with him are all values no gemstone possesses. Yet as we look at him and listen to him and feel his presence in our lives, it is as if we hold a blazing diamond in our hands. It is ours to keep but only for a little while. It is ours to appreciate, love, and share with the world.

Charles R. Paul is a past president of the Birmingham Temple (2000–2001). From 1977 through 2003 he was the editor of *The Jewish Humanist*, the internationally distributed monthly publication of the Birmingham Temple. He also served on the temple board of trustees for many years. He is the president of a marketing and training agency in Farmington Hills, Michigan, and produces videos, manuals, speeches, and presentations primarily for the automotive industry.

A Veritable Pioneer in Spirit and Deed

Felix Posen

Sherwin Wine is now formally established as a pioneer, not in the sense that he has made any scientific discovery or discovered new lands, but as one who has, by his own initiative and intellect, "discovered" the need to describe, organize, teach the practice of, create literature for, and transform an existing phenomenon—one that has been around for a few hundred years but about which nobody bothered to do anything—into a real live option for tens of thousands of Jews.

This pioneering effort is in the area of secular, or Secular Humanistic, Judaism. No one has ever even attempted to properly organize this phenomenon and to simulate what had been done for centuries for other, more traditional (and less traditional—after all the birth of the Conservative and Reform movements had their own very tough beginnings), forms of Judaism. It is a great and historic contribution that Sherwin has made to Judaism by making the Jewish world aware of its largest single component, which was, until recently, referred to simply with silly euphemisms in the hope that it would just wither away.

Until Sherwin decided to create his Secular Humanistic Jewish movement, the concept of secular Judaism was one that was rarely discussed and infrequently debated in newspapers, magazines, or books. To emphasize its non-existence, traditional denominations created the euphemisms of "just Jewish" or "the non-observant Orthodox" in the hopes that "it" would just disappear. The seculars themselves often played along with this game by "pretending" to belong without really belonging to whatever synagogue or temple they were members of.

There were, in fact, some organizations in existence from the middle of the nineteenth century that were secularly oriented, but never just for the sake of secular Judaism per se. I am talking about the Bundists and Zionists, both of whom were overwhelmingly secular but combined their secular Judaism with either a political or sociological philosophy. When their political or sociological *raisons d'être* disappeared, their life expectancy went with it.

After Sherwin received his *s'mikha* at Hebrew Union College in Cincinnati, he recognized and perceived the great need to serve, with complete openness and intellectual honesty, this huge portion of the self-declared secular humanistic American Jewish public who considered themselves Jewish but not religious. Enough clamor from this group, who did not wish to participate in the usual synagogue or temple life offered by the main denominations, gave Sherwin the courage to create a new organization to serve their needs.

With tremendous bravery, Sherwin, together with very few kindred souls, started—without any real financial backing—what was considered a most improbable and unpromising organization, one that is now the largest of its kind in the world: the Society for Humanistic Judaism. After nearly forty years of dedicated hard work, together with some devoted friends, supporters, and colleagues, the society now has about 10,000 members.

A venture capitalist can well understand what this creation, *ab nuovo*, means in terms of difficulty, persistence, hard and dedicated work, and so on.

Sherwin needed to create everything: buildings; forms of services; new literature exploring how to celebrate life-cycle and festival events in a secular manner; intellectual and practical books and forums to help explain and develop this form of Judaism. He needed to create the tools to give it structure and coherence, create new phrases and music—or adapt old phrases and music—to help celebrate and live a form of Judaism that many people yearned for but did not know how to articulate. He became an all-service provider and created a new organization from which arose new and younger leaders to carry on the work.

After a couple of decades Sherwin met with other like-minded souls to start an international organization called the International Federation of Secular Humanistic Jews (IFSHJ), with branches in Israel and Europe. Slowly, but surely, additional groups decided to join and today this growing movement has up to 30,000 members worldwide. Even more important is that there are probably two or three times that number of people in groups operating all around the world who are philosophically allied to the movement without actually being members.

Today, the two main centers of Secular Humanistic Judaism are in America and Israel. This is not surprising as approximately 80 percent of the world's Jews now live in one of these two countries. There are of course other important centers, such as Brussels, and there are some organizations in France. The nature of the activities and needs of the Israeli community versus the Diaspora communities vary substantially, as the challenges of living the life of a secular Jew in Israel versus the Diaspora are hugely different.

> Until Sherwin decided to create his Secular Humanistic Jewish movement, the concept of secular Judaism was one that was rarely discussed and infrequently debated.

We now know that the main forms of practicing secular Judaism in the Diaspora are primarily through the kind of community centers introduced and built up by Sherwin, while in Israel it is primarily through education: both in the school system, and with a sudden rise over the past decade of literally hundreds of learning centers (some with as few as ten members, some with hundreds).

With the sudden "discovery" that the secular Jews, the largest single portion of the Jewish nation, had never been organized and had never had leaders of any kind—be they political, social, or intellectual—came the realization that now, for the first time in history, there are new institutions and centers of learning that, perhaps only a dozen years ago, would have been considered improbable.

During this very short period of time, there is no doubt that Sherwin's impetus led others to promote, particularly in Israel, a veritable explosion of activities such as, among other things, the creation of two colleges devoted to the teaching of secular Judaism; the instruction of teachers in the Israeli school system in teaching our literature, festivals, life-cycle events, and general outlook in a creative and nonreligious manner; the instruction of immigrants and leaders of learning communities in the basics of how to live a rich cultural life as a secular Jew and how to teach Jewish history from a point of view of culture and civilization; the creation of television programs, including secular Seders, *Tikkun Leil Shevuot*, intellectual discussions and debates on general subjects, and talk shows detailing examinations of ancient Jewish literature from the Bible to the Talmud; the gathering of an annual public "marathon" in Tel Aviv consisting of a full day of discussions and lectures by well-known national Israeli speakers, academics, politicians, and the like; the reclaiming of ancient, medieval, and, above all, modern literatures as a common heritage for all Jews; the creation of various websites and now the planning of a major website; the planning of videos and films on the history and development of Jews, including a section specifically of the immense contributions of secular Judaism to Jews and to the world at large; the creation of a new genre of books and magazines in the field of secular Judaism; the creation of new reference works, such as a lexicon on secular Judaism.

In Israel there are now seven institutes of higher learning—including three universities, Hebrew, Bar Ilan, and Tel Aviv—offering bachelor's and master's degrees and Ph.D.s in various aspects of secular Judaism. Courses in secular Judaism are now being offered in some American universities as well.

It is a real reawakening and ideally the beginning of the process of reclaiming a heritage that belongs to all Jews, religious or not. It is a process of development through new articulation, in new genres of literature—to which Sherwin personally has contributed with groundbreaking books—to help this large and alienated portion of the Jewish people reclaim and reconnect to their historical roots. It is a form of Judaism that has existed for hundreds of years, one that has even created fine literature but which has remained quiescent and leaderless until, essentially, Sherwin came along and recognized this lacuna and filled it.

It therefore gives me great pleasure to contribute to this volume in honor of Sherwin. I believe he has done an immense service and a mitsva in clarifying for the majority of Jews what it truly means to be a Jew and remain Jewish without religion: to celebrate, study, debate, teach, and enjoy it, and to wear it with pride.

Humanistic Judaism has existed for hundreds of years, but it remained quiescent and leaderless until Sherwin came along.

This movement of Secular Humanistic Judaism is a most creative exercise in recognizing the obvious, which could have been done long before, but nobody seemed to have thought of it, or bothered about it, or risen to the occasion. Now that Sherwin has initiated the next generation of Secular Humanistic Jewish rabbis, he has created a legacy that, no doubt, will lead to a rich and fulfilled Jewish life for centuries.

Felix Posen is a powerful voice for secular Judaism. His special life interest in higher Jewish education and primarily his quest to determine "what it means to be a Jew in a secular society" has led to the creation of the Posen Foundation, which is the foremost foundation active in the field of cultural, secular, and Humanistic Judaism in Israel and America. He is the energy behind the Posen Bibliography, today's leading world reference work on the subject of anti-semitism. He is the cofounder of Alma Hebrew College and Meitar College of Pluralistic Judaism.

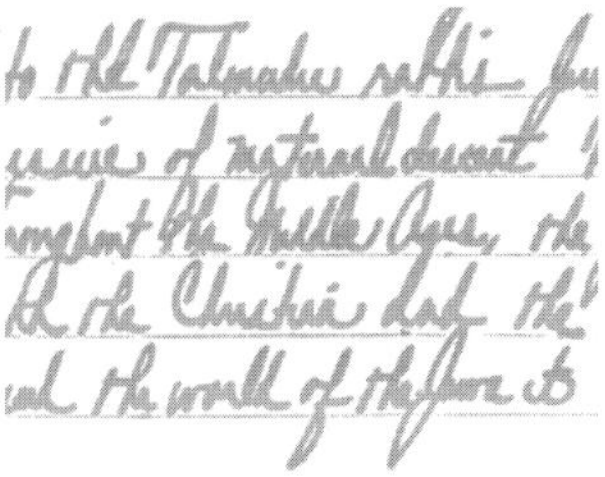

A View from Washington, D.C.

Michael J. Prival

So many people who are active in the Humanistic Judaism movement, including myself, should be deeply thankful to Rabbi Sherwin Wine. After all, if not for Sherwin, we might have gone on to lead normal, productive lives, spending time with our families, going to the movies, watching television, discussing sports and trashy novels with our friends. But this was not to be! Instead, because of this renegade rabbi from Reform, we are up until all hours each night, doing the business of our organizations by e-mail, while Sherwin himself still writes only with a fountain pen (not even a ball point!) and has certainly never mastered the computer keyboard. He, who devours libraries with a knifelike intellect and an airtight memory, has us lesser beings poring slowly, word-by-word, over ancient and modern texts, trying to understand how they can help illuminate the vision of Secular Humanistic Judaism. Because of Sherwin, who inspires us with insights and understanding, we rush home from work so we can spend hours at marathon board and committee meetings, fretting over details of organizational function about which he, of course, will forever remain blissfully ignorant. For all this and more, we are eternally grateful to Rabbi Wine—or at least as eternally as Secular Humanistic Jews are permitted to be grateful.

What is it that makes Sherwin Wine so important in our lives, a person so worthy of respect? We all know that he is a brilliant man who works hard and accomplishes much. But the fact is that the world is full of brilliant and accomplished people. Some of their achievements are important, and some are not. So with Sherwin, it's not his brilliance that we honor, but rather the ways in which he has applied that brilliance. It's not the fact that he has accomplished so much, but the lasting value of those accomplishments.

We honor and respect Sherwin Wine because the expenditure of his formidable intellectual and physical energies has been directed by something far more rare and precious than mere brilliance. And that rare commodity is vision, the unique vision to which he has applied his energy and talents for more than three decades.

Back in the 1960s, when all of this began, Sherwin didn't know more than a few people who were likely to become active in the movement, but he knew we were out there somewhere. He sensed that there were others who hungered to be part of a community that would hold intellectual integrity in the highest esteem. He knew that we wanted a home, a Jewish home, in which we would find no contradiction between our Jewish identity and our secular, humanistic worldview. He was sure that parents wanted a Jewish educational experience that would expose their children to the same kinds of ethical and philosophical messages they received at home. Most daringly of all, he acted on the understanding that secular Jews need the same types of institutions that our more traditionally religious friends, neighbors, and family members enjoy. So Sherwin and a small group of pioneers set out to remake Judaism into something that the largest single group of Jews, those with a secular outlook, could really believe in.

At the same time, he saw that it was not only necessary, but also desirable, to welcome all people who were interested as full and equal participants in that new movement, whether they considered themselves to be Jews, non-Jews, or something in between. (After all, being Jewish is not like being pregnant. You *can* be a little bit Jewish.) This acceptance of all is not a concession to the reality of widespread intermarriage, but rather an affirmation of the supremacy of humanness over ethnicity, of individual choice over conformity to convention. He created a movement that retains its Jewish character and core, while accepting all who are comfortable with what we are doing. Thus, uniquely among the movements of Judaism, we examine neither your genealogy nor your genitals. How could it be otherwise in a movement that calls itself Humanistic?

So we honor Sherwin for his vision of a Judaism that is true to the scientific worldview. We honor him for inspiring the creation of local, national, and ultimately international organizations that foster that vision and make its fruits available to Secular Humanistic Jews around the world.

At the same time, we must also honor him for something else—something as rare as vision and more important than great accomplishments. And that is his personal courage. The struggle that led Sherwin to an understanding of what he really believed was certainly not an easy one. Having reached that understanding within himself, he was able to use it as the basis for establishing a totally new way of being Jewish, as well as a new way of being a humanist. He was able to break his organizational ties to mainstream religion, ties that could have ensured both security and prosperity for one so capable and talented. Instead, he staked his own future to a novel idea and to the encouragement of a very small group of supporters. These were acts of a man who puts principle first, without regard for personal concerns. These were acts of a man who understood all along what it means to live a life of courage.

> Back in the 1960s, Sherwin didn't know more than a few people who were likely to become active in the movement, but he knew we were out there somewhere.

The story of my own family's experience with Humanistic Judaism begins in 1977. At that time, a small group of people, calling themselves the Washington Society for Humanistic Judaism, was beginning to hold meetings in the Washington, D.C., area. While four of these seven people had come to D.C. from the Detroit area, only two, Jules Abrams and Mary Abrams (now Mary Perica), had been members of Sherwin Wine's Birmingham Temple.

By the time I found this group of seven, it had already had a small schism. Apparently another original member, who had also been at the Birmingham Temple, insisted that the new group in the Washington area must use the services and other written materials exactly as produced in Michigan by Rabbi Wine, without modification. The others, however, wanted to adapt and create materials more suitable for their small group in the East. The more orthodox Wineian member declared the others to be insufferable heretics. So Jules Abrams called Sherwin and asked whether they could still be part of the Humanistic Judaism movement even though they were developing their own services. Sherwin's response—"Don't worry about it, Jules. We don't have the machinery for excommunication"—brought down the house when Jules recounted these events to 150 members at the recent twenty-fifth anniversary party of Machar, the Washington Congregation for Secular Humanistic Judaism.

So the inventive group of seven, freed of their more doctrinaire colleague, set out to create something that even they could not imagine. They were people of strong conviction and great energy. Ann and Harold Black had been active parents during the formative days of the secular Jewish Parents' Institute in the Detroit area. Jules also brought in Joe Goodman, with whom he worked, and Joe's wife Mildred. Mary's friend Henrietta Wexler came to a meeting, met Sherwin, and was hooked, as much by Sherwin's sense of humor as by anything else.

At this time, my wife, Joan, and I were wondering what type of Jewish education, if any, we might provide for our children. We knew that we couldn't tolerate any institution with a theistic outlook. We had been to an "open house" at a local Reform synagogue and were astounded to see so many otherwise intelligent people devoting their time and energy to calling out audibly to some imagined unseen supernatural being. It was very strange. We certainly didn't want to expose our children to such unwholesome activities.

I was discussing the dilemma of Jewish education with my friend from graduate school, Sam Fogel, who lived in the Boston area. Sam and his wife, Marge, had found the group that has now grown into the thriving Kahal B'raira, and he gave me Jules Abrams's telephone number. The rest, as they say, is history.

Although the founding members we encountered were somewhat older than we were (and still are!), Joan and I immediately saw that they were trying to build something in which we could truly believe. Henrietta Wexler was the first Sunday school teacher. I followed her in this role, even though our Sunday school had only three students, two of which were my own children. Having been raised in a left-wing secular home in the Bronx, I had almost no Jewish education myself as a child, so teaching was, in fact, an enlightening, learning experience for me. I taught the Bible, and, not suffering from the disability of having read it when I was young, I was able to see it for the first time from a secular, historical, scientific point of view. I had no religious baggage to slough off. These early efforts to explain the Bible to children, from a secular humanistic perspective, eventually led me to write the book, *Learning Bible Today*, published by the International Institute for Secular Humanistic Judaism, or IISHJ.

We were astounded to see so many otherwise intelligent people devoting their time and energy to calling out audibly to some imagined unseen supernatural being.

Back in those days (as we still do), our group placed an ad each year in the *Washington Post* announcing our High Holiday services. While we now are very cognizant of graphic design and the importance of clean copy and white space in our ads, at that time we crammed as many words as we could into the tiny box, trying to explain Humanistic Judaism to those with unusually good eyesight. I suspect that the wordy, hard-to-read style of those early ads inadvertently attracted exactly the type of people we needed—people more focused on content and substance than on form and style, people for whom words that said what they believed were more important than eye-catching graphics. People who responded to those ads exemplify the "type" that formed the core of the group we now call Machar.

Over the years, our style has softened somewhat. We devote a lot more attention to aesthetics at our services, and even to a sort of secular human "spirituality." But in the early years we had mainly a philosophy to offer, and we thrived on what we stood for, even if we sometimes did it without a great deal of grace or eloquence.

We also found that, in addition to our secular humanistic way of being Jewish, we shared a passion for politics and social action. Eventually, Joe Goodman took the initiative to organize and lead Machar's Social Action Committee, which continues to serve as the focus for our unique brand of congregational activism. The high point, I think, came in 1995, shortly after the Republicans swept into Congress with Newt Gingrich as their leader. At that moment, no other point of view seemed like it could be relevant. Even President Clinton whined helplessly, "But I'm still President." Into this complete lack of meaningful political dialogue, Machar stepped boldly with a ten-point platform promoting social justice. Led by Joe with bullhorn in hand, we stood on the Capitol steps and said what no one else seemed to be saying out loud at the time—that the Gingrich "Contract with America" was not acceptable and needed to be stopped. Over the years, Machar has also developed and circulated position statements on a variety of social and political issues, particularly concerning peace in the Middle East. Our website (www.machar.org) outlines our social action activities, which have made our philosophy of Secular Humanistic Judaism relevant and meaningful for our members, particularly for the children of our congregation.

Many years ago I thought it would be interesting to try to write and give a talk for our High Holiday services, based on my understanding of a Bible text. These talks have become a regular feature at our holidays, and I think they led to the next, unexpected step in my association with Secular Humanistic Judaism.

One day I got a call from Grace Avilès, one of the many extremely dynamic older people in our group. She said that she had been called by a couple asking if we had someone who could perform weddings. Grace, always thinking positively, responded, "Of course we do." So I was selected to perform a wedding, though this was years before the leadership program of the IISHJ existed. We then investigated the local law and found that I could indeed perform weddings, based on authorization to do so from our congregation. This led, as you can imagine, to a series of experiences I could never have envisioned in my cloistered life as a research microbiologist—officiating at several weddings a year for many years. Ultimately, I was also certified by the IISHJ Leadership Program. Of course, the intensive weekend seminars required for this certification, many led by Sherwin Wine himself, were exciting and enlightening, one of the best experiences in my relationship with our movement.

So as I finish this piece off at 2:00 A.M., struggling to stay awake, I am grateful to Sherwin Wine for creating something that will live on as a vital, breathing part of Jewish life. I'm happy to point out that the IISHJ-trained rabbis (one of whom, Ben Biber, is now, fortunately, part of Machar) are proof of that. Thank you, Sherwin. You have made it possible for so many of us to move from mundane concerns to a life of passionately held principles and ideas.

Michael J. Prival is a graduate of the International Institute for Secular Humanistic Judaism and a certified *madrikh*. He is one of the founding members of Machar, the Washington Congregation for Secular Humanistic Judaism. He is the author of *Learning Bible Today: From Creation to the Conquest* *of Canaan*, a work explaining how to present the Bible to children. He currently serves on the board of governors of the International Institute for Secular Humanistic Judaism.

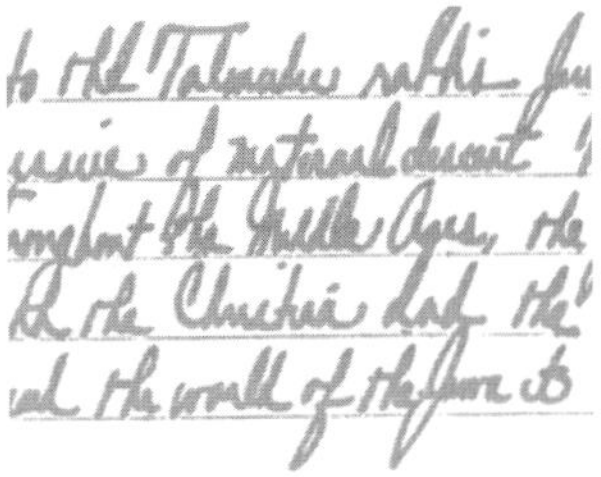

A Celebration of Life

Marilyn Rowens

I know Sherwin Wine is not retiring in June 2003. He is merely changing the location of his desk and moving his collection of Mont Blanc pens.

I have been a "Sherwin Wine watcher and admirer" for more than thirty-eight years. I have watched and admired him as a teacher, as a rabbi, as an organizer of committees and organizations, as a brilliant philosopher and poet of Humanistic Judaism, as a social activist, as a compassionate counselor, as a lecturer who can take the most complicated subject and make it clear and inspiring to his entire audience. I have watched him display extraordinary talent as a positive influence in the lives of all those he has touched.

To pay a valid tribute to Sherwin Wine, it would be necessary to understand the values and philosophy of Sherwin Wine.

It would be necessary to know something about his love and loyal devotion to the Jewish community and the Jewish people. It would be necessary to view his lifelong vision and struggle to develop Humanistic Judaism and to build and organize communities—local, national, and universal—in order to create a meaningful Judaism for the twentieth and twenty-first centuries.

It would be necessary to know something of his passion for philosophy, ethics, and morality, and of his knowledge of historical philosophical thought.

It would be necessary to try to understand his broad and scholarly quest to know the world through study of history, geography, and literature.

It would be necessary to view his constant commitment to freedom, human rights, social responsibility, and social action.

It would be essential to view him as a human being with an extraordinary ability to relate to people in a very positive and personal way, as counselor, philosophic guide, rabbi, and friend.

It would be important to know him as a lecturer who is able to synthesize information from the most simple to the most scientifically complex and to totally engage his audience with clarity, passion, humor, and pleasure.

And lastly, but not finally, it would be necessary to know him through the eyes of friends, congregants, his students, and all those who have learned from him and have been touched by him in their personal lives.

To pay tribute to Sherwin Wine is a challenging task. He does not require tributes. His personal reward seems to come from empowering, enhancing, and serving others. His special talent is the ability to motivate and inspire others to do better, to feel better, and to live with courage and hope.

In any case, I pay tribute to him and thank him for leading the way and motivating me to be part of a movement I have cherished for thirty-eight years.

To have discovered Sherwin Wine and the Birmingham Temple in 1967 was like opening a treasure chest and finding the priceless contents of my Judaism, my humanism, my creativity, my family connections, and my ongoing quest for meaning in life in an identifiable, beautiful space!

Humanistic Judaism connected me to my past. It opened creative doors to the future. It gave me the opportunity to express who I was as a Jew, as a humanist, as a woman. I began learning by teaching a Sunday school sixth grade class entitled "The Celebrations of Life." And I have been celebrating ever since. The world of Humanistic Judaism was my creative marketplace. And the door to that world of Humanistic Judaism was opened by the vision, courage, and influence of Sherwin Wine. I observed and participated in the development, birth, and growth of the worldwide movement of Secular Humanistic Judaism.

I was the ceremonial director for the Birmingham Temple for more than twenty years and created programming that reflected my values of Humanistic Judaism: the need to find the strength within myself to solve the daily problems of life, the need to find truth in the experiences and consequences of human actions, the need to accept the unknown and admit, all too often, that "I don't know." Also, I discovered in my work the essential need to reach out to touch and validate other human beings.

> I know Sherwin Wine is not retiring in June 2003. He is merely changing the location of his desk and moving his collection of Mont Blanc pens.

With Sherwin Wine's continuing encouragement and support and "yes, you can do it" attitude and nudging I created holiday services, puppet shows, children's plays, and holiday stories utilizing our Jewish calendar but emphasizing the importance of connecting our Jewish history with meaningful humanistic values in a way that validated being Jewish in a secular modern world. I treated adult themes with the same purposeful format, reaching out to the women's movement, our aging immigrant community, and our philosophy students, always trying to merge our Jewish heritage with our human need to make sense of the world around us. The timing was essential. Our post-1960s experimentation in Judaism was being absorbed by the seekers who were my peers, those "just Jewish" young adults who were children during World War II. We grew up with Moses, but we studied Freud and Eric Fromm. The Holocaust survivors were still silent, Israel was victorious, and we were struggling with our Jewish identity.

Sherwin Wine's years of vision, encouragement, and motivating all those who came into his philosophic range of influence turned into a growing movement for Secular Humanistic Judaism. I was intricately involved in the outreach that culminated in the Society for Humanistic Judaism and the International Federation of Secular Humanistic Jews. I became the executive director of the International Institute for Secular Humanistic Judaism. We began training leaders and rabbis for our movement.

I am the director of the Rabbinic Program and the Leadership Program and have experienced the practical application of our philosophy in training and creating outstanding leaders and rabbis for our communities. I have seen and felt the impact that Humanistic Judaism has had on so many individuals and groups who are yearning to express their Jewish identity in our rapidly advancing cyberspace world. I have seen them and heard them sigh, "Ahhh, this is what I have been looking for. I can be connected to my Jewish culture, my Jewish roots, my history, my people, and my humanism with honesty, integrity, and hope."

For many years I worked with Birmingham Temple adult confirmation students who discovered or rediscovered their Judaism through study in our adult confirmation class. Rabbi Wine taught a two-year program comprising two classes, the History of the Jews and the Basic Ideas of Humanistic Judaism. After each two-year program ended, I worked with the "graduates" to create a graduation ceremony, a dramatic narrative expressing their Jewish journey. Each group of students over a period of more than ten years had individual stories. Many expressed feelings like, "I never knew I could be Jewish like this." Or, "Now I feel connected to my Jewish heritage with a more positive and deep sense of commitment." Many times I witnessed a non-Jewish spouse who sighed with such a sense of comfort and a real acceptance of Humanistic Judaism. But an underlying and significantly deep result of those two years resulted in a universal feeling of strength and human power that seeped into each student's marrow as the historical material was being taught. Sherwin's special gift of empowering his students was repeated year after year after year. His class on Humanistic Judaism not only opened the way to Jewish history and philosophy but offered skills and tools for living in "a crazy world." Each year the students echoed the same refrain of having been enhanced, enriched, and strengthened in their Judaism and their humanness.

During the process of being involved with the growth and development of our movement, I created for myself a humanistic alter ego, a cartoon stick figure, that observed and expressed not only philosophy, values, and ethical choices, but also deep emotions and awareness of the human condition. The stick figure, appearing monthly in the Birmingham Temple newsletter *The Jewish Humanist* and elsewhere, comments on daily ritual, on human contradictions, on successes and failures of personal relationships, sometimes with the pain of tears but most often with humor and laughter. My stick figure began as a "Happy Humanist" and evolved into a mini-lecturer on the basic vulnerability of the human condition. She is simple in design, a primitive figure. However, her curly hair and large glasses are reminiscent of the person I view in the mirror each morning. Her comments constantly affirm reality, honesty, the need for courage and challenge, the complicated nature of truth, and the need to laugh at the absurdities of life. She speaks in captions and her words reflect her deep commitment to a worldview and practical philosophy that she has developed with time and study and under the powerful influence of a remarkable teacher.

Our post-1960s experimentation in Judaism was being absorbed by the seekers who were my peers, those of us who grew up with Moses but studied Freud and Eric Fromm.

My watchful observations and intense listening have provided me with an overall view of the history of the Secular Humanistic Jewish movement and the personal experience of sharing an effective and working philosophy with my peers and students.

Humanistic Judaism provides a road map for life
With firm parameters for ethical and moral choices
But there are windows to challenge our vision,
Our tolerance, our complacency.
Responsibility and strength do not come easily
They are skills that are learned and practiced.
Failure is not terminal, it is often a rung on a ladder
Upon which we climb two steps up and one step down.
Happiness and beauty do not happen automatically
They are products of human effort, nurturing and creativity.
Reality does not deny fear
Nor does it refuse to smile in the presence of pleasure.
Love is not a mystery
It is the open sharing of intimacy and friendship.
Life and death are part of our existential pattern
And how we face each moment
Is the exciting challenge of being human!

Sherwin Wine had the courage to create an alternative in Jewish life: an alternative that celebrates the Jewish calendar with meaningful ritual that enhances human dignity and strength, an alternative that provides for a strong Jewish identity, an alternative that relies on human responsibility, not supernatural belief. But he also serves as a role model for coping with the daily trials of human choice, confronting the daily pain of human struggle, and encouraging the transcendent power of a natural human spirit.

I feel a sense of accomplishment that indeed our philosophy has reached and validated so many. And after thirty-eight years, I know that I am part of a significant legacy. Thank you, Sherwin. We have touched the future!

Marilyn Rowens is the executive director of the International Institute for Secular Humanistic Judaism. She also serves as the Leadership Program director and the Rabbinic Program director. She was the ceremonial director of the

Birmingham Temple for twenty years. She is the resident cartoonist for the monthly Birmingham Temple publication, *The Jewish Humanist.* She is also the author of many plays and short stories that reflect the human condition.

The Courage of One's Convictions

Peter Schweitzer

"And there was light." Only some take longer to see it than others. In my case, I had a clear vision of it in my adolescence (I was a rebellious teenage atheist), lost sight of it in college (while searching for my roots by *davening* at Hillel), glimpsed it again but dismissed it in rabbinic school, and finally, fortunately, found my way back into the light again some dozen years ago, when I rediscovered the teachings of Rabbi Sherwin Wine, my teacher and friend. It is a great honor to participate in this worthy tribute to Rabbi Wine: he gave us light, now let him bask in the light of our tribute and praise.

When I first heard of Rabbi Wine, I was a student at Hebrew Union College's Cincinnati campus, the same school he had attended a generation earlier. A few of Wine's acolytes were studying at HUC—he hadn't built his seminary yet—and far from being discreet, they weren't shy at all about preaching their mentor's philosophy. They didn't win over too many converts and were generally dismissed as being on the fringe. I personally can't claim to having arrived at a systematic rebuttal to their arguments—my response was more rote than reasoned, more visceral than intelligent. Oftentimes, when our belief systems are threatened, we prefer to put on blinders and write off our challengers as crazy or disturbed. To a dutiful Reform-rabbi-in-the-making like myself, the humanists' godless Judaism seemed quite untenable and misguided. I wasn't exactly raised with God-talk myself, but I was busy embracing God-language in my sermons. Theism aside, it was inconceivable that I would turn away from my roots, which were dug deep in the Reform movement: not only had my father been president of our suburban temple in my childhood, my great-grandfather had led New York City's Temple Emanuel in his day. As far as I was concerned, the Reform movement was modernity's ultimate answer to orthodoxy, and it didn't need any great improvements.

And so it went for a number of years, fifteen in fact, before I rediscovered Humanistic Judaism. As I have written elsewhere (see "A Rabbi's Journey to Secular Humanistic Judaism," at www.shma.com, June 2000), in those early years of the rabbinate, I was too preoccupied with the choreography of the service to actually contemplate its message. I mouthed words I didn't think about. When I did think about them, I grew to disdain them, and I began to reclaim the views of my youth. As my alienation from the theistic message grew more pronounced, I could no longer hide behind my intellectual blinders. I sought alternative approaches to celebrating my Jewish identity. Thanks to a brief foray into Reconstructionism—an unsatisfying return to *davening*, but a very satisfying return to intelligent dialogue—I discovered a reference in one of its journals to Rabbi Sherwin Wine and the Society for Humanistic Judaism. What I had rejected summarily now made clear sense to me. It had taken me years to get the cobwebs out of my brain, and even a few more to put the Reform movement behind me, but I was ready, finally, to see the light, which had been there all along.

Why does Humanistic Judaism work for me, and why has Rabbi Sherwin Wine become my teacher? Because it and he—they are really one and the same—lay out a philosophy and a message that I can embrace without compromise. It is a movement with absolute integrity. It demands nothing less of itself.

Its founder and leader, likewise, is an exemplar of rigorous thinking and intellectual accountability. There is no fudging, no hiding behind loose language.

Rabbi Wine champions the notion that we cope with the travails of life with our endowment of courage, with the support of community, with the honest acceptance that life is not, by definition, fair. In building his movement and his many institutions, he needed his own courage and determination to overcome deterrents and voices of opposition. He also needed the sure conviction that he could stay the course for as long as it took. In this respect, Rabbi Wine has the advantage of being an incorrigible dreamer and optimist, a person who has a vision and breathes life into it by his enthusiasm.

I have relished the clarity of Rabbi Wine's writing. I have been invigorated by the force of his personality. I have been challenged by his example. In tribute to him, I have learned to have the courage to speak more forcefully my own mind. To this end, I append here two messages—made possible by the philosophy of Humanistic Judaism and the inspiration of Sherwin Wine—which I delivered to the City Congregation for Humanistic Judaism, both during Rosh Hashana. The first was delivered in 1999, several months after I had multiple eye surgeries. The second was delivered in 2001, shortly after the terrorist attacks in New York and Washington, D.C., on September 11.

> Humanistic Judaism is a movement with absolute integrity. It demands nothing less of itself.

"THE GOD I DON'T BELIEVE IN" (1999)

The traditional Rosh Hashana Torah reading is taken from Genesis chapter 22 and is known as *Akedat Yitzchak*, or the Binding of Isaac. It is also known as the Test of Abraham, and he is held up each year as the model of obedience and loyalty to God, even to the point of showing his readiness to sacrifice his own son. Isaac, side by side, is no less revered as the willing, unwhining, uncomplaining "sacrificee."

One rabbinic commentary, however, prefers a rather prosaic explanation for this highly touted story of obedience to God. In the alternative account, this whole episode is explained as the result of a bet between God and Satan. It seems they were chatting up in heaven, perhaps over a few schnapps, and Satan said to God, "You know, God, Isaac is a wimp, and Abraham isn't much stronger. When his older brother Ishmael was circumcised he was already a grown man. But Isaac was a mere eight days old when he had it done. Big deal. I bet he couldn't withstand a real test of strength and character."

And so, to prove Satan wrong, God designed the test of Abraham and Isaac.

For my money, the God I don't believe in doesn't put us through the wringer this way. The God I don't believe in does not see how much physical pain and emotional suffering we can stand, does not afflict us with fear and despair and a shattering of safety with chaos, does not play with our bodies and minds to the point of bringing on exhaustion and mental collapse, does not use us to win bets—all for the sake of our personal growth and moral improvement.

For the last seven years, after having surgery for a detached retina in my right eye, I have been trying not to wait for the other shoe to drop—which it did, finally, in April, when the retina detached in my left eye. I greeted that pronouncement with some relief, I suppose, because the waiting was now over, and I also burst into tears, because I felt so overcome by my own fragility and vulnerability, plus the waiting had been exhausting. I really can't thank the God I don't believe in enough for that wonderful day.

In July, when the retina detached again, I barely blinked an eye—pardon the pun—and the doctor couldn't believe how nonplussed I was. Probably a better explanation was shock and incomprehension, and, thanks to the God I don't believe in, a kind of surreal disbelief that this was really happening.

But this was all a mild warm-up for what happened a mere two weeks later when the retina detached once more, but much worse than before. Had I believed in the God I don't believe in I would have cried "Uncle!" and exclaimed, "Enough already. You win. I'm not up to your tests. Please just let me go."

This time I was up in the Adirondacks and hastily went over to Burlington, Vermont, for yet another round of surgery—longer and more complicated this time—and several more days recuperating in local motels so I could be close to my surgeon for frequent post-operative check-ups.

Now it happens that my surgeon and I are born on the same day—I'm a year older—and we also have the same uncommon middle name, so for a moment I thought these might be signs from the God I don't believe in that I was sent to him by one of those obnoxious ministering angels. But not to worry. Fortunately Dr. Millay wasn't left-handed, too, or my disbelief might really have been shattered.

> For my money, the God I don't believe in doesn't put us through the wringer, doesn't afflict us with fear and despair and a shattering of safety with chaos.

The recuperation from this surgery is not pleasant. My eye actually did not hurt too much, but my head and neck and shoulders were in misery because I had to keep my head face-down around-the-clock religiously for nearly two weeks while the retina molded itself into position again. Fortunately, I became acquainted with all sorts of painkillers and sleeping pills and tranquilizers, but I have no thanks to the God I don't believe in for all the unwanted side affects these pills bring in their wake.

I do have thanks for the doctors and nurses who have worked their remarkable ingenuity and skills to fix me up. I do have thanks for the family and friends and even friends of friends I've never met that have held me up and carried me through these very difficult times. I do have thanks for the profound gift of hope and good cheer that we give to each other.

I am reminded over and over again of the final verse of our song "Ayfo Oree," which we sing when we light our candles: "Where is my light / it is in me / where is my hope / it is in me / where is my strength / it is in me, and in you." It's the "in you" that is crucial. Sometimes there just isn't enough hope or strength "in me" alone. The world is too chaotic and our lives are often too frightening to make it through by ourselves. But together, borrowing strength and optimism from one another, we can hope for a brighter tomorrow.

"THE GIFT OF LIFE" (2001)

As I have done every year, I have opened each of our High Holiday services with a brief message intended to set a mood and a context for our celebration and observance.

A week ago, I had one set of thoughts in mind. It had been my intention to share with you some preliminary reflections on my joy and thrill on recently becoming a father and the awe and wonderment I was feeling in the presence of our newborn son. I then wanted to make the connection that these ten days, which stretch between Rosh Hashana and Yom Kippur, are also known as days of awe—only it is a different kind of awe than my sense of amazement at the life and relationship that is unfolding and awakening in front of me.

For religious Jews, these ten days of awe are a time when one stands in fear and trembling before a fierce deity who will decide our fate for the coming year. Our lives, as it were, hang in the balance. So there is awe which is full of worry and trepidation and there is awe which is exciting and life-affirming. In the first instance, we want to bow our head and duck for cover—and plea to the deity to be kind to us. In the latter, we want to stand tall, smile on the world, celebrate our good fortune, and give thanks.

And then, a week ago, our relatively safe and happy world was turned upside-down with an inferno of terror and death and madness. This was no Godzilla movie or blockbuster thriller with all the special effects Hollywood could muster up. This was unfiltered reality—in our own front yard. It did happen here. It did happen to us—to our family, our friends, and the friends of our friends, our business associates, our clients. They and we were there. In the building. Next door. A block away. A borough away. Or just over a bridge, a state away.

And we knew and know shock and panic and sadness and anger and anguish and fear and despair. And we are grieving—personally, for people we knew, and just as powerfully for those we didn't. And we are already attending and continue to attend wakes and funerals and memorial services in the days and weeks to come.

The impulse to give thanks is of particular difficulty to us humanists. How do we give thanks? Who do we thank?

And we also knew happiness and joy for personal survival and reunion with family members and friends, and thanks and gratitude for extraordinary heroism and bravery that lost so many lives in the effort to save others.

This last impulse—to give thanks—is of particular difficulty to us humanists. How do we give thanks? Who do we thank? Our lucky stars? No, thousands were not lucky at all last Tuesday. Our ancestor spirits and the ministering angels? No, they were not particularly kind either.

And what of God—and that wonderful cliché: "There but by the grace of God go I"? This rings hollow and unconvincing and even seems blasphemous to me. Where was grace for the thousands who hung in the balance and didn't make it? What poor taste—to exalt and be grateful amidst those who are mourning.

How else to explain the countless stories of people who should have been in the World Trade Center when it was hit but instead had a doctor's appointment, were detained half an hour with a child at home, or had just stepped out for a cigarette? It wasn't God's benevolence or their own intuition or anything else that spared them. It was just dumb luck.

And if it had all happened just a week later? We shudder to imagine that possibility. The towers would surely have been depleted of Jews attending their holiday observances elsewhere, but this small congregation would have been gathering for our services in the Marriott Hotel next door, in the shadow of the great buildings. Surely we don't believe we were spared by a provident deity we don't exactly rely upon.

This impulse to thank some external power or force for our well-being and good fortune is a subtle way for us to pass the buck: "It is God's will" is another way of saying "Life stinks and I—or we—had nothing to do with it." Or it's a way of saying, "There's a divine plan"—which, of course, we're not let in on, and that's supposed to comfort us, nonetheless, when the plan doesn't seem to be going our way. There's a greater good, in other words, behind all of this, even at the expense of thousands of lives. One of my clients even ventured to suggest that this may be a sign that the Messiah is coming.

An alternative way of thinking, which is no less pernicious, is to assign blame and to find a scapegoat—like the intelligence community for relaxing its guard; like gays, abortionists, and secular humanists for weakening our moral resolve; like American policy generally for its global imperialism.

All of this, I think, is about a desperate way to make order out of a chaotic world. It is about denial and false comfort because if we don't have an explanation, then we don't know how to prevent any of this from happening again. It covers up a harsh, uncomfortable truth: that our lives are very random, often crazy, often unkind, and often very painful.

Too much of what happens in our lives happens to us not from choice or desire. We can and should take pride in our achievements—especially those remarkable acts of heroism and also those everyday acts of human kindness—but at the end of the day we have only so much control over our lives. Far too often, we are reactors, not agents of our own destiny. But even then we have choices: to face adversity with courage or complaints, or, when things go well, to celebrate good times with dignity and humility or with arrogance and bragging.

Far too often, we are reactors, not agents of our own destiny. But even then we have choices.

Which brings me back, finally, to my little child. What I have tentatively figured out is that while we may take some credit for making babies, these new lives basically make themselves in amazing and mysterious ways that far transcend our input. Their creation is simply remarkable and they point us to appreciate what I think of as the awesome miracles of everyday life.

Which also explains why, when I came home on Tuesday night in a state of sadness and anger, my mood was involuntarily lifted when I gazed on my little boy. His tentative smiles were contagious, and despite my effort to suppress my happiness and maintain a somber mood, I couldn't help it. In the midst of madness, he brought me a perspective of joy and light. A few days later, one of our friends wrote, "With the madness around us, it seems like a very good time to be ushering a new life into our community—a reminder that there is a future to be struggled for."

And so now as we enter the New Year I hope you will join me to celebrate the gift of hope and possibility, and the gift of life renewed—not just of the new little life in my life, but of the gift of each of our own lives and the gifts of the lives of all the people we cherish, who give us their gift of life. For each precious day that we and they are alive, let us be very grateful and very thankful.

Peter Schweitzer is the leader of the City Congregation for Humanistic Judaism in New York City, where he has developed liturgy, including a Secular Humanistic Haggada and Shabbat and High Holiday services. He has also developed educational programs for children and adults. He is the vice president of the Association of Humanistic Rabbis. He was ordained as a reform rabbi from the Hebrew Union College–Jewish Institute of Religion and received a master's degree in social work from New York University.

Secularism, Humanism, and Idolatry

Mitchell Silver

Sherwin Wine is the foremost champion of explicit, self-conscious Humanistic Judaism. The existence of multiple institutions testify to his practical leadership: not only was Wine the founder of the first Humanistic Jewish temple, he also was the main force behind the creation of congregational networks, international organizations, educational establishments, and annual colloquia, all devoted to sustaining, promulgating, and studying Humanistic Judaism.

But Wine's central place in the Humanistic Jewish movement is due at least as much to his intellectual and ideological role as to his organizational leadership. Indeed, his intellectual leadership endowed him with the credibility to work so effectively as an organizer. The first task of an organizational leader is to articulate a vision that others find worthy of realizing. Wine, as much as anyone, is the visionary of Secular Humanistic Judaism. His vision is worth exploring.

Wine's thought is wide ranging, but his central vision can be encapsulated thus: 1) Jewish ethnic identity, besides remaining precious to non-religious Jews, is worth maintaining because it has a contribution to make to the world; 2) secular humanism is not only a viable "philosophy of life," it is the most appropriate one for contemporary humanity.

In this essay I will not discuss Wine's views on Judaism or Jewish ethnicity. Nor will I discuss, except as it relates to his humanism, his views on secularism. Rather I will focus on Wine's humanism, which I take to be his core conviction. I will not here argue the points, but I believe that Wine's justification for maintaining Jewish institutions is that they can be made compatible with, and even advance, humanism. His secularism is motivated largely because he believes theism (at least if it is robust enough to be meaningful) is destructive of humanism. Hence humanism is Wine's core commitment, the commitment by which other commitments are judged and justified.

Humanism is easily conflated with secularism. Friends of one are often friends of the other, and the enemies of each use "secular humanist" as a single epithet. Indeed, there are natural connections between the two, but they are logically distinct. Secularism, the claim that this world—the phenomenal, natural world revealed by experience and investigated by science and devoid of gods—is the only world we have reason to believe exists, implies nothing about the value or role of humans, nor about the proper way a human ought to live his or her life. A secularist can consistently hold that humans are worthless beings and that one ought to get as much selfish pleasure as one can without a thought about the needs of humanity. Such a doctrine would hardly qualify as a humanism, in spite of the absence of God.

But though there is no strict logical link, there is a natural connection between secularism and humanism. If there is no God to ground one's values, no God to guide one's life, no God to serve, then "humanity" becomes a plausible candidate to perform those functions. Divine values are replaced by human values, divine commands by human needs, divine service by service to humanity. And therein may lie a rub. Although the religious may rail against secular humanism's dethroning of God, their objections are equally motivated by the coronation of humanity. And this is an objection a secularist can share; one does not have to value or believe in God to question the wisdom of making human well-being one's supreme or sole value. But if one does object to such "humanism," while nonetheless maintaining a secular stance, one must answer the theists' charge that, though not a strict logical entailment, humanism is the natural, invariable alternative to theism.

Wine, however, does not have to answer this charge because he does not find humanism problematic. If humanism is acceptable, the fact that it is the necessary concomitant of secularism is no objection to secularism. So our first order of business is to consider whether Wine is correct in this—if, in other words, there is nothing in humanism a secularist should find disquieting. But before turning to potential secularist worries about humanism, let's further examine the theists' indictment of secularism.

For theists, humanism is simple idolatry. Humanism in effect makes humanity the Supreme Being. Granted, no sane humanism thinks of humanity as having all the properties associated with the traditional Western God. But by elevating human welfare and human taste to be the measuring stick of all value, humanism gives humanity the highest rank in the order of beings. By self-consciously embracing this measuring stick, by advocating its adoption, by ritualizing our devotion to it, we in effect worship humanity, worship ourselves.

> The first task of an organizational leader is to articulate a vision that others find worthy of realizing. Wine, as much as anyone, is the visionary of Secular Humanistic Judaism.

Secularists, of course, don't mind that God is not worshiped. But might we still mind that humanity *is* worshiped? Perhaps worshiping as an activity is objectionable, regardless of the object of worship. Why might this be so? In their survey of Jewish conceptions of idolatry, Moshe Halbertal and Avishai Margalit catalog the various ideas and actions that have been labeled idolatrous.[1] The master notion that seems to unify the sundry ideas is that idolatry consists of worshiping that which is unworthy of worship. Now, what if nothing is worthy of worship? In that case, any act of worship is bound to amount to idolatry, regardless of the reality, goodness, power, or relative metaphysical ranking of the object of worship. The best, the most valuable, of beings might still not merit worship—and so any worshiping turns us into idolaters.

Another objection to worship doesn't depend on the absence of a worthy object, but rather on harmful effects inherent in the activity of worship, in particular the diminishment of the worshiper. The claim is that even a being worthy of worship, if such there be, ought not be worshiped because the activity of worship harms the worshiper without compensating benefits to the object of worship or any third parties.

We deal with the latter objection first. To it the humanist can reply that the worship of humanity has not the harmful consequences of God-worship; if we worship ourselves there is no self-abnegation, no self-debasement. We do not project our own qualities onto some external being, thereby impoverishing our self-esteem to enhance some fantasy figure. Nor must our self-worship involve deceptive self-aggrandizement. We can hold ourselves the supreme being without believing ourselves perfect or attributing to ourselves powers or wisdom we don't actually possess. Saying we are the best does not require that we think of ourselves as very good—only that we think there is nothing better. (Wine is particularly fastidious about recognizing humanity's many limitations in his humanism.) Moreover, worship of humanity may have positive effects, such as helping us to recognize our powers and responsibilities, the better to shoulder them, and filling us with joyful pride that comes not at the expense of anyone else's sense of self worth.

To the first objection, the charge of idolatry, there are two possible humanist replies: the first simply denies that humanism entails worshiping humanity, the second argues that humanity is indeed worthy of worship, so there is nothing idolatrous about worshiping it.

Does humanism worship humanity? Insofar as humanism is made into an organized sect that has ritual celebrations of the value of humanity, makes communal declarations of devotion to human welfare, and proclaims the highest aim in life is the achievement of a human good, it is hard to see how we can deny that humanism worships humanity (unless we stipulate that, by definition, only a supernatural God can be worshiped.) So, to escape the charge of idolatry, an organized humanism, one that engaged in such ritual activities, would need to argue that humanity, or some essentially human attribute, is truly worthy of worship. What does humanism find to worship in humanity?

Up to this point in the discussion I have been a little vague about the nature of humanism. This is because not all humanisms are the same. For Wine, the most valuable aspect of the human being is its capacity for dignity.[2] He recognizes that other things are valuable, such as happiness or pleasure. But ultimately human dignity, which Wine equates with individual human autonomy, is the supreme value, the value to which other values ought to give way. Dignity has a host of implications for Wine—courage, democracy, mutuality, and sensitivity, to name a few.[3] But these are not separately justified values. They are goods derived from dignity. In Wine's humanism, human dignity, understood as human self-sovereignty, human autonomy, is the *summum bonum.* In this humanism, human freedom is the object of worship.

In Wine's humanism, human freedom is the object of worship.

Wine could not have picked a value that has more appeal to secularists, this writer included. If I had to decide on *the* best, most valuable, most precious form of being, human freedom would get the nod. But should I make such a choice? Should I settle on a good that trumps other goods in all situations? Might there not be times that a little less human freedom is worth a lot more human pleasure? Might there not be sound judgments that include some curtailment of human dignity as a price that should be paid to reduce the suffering of nonhuman animals? Might there not even be value in a nonsentient being the realization of which may justify some sacrifice of human freedom? If a small addition of human freedom could be had by the destruction of vast distant galaxies, however devoid of consciousness, is that destruction justified?

I ask these not as rhetorical questions. I am genuinely puzzled about the right answers. On the one hand, when values conflict, how can we make rational ethical decisions if there is no highest value—to serve either as a common denominator to which we can convert other values for the purpose of comparing value quantities, or to serve as the value with the highest rank and therefore the highest priority in cases of value conflict?[4] It seems that a thoroughgoing rational ethics demands a supreme value. On the other hand, our experience and intuitions rebel at having to always defer to a single goal. Ethical life is experienced as more complex, involving many fundamental values that are incommensurable—in other words, a genuine pluralism of values. Wine praises pluralism, but not of this kind. He wants to see many value systems flourish, he wants us to be tolerant of many of those different philosophies of life. He wants a marketplace of ideologies.[5] But in *his* philosophy of life, his humanism, a single value reigns supreme and is indeed the object of worship.

The problem a secularist can have with such a humanism is that it too readily decides the value puzzle. It worships an answer. It makes a difficult and profound question a dogma. Not, to be sure, in a censorious, illiberal way. Humanists are always ready to hear you out. Wine even rebukes "unyielding loyalty to a humanistic tradition."[6] But secular humanists come to the discussion with their fundamental convictions and commitments settled, settled enough to ritually celebrate them, to teach their children to worship them. It is all well and good for secular humanists to deny any dogmatic attitude toward these convictions. But if one is a secular humanist, to reject these values, one must become an apostate. Secularism should be more intellectually unencumbered.

Does that mean that a secularist should have no strong commitments and convictions, no values that they are willing to protect and defend, perhaps at times to the death? No. But it does mean that even when defending things to the death, we secularists should be aware of human fallibility, should have whispering in the back of our minds Oliver Cromwell's voice "beseeching" us "in the bowels of Christ, that Ye might be wrong." It is hard to be genuinely open to the possibility that your answer is wrong if you have been worshiping that answer. Ironically, it is intellectual humility that should make us hesitate in apotheosizing human dignity.

But what are a secularist's alternatives to humanism? (Recall that the theist claimed there were none.) Nihilism is an obvious but not very appealing possibility. The theist would be happy to allow that atheists must choose between having idolatrous values and none at all. A better alternative is to refuse to put anything in God's former role. If there is no worship, there is no idolatry, but there can be still be strongly held values that guide one's life. Indeed a single value can become for a time, perhaps a lifetime, or many lifetimes, the central value. But so long as no value gets enshrined, no value is made immune to change, no value is *worshiped*, secularism can escape the idolatry endemic to religion.

It is hard to be genuinely open to the possibility that your answer is wrong if you have been worshiping that answer.

In fairness it must be said that, in the articulation of his humanistic creed, Wine frequently recognizes and endorses the evolving nature of human values and holds no brief for dogmatism of any kind. But in his eagerness to respond to some of the needs religion has traditionally met, and to put a positive, confident spin on atheism, he elevates his core beliefs and values to a status that I think should give secularism pause.[7] Nothing about these humane values and reasoned beliefs is offensive, and Wine's eloquence on their behalf is a major service to fleshing out a value system for secularist thought. But let it not be *the* value system; let us have secularism with humanistic (among other) values, without having secular humanism.

NOTES

1. Moshe Halbertal and Avishai Margalit, *Idolatry*, trans. Naomi Goldblum (Cambridge, MA: Harvard University Press, 1992).
2. Sherwin Wine, *Judaism Beyond God* (Ktav Publishing; Milan Press, 1995) 42. Wine's assessment of human autonomy as the pinnacle of human moral evolution echoes Erich Fromm's views; see Fromm's *Ye Shall Be As Gods* (New York: Holt, Rinehart & Winston, 1966). Wine doesn't agree with Fromm that this struggle for autonomy has been the underlying true agenda of all religious life—Wine takes a less generous (but more clear-eyed) view of religious history. But I think he would agree with Fromm's thesis that humanism isn't idolatry because in it humankind is finally discovering the appropriate object of veneration.
3. Wine, *Judaism Beyond God*, 44-45.
4. Some philosophers say that sometimes there is no way to make rational ethical decisions—that is what a tragic situation is. See Martha Nussbaum, *The Fragility of Goodness* (Cambridge: Cambridge University Press, 1986).
5. Wine, *Judaism Beyond God*, 133.
6. Ibid., 131.
7. Ibid., 227.

Mitchell Silver is the cultural director of Camp Kinderland and the educational director of the I. L. Peretz School of Workmen's Circle in Boston. Dr. Silver has taught philosophy at the University of Massachusetts in Boston since 1982. He is the author of *Respecting the Wicked Child: A Philosophy of Secular Jewish*

Identity and Education, and he has published works on ethical theory, bioethics, and Middle East politics.

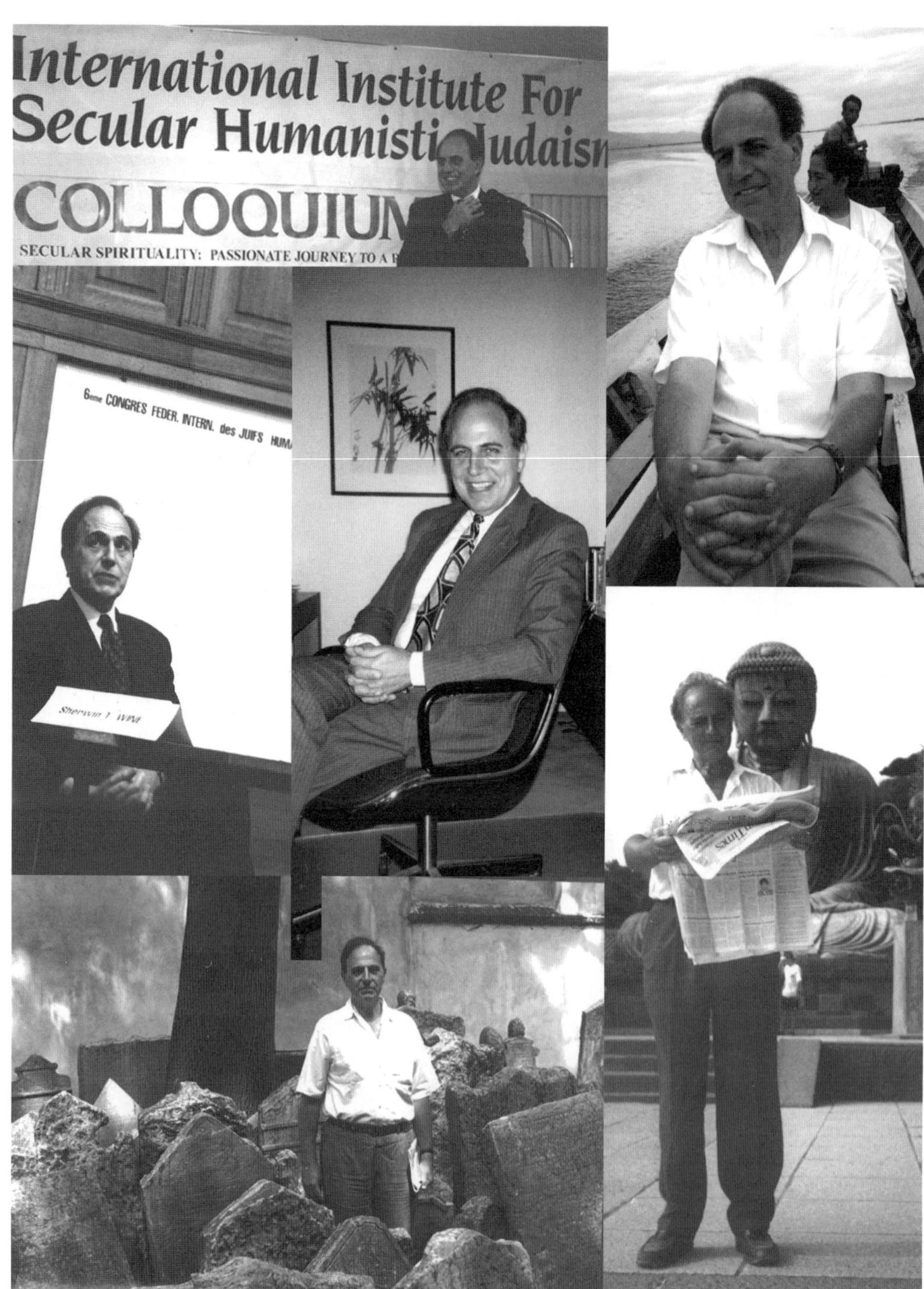
International Institute For
Secular Humanisti
udaism
COLLOQUIU
SECULAR SPIRITUALITY: PASSIONATE JOURNEY TO A
6eme CONGRES FEDER. INTERN. des JUIFS
Sherwin T. Wine

In each of us lies the seed of courage.

Our task is to nourish it

in every moment of our lives.

When we confront the unknown,

when we stand [in] defiance of hate,

disease, and poverty,

our possibility is expressed through the thoughtful

bravery that transcends mere boldness.

To fear is humanly normal.

To conquer fear is humanly noble.

Sherwin Wine

response

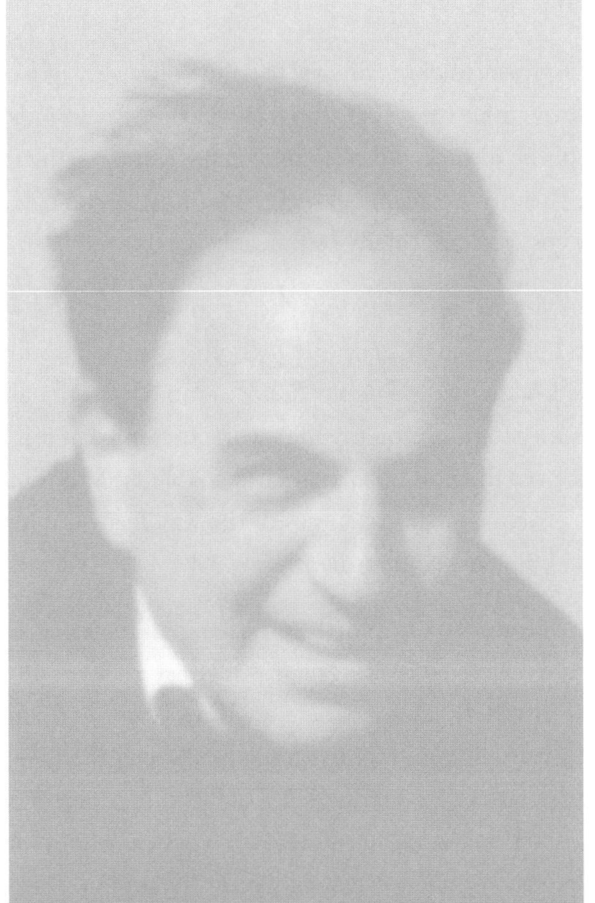

Reflections

Sherwin T. Wine

Reading the story of my life—as seen through the eyes of friends and colleagues—gives me both pleasure and embarrassment. It is wonderful to know that people you admire acknowledge the work that you have done. But becoming the focus of praise and applause can be uncomfortable, especially when you are accustomed to making others the center of attention.

My life has been devoted to growing a movement called Humanistic Judaism. "My" success has always meant "our" success. None of the achievements of our movement would have been possible without the gifts of talent, courage, and devotion of hundreds of "believers," including many of the people who contributed to this book.

One of the greatest pleasures of my life has been the discovery of a community of "believers" throughout the world who have become my friends and co-workers. It was one of the unexpected consequences of pursuing my ideological dream. Among these good friends are Dan Cohn-Sherbok, Harry Cook, and Marilyn Rowens, who are chiefly responsible for this publication.

When Harry Cook first volunteered to write my biography, and when Dan Cohn-Sherbok first proposed this *festschrift* tribute, I was not aware of how important this undertaking would be for me. Responding to the essays has given me an opportunity to reflect on my life's work and on what it is that I believe. Looking back over the past forty years has enabled me to remember the challenges that provoked major changes in the way I saw my Jewish identity and my growing humanist commitment.

My life, like that of most Jews in North America, had its roots in the Ashkenazic nation, in the Yiddish-speaking world of Eastern Europe. My immigrant parents were intensely Jewish. Their Jewishness was both ethnic and religious—and they were not able to distinguish between the two. My father was *halakhically* disposed, but the struggle for survival in America compromised his Jewish satisfactions. A kosher home, no work or school on the holidays, and regular Shabbat attendance at synagogue services in a Conservative shul defined the modern traditional format our family accepted.

Beyond my family existed the Jewish "ghetto" of Detroit, with its bakeries, butcher shops, grocery stores, and public schools. My high school was more than 90 percent Jewish. I could easily have come to believe, like my mother, that most of the people in the world were Jewish. When Rosh Hashana came to Central High School, it was like Christmas in Grosse Pointe.

The Jews in my neighborhood in westside Detroit came in many varieties. There were the bearded Orthodox, whose rejecting children never imagined that eighty years later beards would return with a vengeance. There were the hardworking laborers and merchants who struggled to confront the dangers of the Depression and who found comfort and community in the *davening* world of the local synagogue. There was a sprinkling of German Jews who viewed the "Russian" world with contempt and who found refuge and separation in their Greek Revival temple. There were nationalists and Zionists, reinforced by Hitler hatred, who were fired up by the ideas of Jewish Palestine and *aliya*, but who never succumbed to their passion for pioneering. There were the socialists and communists, often infused with a fanatic secularism, who papered their kitchen floors with either the *Forwerts* or the *Morgen Freihait*. There were the ambitious immigrants and their children who dreamed of fleeing the ghetto and finding success and power in the Gentile world outside. My childhood "ghetto" was rich in Jewish diversity, Jewish anxiety, and Jewish hope. We even had our "Cossacks": Henry Ford and Charles Coughlin.

I loved the intensity and intellectual passions of this world. But I sometimes wearied of the anxiety, which manifested itself in high-decibel living and arguing with no real issues. I sometimes found the sense of vulnerability uncomfortable, especially when it manifested itself in ego-boosting exaggerations. My Hebrew school—and my Sunday school—were filled with claims that we Jews had invented everything from love and social justice to democracy and science. Even when I left the ghetto, these exaggerations persisted. I did not always enjoy being part of a people too needy to face reality. But I thoroughly enjoyed being part of a "race" whose intellectual and economic achievements had aroused the admiration and envy of the world. I often wondered whether Jews could develop a realistic perspective of themselves without the distortions that the threat of antisemitism conferred.

> One of the greatest pleasures of my life has been the discovery of a community of "believers" throughout the world who have become my friends and co-workers.

One of my roots is the Anglo-Saxon world of American culture. My ghetto was Jewish, but my public school teachers, my librarians, my department store clerks, my movie stars, and my language were WASP. I have always valued growing up in America, despite the challenges of the Depression and antisemitism. I liked the calm, the good manners, and the understatement of the Anglo-Saxon world. I also admired the political environment of freedom and opportunity that had its roots in the liberal democracy developed by the English and their American descendants. I do not think that Humanistic Judaism, with its affirmation of human dignity, would have been possible without the setting of America.

My humanistic connections lie deep in my life. They emerged when I was in high school and were refined by my philosophy major at the University of Michigan. I was, in particular, taken by the British empiricists. The idea that truth should be responsible to evidence lies at the foundation of my belief system. I have never been enamored with eternal truths. I have no difficulty living with uncertainty and change. And I would be humiliated to think I would accept an answer to a question simply because it made me feel good. Confronting unpleasant facts is for me the ultimate test of reason. Both liberals and conservatives jump at answers they want to be true.

My choice of the rabbinate seemed bizarre to many of the people who knew me at school. How could an "imperial naturalist" choose to spend time with God? While university teaching in philosophy or history was appealing to me, being the leader of a "philosophic" community was even more appealing to me. I liked the idea of serving families over a long period of time, providing them with both inspiration and information. I enjoyed the poetry of celebration and found that the classroom did not satisfy my aesthetic needs. The closest profession to what I wanted to do with my life was the clergy—and I wasn't going to allow a trivial issue about "believing in God" to prevent me from choosing the clergy, especially since liberal religion had already given permission to everybody to define God in whatever way he wanted to. In a secular age, thousands of smart and talented secular people avoided the clergy because they felt they could not live with God or prayer. Their reluctance deprived hundreds of thousands of liberal people of the best philosophic guidance and counseling that was available to them. The world of religion was left to the second best.

Choosing the rabbinate was a wise choice for me. I have enjoyed rabbinic work since I began this professional adventure, whether I am teaching, counseling, lecturing, or celebrating. I am happy that I was not "called" to the profession like Amos or Jeremiah. I am wary of people who assume roles of power and deny that they want them.

Of course I chose the Reform rabbinate. It was the most liberal option available. At the Hebrew Union College, the Reform school in Cincinnati, I discovered that more than half of the student body were humanists. They proceeded to do what I did—define God in a naturalistic way. For me God became the embodiment of the "ideal man." It certainly was a far-fetched redo of what the word "God" meant in popular parlance. But I was comfortable with my creativity, and I was serving Jews who were interested in being Jewish, but who were not very interested in God.

I am delighted that I went to the Hebrew Union College before the days of the "Great Awakening," which has transformed Reform rabbis into poor imitations of *halakhic* sages. The balance and uniqueness of Reform are gone. They have been swept away in the new frenzy to sacrifice everything for "Jewishness," including truth. When I was at the college, ideology had not yet become the slave of what was perceived to be essential to Jewish survival. Skepticism, rather than faith, was fashionable. The new mystics had not yet arrived. It was a comfortable place for a humanist to study.

I am happy that I was not "called" to the profession like Amos or Jeremiah. I am wary of people who assume roles of power and deny that they want them.

My first seven years in the active rabbinate were problematic. I realized that, for most Jews, "Jewishness," and not truth, was their primary concern in Jewish settings. I spent two years as an army chaplain in Korea. I loved being in East Asia, despite the discomforts. I enjoyed the exposure to segments of the American population I had not known before. I felt fulfilled serving the needs of Jewish men and women exiled from home. But I became aware that Jews, on the whole, preferred salami to prayer, no matter how many rabbinic tirades against "gastronomic Judaism" were delivered. Now, there is nothing wrong with kosher salami. But most Jews no longer saw Judaism as the place where their primary philosophy of life had its roots. The university and the secular world were the settings for that exploration.

When I returned to Detroit and found myself in the functioning world of Reform Judaism—first as the assistant rabbi at a big old temple and then as the organizing rabbi of a small new congregation—I enjoyed my success. But I became increasingly uncomfortable with the intellectual vacuity of it all and with the rationalization about God I had offered myself when I entered rabbinic training. I found the discrepancy between the symbols of Reform Judaism and the obvious beliefs of its members to be more than annoying. Making the Torah the central symbol of Reform even when the Torah lifestyle had vanished from the lives of Reform Jews lacked integrity in my eyes. I wanted an environment where conviction, not symbols, counted. A tenuous continuity, without integrity, was not enough to fire up my rabbinate.

In 1963 I made the break. Friends seeking to establish a new "Reform" congregation in suburban Detroit offered me the opportunity to lead, and not to follow. Within the first year of the existence of the new congregation we had laid the foundation of a new movement in Jewish life and we had given it a name—Humanistic Judaism. We faced many challenges. The most pressing one was the intense hostility we experienced in the Jewish community when we went public with our ideology. We thought that we were simply giving voice to what most Jews believed. We discovered that they viewed our role differently. Ironically, our emergence triggered a rare opportunity for the Jewish world in America to discuss an issue of personal philosophy, rather than the usual unresolved discussions about Jewish identity and Jewish survival.

The evolution of Humanistic Judaism—both in the Birmingham Temple and in the new communities that followed—is the story of confronting challenges other than hostility. I discovered that while I did not like or seek out rejection, I could live with large amounts of it so long as I felt useful and supported by friends. Hostility did not diminish my optimism. It only made me more determined to succeed. I was particularly amused by the fact that the most hostile people were not the Orthodox, but rather Reform rabbis. Orthodox leaders sometimes applauded our honesty in contrast to the religious pretensions of the liberals. But the liberal religionists were threatened by the fact that we were saying out loud what many of their own congregants really believed.

Yet my greatest anxieties were directed to more substantial challenges—philosophic and pragmatic. These challenges are still around. They help to mold the character and direction of our movement. Some of these challenges appear in the wonderful essays that were contributed to this work.

I want to deal with each of these challenges, one by one.

ATHEISM

In North America, atheism is a problematic allegiance. Even if you call yourself an "agnostic" or a "humanist," living your life publicly without God is a provocation. Everything from immorality to hedonism is attached to this ideology. In Europe, atheism is widespread and even, in many circles, fashionable. Religious people are sometimes regarded as eccentric—but not in America, where religious affiliation confers respectability and where Christian fundamentalism has its homeland.

From the very beginning, Humanistic Judaism had to deal with the accusation that it was atheistic. For the enemies of our movement this assault was the most popular. The "God" issue was the primary focus of those who hated us. "How can you be Jewish if you do not believe in God?" "How can you be ethical if there is no divine authority?" "How can you explain the existence of the universe without God?" The God questions were always there in the forefront, even though the God issue was not the central question of Humanistic Judaism. From the beginning we faced this hostility and anxiety, even from people who did not believe in God but who felt vulnerable saying so.

There are different kinds of atheism. The most popular kind is "ontological" atheism, a firm denial that there is any creator or manager of the universe. There is "ethical" atheism, a firm conviction that, even if there is a creator/manager of the world, he does not run things in accordance with the human moral agenda, rewarding the good and punishing the wicked. There is "existential" atheism, a nervy assertion that even if there is a God, he has no authority to be the boss of my life. There is "agnostic" atheism, a cautious denial that claims that God's existence can be neither proven nor disproven; this type of atheist ends up with behavior no different from that of the ontological atheist. There is "ignostic" atheism, another cautious denial, which claims that the word "God" is so confusing that it is meaningless; this belief, again, translates into the same behavior as the ontological atheist. There is "pragmatic" atheism, which regards God as irrelevant to ethical and successful living, and which views all discussions about God as a waste of time.

Most Humanistic Jews are "atheists" in one of these senses. But for all Humanistic Jews, atheism is not at the heart of their belief system, especially in a liberal theological world where the word "God" can mean anything you want it to mean. At the heart of Humanistic Judaism is a positive answer to the central question of all historic religions and pragmatic philosophies: Where do we find the source of power, strength, and wisdom to cope with the problems of life? The central focus of humanism is people and the forces of the natural world. We are not Atheistic Judaism. We are Humanistic Judaism.

Refocusing the challenger—and sometimes even our own adherents—is a formidable job that never goes away.

JEWISHNESS AND TRUTH

The greatest challenge to Humanistic Judaism has been the indifference of most Jews to matters of belief and philosophic consistency. What they believe and what they do as Jews have no connection with each other. One is the pursuit of truth; the other is family loyalty.

Humanistic Judaism is only of interest to Jews who are interested in the world of ideas. If the words you say in Jewish celebrations are only a matter of tribal allegiance, then what you say is of no consequence as long as it is perceived as Jewish. How many times have I been invited to recite the traditional Kaddish by atheists who are annoyed by my refusal to do so! For them the words of the Kaddish have nothing at all to do with truth. It is just a way loyal Jews express their loyalty to the dead.

There was a time when things were different, when the truth and Jewishness went together. In pre-Enlightenment days, during the many centuries of the Age of Faith, the words of the Bible and the prayer book corresponded to what most Jews really believed. The recitation of prayers featured passion and fervor because the ideas behind the words struck chords of belief that gave the experience the virtue of integrity. Belief and loyalty went together.

Today a clear dichotomy exists. The Enlightenment and secular education have eroded the core of traditional belief. Today all that remains, for most Jews, are the words. Most Jews are reluctant to change the words, even if these Jews are very secular, because they want to say what their ancestors said. They do not want to engage in philosophical speculation. They do not want to fit their Jewish experience into their belief system. They just want to feel connected. That is all they have time for. Religion is an act of ancestral loyalty. It has nothing to do with personal conviction.

Even if you call yourself an "agnostic" or a "humanist," living your life publicly without God is a provocation.

My experience is that ancestral loyalty, not personal conviction, sustains most Jewish religious communities today. The dichotomy is acceptable because the words are Hebrew and the worshiper is reciting nonsense syllables, or the words are rote recitations that repetition has turned into nonsense syllables. Often, the sound of Hebrew is enough to convey roots and to evoke tears.

Our humanistic road is a much harder road to travel. It takes time, introspection, and endless dialogue. It features the painful experience of having to reject familiar words because they do not correspond to convictions and the exhausting search for alternatives that provide integrity. It forces people to explain why they are different and to justify their difference. Most Jews are not willing to invest the time and energy that such a transformation would require. For those of us who have traveled this difficult road, the rewards are astonishing, the experience is liberating. But then, we are interested in the world of ideas.

KOSHERIZING

When I was a rabbi in the Reform movement I was impressed by how much time we spent proving that what we taught was ultimately consistent with the Torah. Preaching was built on the premise that every Torah verse could yield a Reform conclusion—and that the underlying principles of the Torah were essentially the basic principles of Reform Judaism. We struggled to find Torah quotations that would back up conclusions that we had already arrived at through our own personal reason. We were the desperate victims of a liberal religious disease called "kosherizing."

The Reform movement was a radical departure from rabbinic Judaism, and certainly from the priestly Judaism that preceded it. It rejected authoritarian religion and appealed to reason as the ultimate criterion of truth. It abandoned most of the "ritual" requirements of both the Torah and the Talmud. In time it embraced "progressive revelation," which placed the Torah at the beginning of a long line of developing wisdom. But it did not escape the disease of "kosherizing"—the desperate need to find the approval of the Torah. In the end, Reform chose the Torah as the central symbol of its "religious faith," just as its Orthodox rivals had done centuries before.

The ritual of praising the Torah and simultaneously distorting the Torah to fit the praise is one of the major reasons I departed from the Reform movement. It was an ethical issue. I believed that the writers of the Torah were entitled to be heard in the way they intended to be heard. They were not mouthpieces for succeeding generations who would use their words to say what the writers did not intend. If the Torah is a fallible human creation—and even Reform conceded that—then it does not have to pretend to be the be-all and end-all of wisdom. It does not have to be exploited to confer divine authority. It can be important Jewish literature reflecting the times in which it was created. It can be an open door to listening to and understanding the Jews who lived in those centuries. Are not the dead entitled to have a voice? Or is the Torah commentary a form of ventriloquism where the dead say what we want them to say and then we turn around and pretend to revere our puppets?

This struggle is endless. There are many Humanistic Jews who want to be "kosherized" by the past, who want to feel that our ancestors were essentially humanist, who want the Torah to be a humanistic document. But becoming a Humanistic Jew is an act of liberation, freedom from needing the approval of the past in order to understand the past. The Torah as a symbol of Jewish literature is appropriate. The Torah as a symbol of humanism is not.

We need to avoid the dilemma of Reform and all other liberal religious movements. If the Torah is the heart of Judaism, then we have handed over our own authority to the Orthodox. As everybody knows, only they really obey these voices of the past. That mis-chosen symbol now becomes the vehicle of "returning" Reform to what it never was.

For those of us who have traveled this difficult road, the rewards are astonishing, the experience is liberating. But then, we are interested in the world of ideas.

RELIGION

Shimon Dubnow, the first great secular Jewish historian, and Mordecai Kaplan, the founder of the Reconstructionist movement, performed an important service for us. Looking at Judaism, they denied that it was the religion of the Jews. Preferring a broader definition, they chose to define it as the "culture and civilization" of the Jewish people. Their definition is a comfortable one for us as Humanistic Jews.

But, in North America, Judaism means religion to the overwhelming majority of Jews and non-Jews. That definition is comparatively new. For most of Jewish history the Jews were viewed as a nation, not a religious denomination. Initially there was great diversity of religious belief and practice. Polytheists and monotheists shared Jewish identity. Many Jews may have deplored the religious behavior of their Jewish neighbors, but they never denied their Jewish identity. When priestly and rabbinic Judaism appeared, the clerical leaders demanded behavioral conformity, but they never defined Jewish identity by religious behavior. According to the Talmudic rabbis, Jewish identity is a matter of birth, an issue of maternal descent. The criterion is "racial," not religious. Throughout the Middle Ages, the Jews functioned as an alien nation in both the Christian and the Muslim worlds. If Judaism encompassed the world of the Jews, it was always more than a religion.

The change goes back 200 years. The emancipation of the Jews at the beginning of the nineteenth century provided a dilemma. Since Jews became citizens of the nations where they lived, they were now confronted with a pressing question. "Can Jews be members of two nations? Can they be both French and Jewish?" The heightened nationalism of the period precluded this option. The price of freedom was that they had to become "Frenchmen of the Jewish faith," even though most Frenchmen still viewed Jews as a "race."

The early Reform movement in Western Europe and North America championed the change. Assimilation was desirable and required total patriotism as the price of acceptance. Jews were not analogous to the French and Germans. They corresponded to Catholics and Protestants. Being Jewish was only a matter of religious belief. Once you stopped "believing" or converted, you ceased to be Jewish. Once Cohen and Lipshitz became atheists, they ceased to be Jewish. Since Reform became the dominant form of Judaism in America, the Jews of America accepted it as the norm and enthusiastically supported it. The religious definition of the Jew enhanced their self-image of American patriotism and gave them a sense of security and belonging. From that point on Judaism became a matter of faith, even though unofficial America still saw the Jews as ethnic.

One of the constant assaults by enemies is the question, "How can you be Jewish if you do not believe in God?" The absurdity of excluding Einstein, Freud, and Herzl seems to escape them. Even Zionism and Israel cannot change their perception. In recent years, however, many Jews who have lost their theological convictions have been identified in North America as "cultural."

This change coincides with another change. During the Vietnam War, the Supreme Court ruled that it was possible to be religious without believing in God. Strong ethical convictions were an appropriate substitute for theistic beliefs when claiming conscientious objector status. All of this development was preceded in liberal circles by the emergence of a concept of a nontheistic religion. Ethical Culture laid claim to that distinction. In recent decades the phenomenon of Eastern religion has presented us with the concept of an "atheistic Buddhism." This broader definition of religion includes any philosophy of life that features community and ceremonial life. Just as the cultural definition of the Jew and Judaism has achieved acceptance, the acceptance of Humanistic Judaism as a religion is also in the works.

Are the two designations compatible? Of course. Judaism remains the culture of the Jewish people. Within that culture there are many philosophies of life, including humanism. Any philosophy of life that features community and a ceremonial life is a religion. Humanistic Judaism qualifies on both counts. If nontheistic approaches to life become increasingly accepted as religious, however, old-line secularists will have a fit. But the opportunities for dialogue and acceptance are irresistible.

> Is the Torah commentary a form of ventriloquism where the dead say what we want them to say and then we turn around and pretend to revere our puppets?

OLD SECULARISM

Some of our fiercest critics did not come from the religious side. They were the secular survivors of a century-old movement that had pioneered the way for Humanistic Judaism. They were devotees of Jewish culture. They were lovers of Jewish languages, turning Yiddish into a literary language and Hebrew into a spoken one. They were the creators of Jewish music and Jewish poetry who found nothing more wonderful than organizing reading circles where Jewish books, Jewish history, and Jewish politics were heatedly discussed. They were the passionate workers of an idealistic socialism that produced armies of strikers and demonstrators to fight for equality. They were the drainers of swamps and the builders of cities who transformed a problematic territory into a homeland.

Secular Jewish nationalism became the most powerful Jewish movement in the Jewish world in the twentieth century. In response to both the Enlightenment and antisemitism, the nationalists crafted a powerful Jewish identity that saw the Jews as a nation and not as a religious denomination. Jewishness lay in speaking Jewish languages and celebrating Jewish culture, not in praying, attending synagogue, or studying religious texts. Like many of its European counterparts, Jewish nationalism championed a militant anticlericalism that saw religious institutions and clergy as enemies of progress and emancipation. This "old secularism" went out of its way to avoid any activity, any profession, or any building that could be connected in any way with the old religion. Only a powerful break with the "superstitions" of the past could yield the "new Jew." For many of them, Judaism was a designation of religion. They were more comfortable with "Jewishness."

Humanistic Judaism rests on the old secularism. But it is different from it. If secular nationalism was a "first-wave" cultural Judaism, then Humanistic Judaism is the "second wave." Old-line secularists see no value in creating congregations and training rabbis. They are uncomfortable with "services" and "spirituality." They feel betrayed by viewing a secular Jewishness as a fifth denomination in the spectrum of Judaism. They want the distinction between secularism and religion to be clear and the boundaries to be wide. The new search for personal fulfillment and self-actualization leaves them bewildered. They are not quite sure how that fits into the struggle for creating and maintaining a strong national culture. The old nationalism always asked the collectivist question, "What have you done lately for the Jewish people?" It rarely asked the individualist question, "What have the Jewish people done for me?"

The old secularism had its roots in the poverty and preservation of Eastern Europe. The new humanism emerges from the new freedom and ambitiousness of North America. In America religion is powerful, but no single religious hierarchy dominates public life. Religion is part of the free enterprise system of choice. And liberal religion has adopted a secular agenda of ethics and personal fulfillment. America is a very different environment from the old Eastern Europe and the old Israel. But the new Eastern Europe, and especially the new Israel, are changing in the American direction.

When Humanistic Judaism began, many old-time secularists viewed it negatively. While some of our critics called us "atheists," old-time secularists called us "too religious." They equated congregations, rabbis, and services with theistic religion. They saw the project of developing a personal philosophy of life as a silly diversion from the primary task of learning Jewish languages and participating in Jewish culture. They prided themselves on the purity of their secularism. Some of them joined Humanistic Jewish communities and wanted them to be like old-line secularist reading circles and schools.

The old secularism had its roots in the poverty and preservation of Eastern Europe. The new humanism emerges from the new freedom and ambitiousness of North America.

But Humanistic Judaism regards this approach as no longer useful. While many institutions in the old authoritarian religion were harmful, not all of them were. Congregations and rabbis were useful inventions. Secular Jews need full-service communities, and they need trained leaders who can respond not only to their Jewish cultural needs but especially to their human needs for coping with the human condition. Suffering and death are also Jewish. Struggling for happiness is also Jewish. In many ways Humanistic congregations function in the lives of their members in the same way as Reform, Conservative, and Reconstructionist synagogues do. They provide the same services, ask the same questions—even though they provide different answers. We are part of the Jewish spectrum. We have a right to sit at the center table, not a peripheral table of our own creation.

The old-line secularists are fading away, even in Israel. Their grandchildren find the old nationalism wanting, too impersonal and too collectivist. They are searching for paths to personal happiness and even "spirituality." They are not caught up in the arguments and slogans of the secular past. Humanistic Judaism will never be fully compatible for old-time secularists. But it may be comfortable for their grandchildren and great-grandchildren.

"JEWISH HUMANISM"

Are we "humanistic Jews" or "Jewish humanists"? That question appeared very early in our development and remains persistent. We have two powerful connections—one Jewish and one humanistic. Which is primary? Or are they both of equal significance?

The people who join our movement have minds of their own. They do not easily fit into formulas that we may choose to create. Most people who join want to find a way to live their lives Jewishly with integrity. Others who enter our movement enjoy Jewish culture but the message of humanism is what motivates them to stay. Both groups are legitimate parts of our movement. Frequently, in the case of intermarriage, the non-Jewish partner will be a humanist. (We designate these couples as intercultural rather than interfaith.) If the humanist partner joins the community, the humanism generally will be of greater interest to him than the Judaism, though I know of many cases where non-Jews are enamored of Jewish culture and want to be part of a Jewish community.

Frequently people who are members of humanist groups will challenge me. They want to know why our communities have this parochial interest in

Jewish culture when they should be promoting a universal humanism. They claim that our Jewish loyalty diminishes or is incompatible with humanism.

From the beginning we have been Humanistic Jews, rooted in the history and culture of the Jewish people. Our humanism has always been enhanced by our Jewish connection, because the message of Jewish experience is that we cannot rely on the kindliness of the fates. Most of us are humanists because the memories of Jewish history are "in our bones." The rabbinic establishment may have told us that we are the Chosen People. But our memories tell us that we are the victims of a cruel destiny. If the Jewish people survived, it was only because of human self-reliance, courage, and cooperation. Our survival is a tribute to people power.

We are part of the Jewish world. Even when other Jews do not share our philosophy of life, they share our culture—and we share the social fate to which all Jews are subjected when society is in turmoil. Judaism has evolved over many centuries and provides us with roots and with a distinctive place in human culture.

Most cultures and religions accommodate different philosophies of life. Christianity, even if it did not begin as a nation, has roots in the Greco-Roman world, which embraced and molded its teachings. In many ways it has its own culture, independent of any specific ideology. In modern times, the battle over the Enlightenment has splintered the church into many ideological factions. Like Judaism, it has become a culture with great ideological diversity.

If the Jewish people survived, it was only because of human self-reliance, courage, and cooperation. Our survival is a tribute to people power.

The main divide in religion today is between the humanists who explicitly embrace the Enlightenment and the fundamentalists who reject it. In the middle lie the overwhelming majority of adherents who linger in the limbo of confusion and ambivalence, paying lip service to old creeds they have ceased to believe in and feeling apprehensive about change. Humanistic Christians find it easier to talk to Humanistic Jews than to talk to fundamentalist Christians (witness Ron Modras and Harry Cook). Humanistic Jews find it easier to talk to humanistic Christians than to converse with Orthodox Jews. The ideological divide is no longer "vertical," following the old religious divide (Jew/Christian/Muslim/Buddhist). The ideological divide is "horizontal," crossing through the middle of all religions and cultures, splitting each group into liberals and conservatives, humanists and traditional theists.

Traditional theists, whether they be Jewish, Christian, or Muslim, share the same kind of salvation connections. Sin and repentance, reward and punishment, the afterlife and Messianic rescue are fundamental to all of them. Liberal religionists have a secular "thisworldly" focus with a strong emphasis on a compassionate ethics. The two ideologies are incompatible. But they exist in the same cultural and "religious" system. For most people the cultural system is primary. The ideological system is important but secondary.

Most humanists who choose affiliation will be Humanistic Jews or humanistic Christians or humanistic Buddhists. Some will choose groups with strong ideologies but shallow cultural roots. Jewish humanists may be comfortable there. Be we have chosen to be Humanistic Jews.

PEOPLE

Are people an appropriate substitute for God? I get that question all the time. It is usually accompanied by the comment that "If you can't believe in God, you certainly can't believe in people." The hidden premise in that assault is that Humanistic Judaism substitutes people for God. If we do not worship God, then we must worship people.

Mitchell Silver, in his essay, suggests that that is what humanism does. While he is perfectly comfortable being a secular or naturalistic Jew, he is not sure that he would be comfortable being a humanistic Jew. Worshiping man, for him, would be as uncomfortable as worshiping God.

This view of humanism as the worship of man has some basis in the excesses of early humanism. The most strident of the early humanists was the French philosopher August Comte. In addition to developing a somewhat contrived view of human development, especially the development of human thinking, he conceived of something called the Religion of Man. This new religion would discard the metaphysical and theological premises of the past and would place its foundation in the positivist and empirical world of modern science. This transformation would enable man to fulfill the enormous potential he possesses. Reborn man now becomes the focus of celebration and even adoration. Comte imagined that by the end of the nineteenth century, Notre Dame de Paris would be converted into the cathedral of the Religion of Man.

Of course, this absurd scenario is pure Comte, who was such a colossal failure that he was supported for a good part of his life by the generosity of the English humanist philosopher John Stuart Mill. Mill wrote about a humanistic religion. But he lacked the pretensions of Comte.

The reality is that the Comtian excess is atypical of humanism and humanist writers. Once the flamboyance of the French departs, more sober English and American philosophers follow. For a true empiricist, worship of any kind is absurd. In a world of tentative answers and no perfection, reverence is ludicrous. In the real world, godlike men do not exist. The human condition is one of struggle and limitation, every seeming progress leading to more problems. Humans are certainly far more than dust and ashes. But they certainly are not God.

In a world of tentative answers and no perfection, reverence is ludicrous. In the real world, godlike men do not exist.

In the world of twentieth-century humanism, human power is seen as limited and human nature as morally ambiguous. The only seeming deviation is when Sartre (who is reluctant to call himself a humanist) describes the project of man as becoming God. Sartre means by this that, like God, man should assume full responsibility for all his actions and that no fixed human nature limits human ambition. But, barring the Sartrian excess, the humanist world is fairly sober.

For contemporary humanism, eliminating God requires no substitute. God is a harmful idea because it provokes worship and then obedience. It conjures up the categories of the sacred and the holy and discourages skepticism. Having eliminated God, humanists want no substitute for it.

Humanism has no object of worship. It simply encourages people to confront the human condition with whatever limited knowledge and power that they have. Above all, there are no guarantees. The Messianic pretensions of Marx with all their assurances of happy endings are no longer sustainable.

Humanists learn from experience. They are empiricists. They want no authoritarian government claiming perfection either on earth or in heaven. But neither do they want a slavish man who discourages his desires and denies his power. The ideal is somewhere in between. The choice of the word "humanistic" for our movement was to express this ideal. The basic power for solving human problems, however limited, lies within human beings. It is our job not to exaggerate or demean our power, but to discover it.

LEGACY

One of the sources of Jewish pride in modern times is that we believe we invented monotheism. You often hear that the greatest gift of Jews to the world is the idea of the "one God." Even a secularist like Abba Eban, when he wrote his history of the Jews, made that statement.

Well, if monotheism is the greatest contribution of the Jews to humanity, Humanistic Judaism seems to have blown up the pillar of Jewish significance. If Jews derive their sense of importance from their connection to God, we may be guilty of destroying Jewish self-esteem. In North America, where this claim circulates heavily in the interfaith banquet scene, monotheism is touted as our special gift. And there have been many times at public lectures when members of the audience have accosted me on this issue.

There are two kinds of monotheism. One is philosophic monotheism. Plato and Aristotle, philosophers of ancient Greece, had already arrived at monotheism in the fourth century B.C.E. For Plato it was the Good; for Aristotle it was the First Mover. In either case, it was universal, with no revelations or worship attached. The other kind of monotheism is cultic monotheism. A particular god is elevated by his priests and devotees to the status of supreme god, so supreme that lesser gods can no longer be considered to be gods. In fourteenth-century-B.C.E. Egypt, Atun was so elevated by the Pharaoh Akhnaton. In sixth-century-B.C.E. Persia, Mazda received a similar honor. In sixth-century-B.C.E. Judea, Jahweh was raised to supreme status by some of his prophets.

In all cases of cultic monotheism, access to the one God is only possible through his cult and through his name. Jewish monotheism is not universal monotheism. It is particularistic. If you call the one God by the name of Atun or Mazda you cannot receive the benefits of his power.

Monotheism, as a doctrine, is a heavenly counterpart to an earthly political development. World empires feature world gods. The world emperor ultimately yields a world god. The Persian "king of kings" derives his authority from "the king of the king of kings." When world empires appear, monotheism appears, whether in Assyria, Egypt, or Persia.

For contemporary humanism, eliminating God requires no substitute. Humanism has no object of worship.

Traditional Jews trace monotheism back to Abraham in the eighteenth century B.C.E., giving him a head start on all rival claims. But modern historical scholarship renders Abraham a mythical figure and pushes the origin of Jewish monotheism forward to the seventh or sixth century B.C.E. If that is true, the Egyptians have won the sweepstakes.

But the "Who did monotheism first?" question is a less interesting focus than "Why is monotheism so terrific?"

Once you accept the validity of the God hypothesis, one god is no more rational than many gods. In the corporate and scientific worlds, teams and committees are generally more effective than single individuals operating alone. A committee of cooperating gods is no less effective than a single divine dictator. In fact, a single divine dictator deprives you of options. In a polytheistic world, if you are dissatisfied with the performance of one god, you can always choose another. This freedom lies at the foundation of a free society. But with a single divine authority, you are stuck with his dictatorship. You do not even have the privilege of complaining about his ineffectiveness. You are compelled, in order to save his reputation, to apologize for him and to call his injustice a mystery.

The God hypothesis, whether polytheistic or monotheistic, adds no useful information about how to deal successfully with the world we live in. But if you are already making choices within the system, a decentralized polytheism gives you greater opportunities for freedom and dignity.

The greatest gift of the Jewish people to the world is not monotheism. It is the transformation of a territorial nation into a Diaspora world people. In a modern secular world, where national boundaries have become increasingly irrelevant and where technology will make mobility universal, the Jewish model will be a paradigm for the future of all nations. The state of Israel is wonderful. But it would be ordinary without its Diaspora. It is the Jewish people, not God, which is extraordinary.

BALANCING ACT

Life is juggling incompatible agendas. From the moment we are born, we discover that desire presents no single goal. It taunts us with having to make choices. We would love to "have our cake and eat it," but reality intrudes.

Every day we struggle with how much to give to "me" and how much to give to others. The prudential pursuit of my welfare is not always compatible with the ethical pursuit of the welfare of others. Between being a sociopath and a martyr doormat, there is a wide range of options. Finding an appropriate balance is a personal choice without fixed formulas.

In addition to the prudentially ethical balancing act, there are two balancing acts that consume a lot of time in Humanistic Judaism. Their challenge has existed from the very beginning of our movement.

The first is the balancing act between the past and the present, between tradition and creativity, between continuity and integrity. How can I be fully Jewish if I do not feel deeply connected to the culture of my past? But how can I feel honest if I am forced to say words and use literature that does not completely fit what I believe as a humanist? This balancing act is one of the hardest we have to engineer. Some people favor continuity over integrity. Others favor integrity over continuity.

The Reform movement has opted for continuity. The choice of the Torah as the symbol of Reform belief and commitment is problematic from the integrity perspective. The Reconstructionist movement, with its humanist ideology, has made a similar choice. Turning the Torah and the prayer book into humanist documents requires intellectual and philosophic acrobatics that defy reason. But continuity is the reward. For Mordecai Kaplan, continuity was a supreme value. The integrity of words was important, but far less important.

> The state of Israel is wonderful. But it would be ordinary without its Diaspora.

Rabbi Chalom raises this issue in this book with regard to Humanistic Judaism. Have we not in the past pursued integrity at the expense of continuity? And do we not now need to adjust the balance in order to strengthen our Jewish roots? My response is, of course, yes. The balancing act never ends. But for us, integrity always takes priority over continuity. That is a fundamental difference between Humanistic Judaism and its liberal opposition in Reform and Reconstructionism. If the occasion is celebratory of what we believe in, then integrity prevails. If the occasion is educational, then there are no boundaries. We simply want to listen to what our Jewish brothers and sisters have to say. I suspect that when we celebrate, the overwhelming majority of the prose and poetry will continue to be contemporary, simply because there are not many traditional texts that pass our test of integrity. The best way to introduce our members to the Jewish past is through the educational format.

The second balancing act is between Jewish and non-Jewish wisdom. As Humanistic Jews we do not believe that all wisdom necessary for human survival and happiness is contained in the Torah or in the sacred texts of traditional Judaism—not even in the contemporary texts of the secular Jewish world. Most of the great humanist philosophy extant today was created by non-Jews, whether they be prose writers or poets. Epicurus, Lucretius, Omar Khayyam, John Stuart Mill, Bertrand Russell, John Dewey, and Albert Camus (among hundreds of others) speak truths that we need to hear. Translating them into Hebrew will not make them Jewish.

If our commitment were to Jewish culture alone, then the wisdom of non-Jews could be legitimately excluded. But if our commitment is also to a humanistic philosophy of life, then such an exclusion is harmful. Our Jewish identity is overwhelmingly important. And so are the humanist resources within Jewish culture. But we cannot be fully developed human beings if we cannot dip into the pool of universal creativity for inspiration.

"FLESH ON THE BONES"

Ideology is never enough for a philosophic or religious movement. It needs to be translated into activity. Some of that activity is prudential, connected to personal development. Some of that activity is ethical. And some of that action is celebratory, strengthening the community through art, music, and literature. Holidays become the special times for celebration.

Our ideology, from the beginning, eliminated the use of traditional formats and traditional liturgies. Prayer and *davening* were out. Elaborate readings from the Torah were out. Lectures were fine as an educational component, but not enough. We were constrained by a very demanding principle. We were not prepared to say anything that we did not believe. We were literally starting from scratch.

In this book, Judith Goren has vividly described the early history of the Ritual Committee of the Birmingham Temple. It was exciting to be pioneers. But it was a daunting challenge to invent a new format for Jewish celebration, a format that would be rooted in the past but that would simultaneously be faithful to what we believed. We faced one more demand. Since the ideology was new, the celebrations needed to explicitly reinforce the principles we had chosen. There had to be a certain didactic element to the celebrations so that members could receive words to frame and dramatize their convictions, and prospective members could easily understand what we were about.

While there were some humanistic selections from biblical and rabbinic literature that could be read or sung, the overwhelming majority of available celebration material that was appropriate was contemporary. The poets and songwriters of modern Israel, with their strong secular and humanistic convictions, were a favorite source of inspiration. We used them often and effectively. We also used our own words extensively. We had the right to participate in the creation of Jewish literature—a literature that would clearly and explicitly reflect what we believed and felt.

> Ideology is never enough for a philosophic or religious movement. It needs to be translated into activity.

One of the problems we faced—and still face—is redoing the words of famous Jewish liturgical rubrics. Can you take something as famous and sacred as the Sh'ma and the Kaddish and revise the lyrics? Our initial response was not to do it. It appeared too insulting to traditional sensibilities and too contrived to be taken seriously. We did not want people to be outraged or to laugh. But, as time went on, it was clear that some communities needed this reassurance of continuity. Today several humanistic Sh'mas and Kaddishes circulate in the Humanistic world. They have been well received.

Of all my creations for these new liturgies, my favorite is the song "Ayfo Oree." The words are mine; the music was by Dorian Samuels. I wanted to write short lyrics that would summarize the essence of Humanistic Judaism and its message of personal empowerment and ethical responsibility. "Where is my light? My light is in me. Where is my hope? My hope is in me. Where is my strength? My strength is in me. And in you." It will never make Deuteronomy. But it may help adults and children celebrate our message.

SPIRITUALITY

If there is a word that old-line secularists detest it is "spirituality." The word is connected, in their minds, with the worst excesses of old-time religion, with dealings in the spirit world, and with a deep attachment to the supernatural realm of God. It reeks of piety.

But, in the past four decades, the word has become a favorite among young people, most of whom lead secular lifestyles. The phenomenon of new-age religion produced an abundance of sects and groups who used this word to describe the ultimate experiences of life. Many of these people were theistic. But many of them were essentially secular. This second group did not use this word in any supernatural sense. Rather they were talking about serenity, or extraordinary experiences of empowerment, or inspiring moments of transcendence. By "transcendence" they meant feeling part of something greater than oneself.

During the 1980s Humanistic Judaism confronted the "spirituality" controversy. There were many members of the movement who wanted to use the word and who wanted more "spirituality." The old-line rationalists fussed and fumed and declared the word to be humanistically *trayfe*, or non-kosher. The battle was on; the arguments were fruitless. Neither side really listened to the other. One side imagined an invasion of religious supernaturalists and the other side believed that the opposition was committed to a cold frozen intellectuality.

Since that time, things have calmed down. "Spirituality" is frequently used and the opposition has thrown up its hands in resignation.

While I was not initially comfortable with the word for all the reasons cited above, I saw no reason for driving out secular people who were using the word to describe secular experiences. If they were talking about personal empowerment, what is more humanistic than empowerment, as long as no supernatural or magical force does the empowering? If they are talking about the serenity that comes from stress relief through introspective meditation, what humanist can be opposed to stress relief? And if they are describing a natural sense of transcendence, we need it. We cannot have ethics without feeling part of something greater than ourselves—our family, our community, our nation, humanity. Enlightened self-interest is not enough to ensure ethical behavior. People who are not sociopathic have a strong sense of identification with the groups to which they belong. The welfare of their group may become as important as their own personal welfare.

Even nature offers its opportunities for a natural transcendence. Evolution tells us that we are part of a chain of life that extends back more than four billion years. All the organisms in the world are our "relatives." Even the universe contains the elements out of which all things are made. Scientific knowledge is filled with moments of transcendence.

In the end we need the "hardliners" to keep us from straying into dangerous waters. But we need the romantics to open our eyes to the wonders of the world.

We cannot have ethics without feeling part of something greater than ourselves—our family, our community, our nation, humanity.

INTERMARRIAGE

Intermarriage among ethnic and religious groups is inevitable in a dynamic, secularized, urban society, where mass mobility produces mixing. Mixing and science take the edge off old religions and racial intolerance and produce the world we now live in. In North America more than 50 percent of Jews who choose to marry, marry non-Jews.

For traditionalists this development is disastrous. Gentile mothers will render the children of such unions Gentile. For nationalists this development is equally disastrous. If a child is only half-Jewish his motivation to remain

Jewish will be diminished. It is "bad enough" that a free secular society diminishes an interest in traditional religion and ethnic identity; intermarriage will only aggravate these problems.

No matter what resolutions are preached, no matter what punishments are threatened, no matter how much Jewish education is provided, intermarriage will increase in a free society. Only a return to a repressive and segregated society will reverse the trend. The future in North America and the Diaspora is one with many "half-Jews" and "quarter-Jews" with diverse ethnic and religious backgrounds.

This development raises an ethical and political issue which we, as Humanistic Jews, have had to confront since the beginning of our movement. Over the past forty years, desperation has forced a change in the response of Jewish leaders. The first response was outright condemnation and the refusal to serve the needs of intermarried couples, including marrying them. The second response was disdainful toleration. Intermarriage was condemned, but intermarried couples were reluctantly accepted into congregations with the ultimate expectation of conversion for the Gentile spouse and the "Gentile" children. The third response was the Reform movement declaration that fathers also could confer Jewish identity on their children, solving the problems of child conversion for liberal Jews. The fourth response is the increasing willingness of liberal rabbis to officiate at intermarriage wedding ceremonies and to provide a more welcoming environment in their congregations for intermarried couples.

But there has been only one Jewish movement which, from the beginning, has unequivocally volunteered to serve the needs of intermarried couples without negative judgment and with loving support. That decision was not based on Jewish survival reasons. It may be the case that intermarried couples who are treated with dignity will choose Jewish identity. But even if they do not, their right to be treated with dignity is humanistically obvious. People have a right to marry the people they want. Jews have a right to marry the partners they choose. And Jewish leaders, as ethical leaders, have an obligation to help them if they can. The issue is moral, not narrowly pragmatic.

We certainly knew from the beginning that being nice would enhance the choice of Jewish identity to intermarried couples. But that was not the primary reason. The primary reason was ethical.

A free and open society presents many dilemmas for the Jews. It offers opportunities for dignity and success to individual Jews that a repressive and closed society cannot offer. It has been irresistibly attractive to most Jews. But a free and open society breaks down the barriers between ethnic and religious groups and mixes people, eliminating old identities and forging new ones. Above all, it creates the "autonomous" individual who refuses to be dictated to by any group.

Without the free and open society, neither Reform, Conservative, Reconstructionist, nor Humanistic Judaism would have come into existence. Without the free and open society, most Jews would be enormously unhappy. Without the free and open society, the success of the Jews in all the major professions would never have taken place. But the price is a more chaotic, unstable, ever-changing world. Nothing stands still, including the Jewish people.

> No matter what resolutions are preached, no matter what punishments are threatened, no matter how much Jewish education is provided, intermarriage will increase in a free society.

Moaning about Jewish survival will not change things. Most Jews, whatever their anxieties, will choose the free and open society. All we can do is to serve the Jewish needs of people who want to be Jewish in the best way we know how and to treat all people with the dignity they are entitled to. Things change so fast that we cannot know what will happen in ten or twenty years. But we can take the energy we devote to this useless anxiety over Jewish survival and turn it into training Jews to live productive, ethical, and culturally Jewish lives in a free society.

"RETURN"

There is much talk these days about the "return" of Jews to tradition. Thousands of young Jews have chosen the path of ultra-Orthodoxy, a visible army of black hats, fringes, wigs, and yeshivas. Hasidic sects are flowering and expanding. The Lubavitchers are ubiquitous, raising millions of dollars and taking control of hundreds of Jewish communities. Reform has repudiated its classic beginnings and is running headlong into the arms of the *halakha.* The Kabbala has seized the attention of the Jewish and general public, hungry for mystical opportunities. In the media, the Judaism that now receives the most attention is traditional.

What a surprise! Liberal Jews imagined that all this "superstition" would evaporate before the sun of the Enlightenment. But it did not. It revived with a vengeance and stole the technology and marketing techniques of the secular world to strengthen its own forces.

Many people now accost me and say that the energy of the Jewish and general world is moving in a direction opposite to that of humanism. They see this new development and claim that the future of Humanistic Judaism will only be more uphill.

But reality intrudes. The traditional revival is not a sign of the demise of the secular world. It is a tribute to its success. Modern fundamentalism is a rebellion against the relentless secularization of our entire planet through science, the new technology, secular education, capitalism, and urbanization. It is a protest movement, not a majority movement. A significant minority of people on this planet, even in the Western world, do not like the modern secular world. They do not like the stress of continuous change, personal responsibility, and democratic chaos. They romanticize the past and imagine that their ancestors have the answers to the problems of the human condition. They will not vanish. They will be a chronic thorn in the side of the advancing new world. But they will not take over, even if they choose terrorism. Traditional lifestyles and government by the clergy cannot guarantee jobs and economic security. Whenever they govern in the modern world, they fail. They are only good at being protest movements.

In America the Christian Right is corrupted by compromise. They want to have their cake and eat it, too. They want both the freedom of the consumer society and the stability of traditional societies. But their ranks are filled with the same divorce, alcoholism, abortion, homosexual behavior, child defiance, and female assertiveness that they deplore in their enemies.

Among the Jews, only 5 percent have chosen the traditional lifestyle. Their numbers seem greater because they are so visibly different. Their growth is less through "conversion" than through a spectacular birthrate. As for the new Reform traditionalists and Kabbala lovers, there is no indication that their lifestyles have radically changed. Their ranks still feature major intermarriage and eclectic borrowing from other cultures. The "return" is more intensive hype and periodic dabbling in tradition than it is substance. The new traditional Reform rabbinate is now moving in a direction opposite to that of its laity.

The secularization process will continue and expand because it provides personal power, prosperity, and options that its chronic opposition cannot create. The opposition can only work if it is in opposition.

The traditional revival is not a sign of the demise of the secular world. It is a tribute to its success.

In the coming years the aggressive tactics of the ultra-Orthodox in both Israel and America will produce an unbridgeable dichotomy in Jewish community life. On one side will be the traditional dissenters. On the other side will be the overwhelming majority of the Jews. This majority will, in turn, be divided between those who are ambivalent, embracing the modern world and complaining about it all the time, and those who accept it as the best of all possible available alternatives—a world of stress and change and positive excitement. The second group is our group.

"BELIEVERS"

Most secularists live with the designation of "non-believers." They accept the label their enemies give them. They also live up to the label. When strangers ask them what they believe, they always answer negatively. They prefer to tell others what they do not believe rather than telling them what they do believe. Since "God" is usually associated with "believers," they announce that they "do not believe in God."

Negative answers are never as effective as positive answers. They always define you against the beliefs of others. Your opposition has beliefs. You do not. Having no connections is a weakness; it is also an impossibility. All people act on their understanding of the world, whether they can articulate this understanding or not. But they are easily intimidated into being non-believers, especially when an aggressive majority tells them that they are.

From the beginning, negative answers have dogged our movement. "Non-believers" have nothing positive to offer anybody who follows them. But the reality is that humanists and Humanistic Jews are loaded with beliefs—beliefs about the universe, people, and survival. While they have strong beliefs, they do not have absolute beliefs. Their minds are open to revise their convictions on the basis of new experience and new evidence.

Saying that we do not believe in God is less effective than saying that we believe in people power. Saying that we do not believe in faith is less effective than saying that we believe in reason. Saying that we do not believe in the importance of the Torah does not work as well as saying that we believe in the importance of Jewish literature and Jewish culture. Sometimes negative answers are unavoidable. But they must never become a lifestyle.

Positive answers are personal. They do not establish invidious and assaultive comparisons with others. They strengthen connections because they make us aware of them. They also strengthen self-esteem because we are affirming who we are and not who we are not. With positive answers we feel less vulnerable, less subject to intimidation.

It is important to remember that we are "believers." If there are non-believers, they belong to our opposition. To be a believer requires hard work. We have to stop thinking of ourselves only as a respondent to the opinions of others. We have to look at our behavior and induce the convictions that govern it. We have to sort through all of our negative responses to life and discover what it is that we value, respect, fear, and love. We have to discipline our speech, choosing to avoid assaults on other people's beliefs and calmly accenting our guiding principles.

When you finally get the hang of it, being a believer can give you the dignity you deserve.

CONCLUSION

The foundations of Humanistic Judaism have been established. There are communities and congregations to serve the needs of Humanistic Jews. There is a body of literature to articulate the message. In North America there is the Society for Humanistic Judaism to serve the needs of the communities and to raise their visibility. There is the International Institute for Secular Humanistic Judaism to train rabbis and leaders. There is the International Federation of Secular Humanistic Jews to coordinate the work of our national organizations throughout the world. There is the Leadership Conference of Secular and Humanistic Jews and the Association of Humanistic Rabbis to provide a voice for the professional leaders of our movement. There is recognition by the United Jewish Communities of our place in the Jewish world as a fifth denomination of Judaism. There is the legacy of important leaders and thinkers all over the world, like Shulamit Aloni, Yehuda Bauer, Yaakov Malkin, Albert Memmi, Felix Posen, Egon Friedler, and Dan

"Non-believers" have nothing positive to offer anybody who follows them. But the reality is that humanists and Humanistic Jews are loaded with beliefs—beliefs about the universe, people, and survival.

Friedman to provide inspiration. There are the creative voices of our present and future—Rabbi Tamara Kolton, Rabbi Adam Chalom, Rabbi Miriam Jerris, Rabbi David Oler, Rabbi Binyamin Biber, and Rabbi Peter Schweitzer—to enrich our message. There is the promise of future significant contributions from the students in our rabbinic and leadership training programs who have made a strong commitment to Humanistic Judaism. There is the worldwide humanist movement exemplified in the work of Khoren Arisian, Edd Doerr, Roger Greeley, and Joe Chuman to offer us support. There is the unending devotion of "believers" like Charlie Paul, Helen Forman, Judith Goren, Ruth Feldman, and Michael Prival to emulate.

Above all, there is a large mass of unaffiliated cultural Jews out there who will choose to be Humanistic Jews when they discover that we can serve their needs.

The lifestyle of Humanistic Judaism is the life of courage. In the problematic world of the twenty-first century, that message will be needed.

The International Institute for Secular Humanistic Judaism

Secular Humanistic Judaism embraces a human-centered philosophy that affirms the power and responsibility of individuals to shape their own lives independent of supernatural authority. It maintains that ethics and morality should serve human needs—chiefly the preservation of human dignity and integrity—and that behavior (ritual or otherwise) should reflect belief. Secular Humanistic Jews value their Jewish identity and the aspects of Jewish culture that offer a meaningful connection to the past and a genuine expression of their contemporary way of life. Secular Humanistic Jewish communities celebrate Jewish holidays and life-cycle events (such as weddings and bar and bat mitsvas) with inspirational ceremonies that draw upon, but are not limited to, traditional literature.

Secular Humanistic Judaism is a growing force within North America today. Meeting the needs of those who see a Judaism consistent with their contemporary lifestyle and values, providing a Judaism that is compatible with the secular perspective of young people today, offering a meaningful

way for those who identify themselves as "just Jewish" to celebrate their Jewish identity, providing a welcoming environment for the intermarried to affirm their attachment to Jewish culture and community, creating a path back to Judaism for the unaffiliated who do not join traditional communities, Secular Humanistic Judaism is the best hope for Jewish survival in the twenty-first century.

The International Institute for Secular Humanistic Judaism is the educational arm of the International Federation of Secular Humanistic Jews, an association of national organizations from the United States, Canada, Israel, Belgium, France, Great Britain, Italy, Australia, Argentina, Uruguay, Mexico, and the countries of the former Soviet Union. As the intellectual and teaching center of the movement, the institute sponsors programs in Israel, Eurasia, and throughout North America for professional lay leaders, educators, and individuals interested in learning more about Secular Humanistic Judaism. The institute also trains rabbis, leaders, music directors, and educators.

The institute's commitment to Jewish identity and continuity forms the foundation of its programs. Secular Humanistic Judaism sees pluralism as the best guarantee of Jewish survival. By training rabbis, leaders, music directors, and educators for communities, by publishing philosophical and celebrational texts, by offering adult outreach and children's programs to the world Jewish community, the institute serves as a positive force for the continuation of the Jewish people, enriching life for all Jews.

The Writings of Sherwin T. Wine

BOOKS

A Word from the Rabbi. Farmington Hills, MI: Birmingham Temple, 1966.

Sabbath Services. Farmington Hills, MI: Birmingham Temple, n.d.

Meditation Services for Humanistic Judaism. Farmington Hills, MI: Birmingham Temple and Society for Humanistic Judaism, 1976.

Humanistic Judaism. Buffalo, NY: Prometheus Books, 1978.

High Holidays for Humanists. Farmington Hills, MI: Birmingham Temple and Society for Humanistic Judaism, 1979.

Celebration: A Ceremonial and Philosophic Guide for Humanists and Humanistic Jews. Buffalo, NY: Prometheus Books, 1988.

The Pursuit of Happiness. Birmingham, MI: Center for New Thinking, 1989.

Judaism Beyond God. Hoboken, NJ: KTAV Publishing House, 1995. Published in Russian as *Norvey Put ov Yudaism* (A New Way of Judaism; Moscow: Association of Humanistic Judaism, 1998).

Staying Sane in a Crazy World. Birmingham, MI: Center for New Thinking, 1995. Published in Spanish as *Como Mantener La Cordura En Un Mudo Loco* (Birmingham, MI: Center for New Thinking, 2000).

CONTRIBUTIONS TO BOOKS

"Humanistic Judaism and the 'God is Dead' Theology." In *The Ghetto and Beyond.* New York: Random House, 1969.

"Jewish Humanism." In *The Book Your Church Doesn't Want You to Read.* Dubuque, IA: Kendall/Hunt Publishing Company, 1993.

Foreword and preface to *Judaism in a Secular Age.* Hoboken, NJ: KTAV Publishing House, 1995.

"Perspectives on the 21st Century." In *Colloquium '95.* Farmington Hills, MI: IISHJ and the Milan Press, 1997.

"The Humanistic Alternative." In *Colloquium '99.* Farmington Hills, MI: IISHJ and the Milan Press, 2001.

"Now What Do We Do?" In *Colloquium '01.* Farmington Hills, MI: IISHJ and the Milan Press, 2003.

ARTICLES

"What Is a Jew?" *The Humanist* (July/August 1970).

"Bar and Bat Mitzvah, The Humanistic Way"; "A Mitzvah Service." *Humanistic Judaism* 10, no. 4 (winter 1983).

"Anti-Semitism and Jewish Humanism"; "Why *Jewish* Humanism," with Rami Shapiro. *Humanistic Judaism* 11, no. 1 (spring 1983).

"Symposium: The Torah: Its Place in Humanistic Judaism." *Humanistic Judaism* 11, no. 2 (summer 1983).

"Hanukka: How It Happened"; "National Liberation: The Hanukka Question"; "Celebrations: Hanukka Services for Home"; "The Hanukka Bandit," with Marilyn Rowens. *Humanistic Judaism* 11, no. 3 (autumn 1983).

"The New Egalitarianism and the Death of Deference." *Humanistic Judaism* 12, no. 3 (autumn 1984).

"Anti-Semitism—A Force for Jewish Survival." *Humanistic Judaism* 13, no. 1 (spring 1985).

"Judaism Beyond God: Excerpt: Jewish Identity"; "The Meaning of Jewish History"; "Jewish History—Our Humanist Perspective." *Humanistic Judaism* 13, no. 3 (autumn 1985).

"A Secular Yeshiva." *Humanistic Judaism* 13, no. 4 (winter 1985).

"Secular Humanistic Judaism—Continuation of Jewish Civilization." *Secular Humanistic Judaism* (Jerusalem, IISHJ) no. 1 (February 1986).

"A Short Humanistic History of the High Holidays." *Humanistic Judaism* 14, no. 2 (summer 1986).

"Reason and Emotion"; "Celebrations: Reason and Emotion." *Humanistic Judaism* 14, no. 3 (autumn 1986).

"Building Communities for the New American Jew"; "Atheism in the Soviet Union." *Humanistic Judaism* 14 and 15, nos. 4 and 1 (winter 1986/spring 1987).

"Afterthoughts: Four Humanist Leaders Appraise Soviet Atheism." *The Humanist* (January/February 1987).

"Jewish Identity in the Contemporary World." *Humanistic Judaism* 15, no. 2 (spring 1987).

"Marriage and Humanistic Judaism." *Humanistic Judaism* 15, no. 3 (summer 1987).

"Jewish Identity in the World Today." *Secular Humanistic Judaism* (Jerusalem, IISHJ) no. 2 (August 1987).

"Humanistic Judaism and Tradition." *Humanistic Judaism* 15, no. 4 (autumn 1987).

"Circumcision." *Humanistic Judaism* 16, no. 3 (summer 1988).

"The Birmingham Temple's First Quarter-Century"; "Who Is a Jew?"; "Celebrations: We Believe." *Humanistic Judaism* 16, no. 4 (autumn 1988).

"Fundamental Issues." *Humanistic Judaism* 17, no. 2 (spring 1989).

"Cremation"; "Remembering the Dead." *Humanistic Judaism* 17, no. 3 (summer 1989).

"Intermarriage." *Humanistic Judaism* 18, no. 1 (winter 1990).

"The Spiritual Dimension"; "Latin America, Moscow, Israel"; "Responsa." *Humanistic Judaism* 18, no. 2 (spring 1990).

"A Humanistic View of Sukkot"; "Our Dietary Laws." *Humanistic Judaism* 18, no. 3 (summer 1990).

"Humanistic Judaism Makes a Difference"; "Exploring Humanistic Judaism for Old-Timers." *Humanistic Judaism* 18, no. 4 (autumn 1990).

"Secular Humanistic Jewish Ideology: Addressing the Needs of the Future." *Humanistic Judaism* 19, no. 1 (winter 1991).

"The Use and Abuse of the Holocaust"; "Remembrance Day." *Humanistic Judaism* 19, no. 2 (spring 1991).

"What Could Be More Humanistic Than Jewish Humor"; "Responsa." *Humanistic Judaism* 19, no. 3 (summer 1991).

"Purim"; "A Purim Adult Service"; "A Purim Youth Service." *Humanistic Judaism* 20, no. 1 (winter 1992).

"Professional Leaders: Why and How." *Humanistic Judaism* 20, no. 2 (spring 1992).

"The Return to Tradition"; "Responsa." *Humanistic Judaism* 20, no. 3 (summer 1992).

"The Rational Life." *Humanistic Judaism* 20, no. 4 (autumn 1992).

"Tu Bi-Shevat, Earth Day, and Environmentalism." *Humanistic Judaism* 21, no. 1 (winter 1993).

"Being a Secular Humanistic Jew in the Diaspora"; "What Makes Humanistic Judaism Jewish?"; "Responsa." *Humanistic Judaism* 21, no. 2 (spring 1993).

"Demystifying Family Values"; "Responsa." *Humanistic Judaism* 22, no. 1 (winter 1994).

"The Significance of Shabbat, Past and Present"; "Secular Humanistic Judaism: A Shabbat Service." *Humanistic Judaism* 22, no. 2 (spring 1994).

"Studying Jewish History"; "Responsa." Humanistic Judaism 22, nos. 3–4 (summer/autumn 1994).

"The Outlook for Peace in the Middle East"; "A Gamble That Paid Off." *Humanistic Judaism* 23, no. 1 (winter 1995).

"The Blue Dress," with Marilyn Rowens; "Rethinking Shavuot"; "A Shavuot Youth Service"; "A Shavuot Service." *Humanistic Judaism* 23, no. 2 (spring 1995).

"Confronting the Religious Right"; "Palestine and Jordan." *Humanistic Judaism* 23, nos. 3–4 (summer/autumn 1995).

"Ten Humanistic Disciplines"; "The Unaffiliated Jew." *Humanistic Judaism* 24, nos. 1–2 (winter/spring 1996).

"Israel after the Election." *Humanistic Judaism* 24, no. 3 (summer 1996).

"Assisted Suicide: Ethical Issues." *Humanistic Judaism* 24, no. 4 (autumn 1996).

"Our French Heritage"; "The Lesson of Evita"; "Homosexuality: A Challenge to Traditional Morality." *Humanistic Judaism* 25, nos. 1–2 (winter/spring 1997).

"New Ethnic Realities and the Jewish Future." *Humanistic Judaism* 25, no. 3 (summer 1997).

"Women and Humanistic Judaism." *Humanistic Judaism* 25 and 26, nos. 4 and 1 (autumn 1997/winter 1998).

"After the Colloquium"; "The Irony of Jewish Survival." *Humanistic Judaism* 26, no. 2 (spring 1998).

"Israel: How It Has Changed." *Humanistic Judaism* 26, no. 3 (summer 1998).

"Meeting the Challenge of Renewal." *Humanistic Judaism* 26, no. 4 (autumn 1998).

"The Continuing Symposium on Humanist Manifesto II." *The Humanist* (November/December 1998).

"Bar and Bat Mitsva, the Humanistic Way"; "Marriage and Humanistic Judaism"; "Intermarriage"; "Cremation"; "A Sample Funeral or Memorial Service"; "Remembering the Dead." *Humanistic Judaism* 27, nos. 1–2 (winter/spring 1999).

"The Future of Israel." *Humanistic Judaism* 27, no. 3 (summer 1999).

"The Millennium: Where We've Been and Where We're Going." *Humanistic Judaism* 27, no. 4 (autumn 1999).

"An Introduction"; "Beyond Tradition: The Humanistic Alternative." *Humanistic Judaism* 28, nos. 1–2 (winter/spring 2000).

"Evolution Is Our Story"; "Tribute to Daniel Friedman," with Louis Altman. *Humanistic Judaism* 28, no. 3 (summer 2000).

"Going Mainstream: The Fifth Branch"; "The Mideast Crisis: Humanistic Jews Respond," with D. Oler, T. Kolton, G. Feldman; "The U.S. Election: Our Rabbis Comment," with D. Oler. *Humanistic Judaism* 28 and 29, nos. 4 and 1 (autumn 2000/winter 2001).

"A Ninefold Path for Humanistic Jews." *Humanistic Judaism* 29, no. 4 (autumn 2001).

"Going Mainstream: The Fifth Branch." *Contemplate* no. 1 (autumn 2001).

"Two Kinds of Religion." *Humanistic Judaism* 30, no. 1 (winter 2002).

"Spirituality As Empowerment." *Humanistic Judaism* 30, nos. 2–3 (spring/summer 2002).

"Jews and Arabs." *Humanistic Judaism* 30, no. 4 (autumn 2002).

"Arabs and Jews." *The Humanist* (September/October 2002).

"Nove 'Piste' Per Gli Ebrei Laici." *Keshet* (Milan, Italy) 1, nos. 4–5 (November/December 2002).